Electri

Electric Trucks

*A History of Delivery Vehicles,
Semis, Forklifts and Others*

KEVIN DESMOND

Foreword by UMBERTO DE PRETTO

McFarland & Company, Inc., Publishers
Jefferson, North Carolina

Library of Congress Cataloguing-in-Publication Data

Names: Desmond, Kevin, 1950– author. | De Pretto, Umberto,
  writer of foreword.
Title: Electric trucks : a history of delivery vehicles, semis, forklifts
  and others / Kevin Desmond ; foreword by Umberto de Pretto.
Description: Jefferson, North Carolina : McFarland & Company, Inc.,
  publishers, 2020 | Includes bibliographical references and index.
Identifiers: LCCN 2019029152 | ISBN 9781476676159 (paperback : acid free paper) ♾
Subjects: LCSH: Industrial electric trucks—History.
Classification: LCC TL223 .D48 2020 | DDC 629.22/93—dc23
LC record available at https://lccn.loc.gov/2019029152

British Library cataloguing data are available

ISBN (print) 978-1-4766-7615-9
ISBN (ebook) 978-1-4766-3618-4

Front cover: *Insets, left to right,* In the days before refrigerators, huge blocks
of ice would be delivered by firms such as the Standard Plate Ice Company
and Consolidated Ice, using Edison batteries (U.S. Department of the
Interior, National Park Service, Thomas Edison National Historical Park);
between 1938 and 1941, over seventy DV4 4-ton refuse trucks were purchased
by the City of Birmingham Salvage Department (Transport Museum Wythall);
background, Elon Musk's Tesla Semi prototype (author collection).

Printed in the United States of America

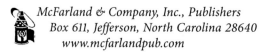

McFarland & Company, Inc., Publishers
  Box 611, Jefferson, North Carolina 28640
    www.mcfarlandpub.com

To
Ἑρμῆς (Hermes, Greek god of commerce)
Ἠλέκτρα (Elektra)
Πύρο, Αἰο, Φλέγκον, Αἔθων
(Pyrois, Aeos, Phlegon, Aethon,
the four horses of Helios)

Acknowledgments

The author would like to thank the following for their kind help in this book:

Ann de Astui; Fondation Automobile Marius Berliet; Courtney Cesar (Antique Truck Historical Society); Lucien Chanuc; Patrick Collins (National Motor Museum Trust); Kendra Cook (Boyertown Museum of Historic Vehicles); Jay K Crist; Barbara Davies (Clarendon Hills Historical Society); Leonard DeGraaf (Thomas Edison National Historical Park); Alison Duce (Kelham Island Museum); Paul Grey (Transport Museum Wythall); Bob Hakewill; Stan Howell Harold (Washington Library Center; Chicago Public Library); Craig Harman (The Lincoln Highway National Museum & Archives); Senator John Heinz History Center; Ted Kemp (IEET); Deb Henderson (Shell International Ltd.) Leslie M Kendall (Petersen Automotive Museum); Damien Kuntz (Musée EDF, Electropolis); Florian Martini (Siemens AG); Gijs Mom (Technical University of Eindhoven); Stuart Ray (Ipswich Transport Museum); Jean-Noël Raymond; Keith Roberts, Valerie Shoffner; Westinghouse Electric Corporation Photographs, Detre Library & Archives, Heinz History Center; Sebastian Wormell (Harrods Corporate Affairs).

Thanks also to my wife Alexandra and Kathryn Cooper (my indexer and proofreader).

Table of Contents

A well-known operator once said that his idea of a commercial vehicle was a box on wheels.

— "The Commercial Motor," April 27, 1945

The electric vehicle since its very first existence has always been a "véhicule utilitaire" in the meaning that one must give to this phrase.

—Louis Kriéger, Honorary President of the French Syndicate of Electric Vehicle Builders

I believe that ultimately the electric motor will be universally used for trucking in all large cities, and that the electric automobile will be the family carriage of the future. All trucking must come to electricity. I am convinced that it will not be long before all the trucking in New York City will be electric.

—Thomas Alva Edison in an interview with Automobile Topics *in May 1914*

In a short time the use of horse drawn truck wagons for Company work will be as rare as the dodo bird and the left-handed monkey wrench. You'll see a pair of horses drawing one of our rigs about as often as you see a gas jet illuminating the Edison Building. Every vehicle engaged in Company business including dump wagons and pole wagons will be operated by electricity by the first of the year.

—Edison Round Table, 31 October 1921, from Technology and Culture, *July 2001*

Foreword
by Umberto de Pretto

Most vehicle manufacturers are working hard on research and trying to outpace their competitors in bringing viable, consumer-friendly, mass-produced electric vehicles to the market.

What this book reminds us is that electric trucks are also part of our past as well as our present. It tells us that electricity became the fuel of choice for short-haul deliveries as horses became obsolete. The combustion engine eventually took over, as we all know, though it was normal to see electric-powered vehicles delivering milk in UK cities until relatively recently, and many types of electric vehicles are still used extensively in warehouses, ports, airports, terminals and factories around the world.

I'm honored to be writing this foreword because road transport is both my job—I'm Secretary General of IRU—and, more importantly, my passion.

IRU's members represent close to a million road haulage companies, from the smallest to the largest, and from across the globe. The organization has been around for 70 years and we've seen a huge amount of innovation in that time. Technology, for example, has helped cut toxic emissions from trucks by up to 98 percent from diesel engines. But there's more to do.

As Kevin Desmond tells us, there has been significant progress in the development of the new generation of electric trucks, helped by lithium-ion battery technology. However, it looks like we're going to have to work even harder because long-haul journeys, even with lithium-ion, still aren't viable.

Indeed, when I first joined IRU in 1995, a 20-tonne battery would have been required to provide the same energy needed to operate a 40-tonne diesel powered truck. Today that figure has dropped to 9 tons. But that's still nine tons of goods that are not being transported. The challenge to the road trans-port industry, and beyond, is to keep pushing the boundaries, so we must keep searching for new innovations.

1

That is a lesson I learned growing up in Canada. It's a big, wild place and a major part of being Canadian is the philosophy of protecting and preserving nature. Road transport is also important there because we need to move things, and people, across vast distances. Perhaps that's why I've been a transport geek since I was very young. There's hard evidence: my office is full of model trucks, buses, coaches and taxis both modern and antique.

What I've always found particularly fascinating is technological development. This must have been ingrained in me when, at 16 years old, I rebuilt (or rather I helped my good friend who knew what he was doing) my father's 350 cubic inch Oldsmobile Cutlass motor to increase the stock horsepower from 260 to around 350. What I learned the hard way is that my fuel consumption increased dramatically to 38 litres/100km! Today that sort of horsepower can be achieved with less than 6 litres/100km. That's the huge difference technology makes.

Enjoy reading this book and see what the future could hold for electric vehicles.

Umberto de Pretto is secretary-general of the International Road Transport Union (IRU), a global industry federation of national member associations and associate members in 73 countries on the five continents, that represents the interests of bus, coach, taxi and truck operators worldwide.

Prelude

In my childhood and youth, we regularly borrowed books from the nearby Wallington Library, in Surrey, England. In the library grounds, next to the car park, were two very old iron rails, each with three stone sleepers. Next to them, a little panel reads:

> The Surrey Iron Railway. Opened in 1803, ran from Wandsworth to West Croydon and had a branch from Mitcham which terminated in this Borough in 1804. The first public railway in the world, was horse drawn, carried only freight and operated until 1846.

Benjamin Outram's Iron Railway was a toll plateway on which carriers used horse traction. The chief goods transported were coal, building materials, lime, manure, corn and seeds.[1]

In 1821, the English landscape painter John Constable completed a six-foot painting called *The Hay Wain*. It depicts a rural view from Flatford Mill on the River Stour between the English counties of Suffolk and Essex. Painted in oils on canvas, its central feature is three horses pulling what in fact appears to be a wooden wain, or large farm wagon, across the river. At the time, horse-drawn wagons were considered the only effective method of goods transport. The Dutch word *waghen* dates from the early 16th century. Another new word around was *truckle*, or wheel pulley, used to carry the heavy guns on His Majesty's warships. This was soon shortened to truck.

Since the earliest civilizations in Mesopotamia, 7000 BCE, heavy loads had been carried by such vehicles, first pulled by oxen and then by draft horses. These beasts of burden were not the most sanitary because of their daily habits of relieving themselves anywhere they felt like it. In the Book of Numbers in the Hebrew Bible, one reads, "When they brought their offering before the LORD, six covered carts and twelve oxen, a cart for every two of the leaders and an ox for each one, then they presented them before the tabernacle."

In the 13th century, Roger Bacon (also known as "Frater Rogerus"), a

The Hay Wain, or wagon, in John Constable's 1821 work depicted a horse-drawn truck in existence for centuries, the Dutch word *waghen* dating from the early 16th century. The year before Constable died in London, John Daniell invented an improved electrical battery.

Franciscan friar in Oxford contemplating the mechanics of the cosmos, wrote "The Letter on the Secret Workings of Art and Nature and on the Vanity of Magic" ("Epistola de Secretis Operibus Artis et Naturae et de Nullitate Magiae"): "chariots that shall move with unspeakable force, without any living creature to stir them."

In 1478, Leonardo da Vinci, the Italian polymath genius, took a new page of his notebook and did a drawing of a driverless cart, powered by coiled springs and also featuring steering and brake capabilities. When the brake was released at a distance by an operator with a hidden rope, the car would move forward, while the steering was programmable to go either straight or at pre-set angles. It was conceived as a special effect for Renaissance festivals. Leonardo's cart design was so ahead of its time that its exact workings baffled scholars until late in the 20th century. In 2006, Italy's Institute and Museum of the History of Science in Florence built a working model based on Leonardo's design and, to the surprise of many, the cart actually worked.[2] To move wagons without horses would require a different method of propulsion. In the 1780s, James Watt and Matthew Boulton, steam engine pioneers of Birmingham, England, faced a problem. They had previously agreed to take royalties of one third of the savings in coal from the older Newcomen steam engines. This royalty scheme did not work with customers who did not have existing steam engines but used horses instead. One of Watt's first customers, a brewer, specifically demanded an engine that would match a horse, but tried to cheat by taking the strongest horse he had and driving it to the limit. Watt, while aware of the trick, accepted the challenge and built a machine which was actually even stronger than the figure achieved by the brewer, and it was the output of that machine which became the "horsepower." Watt determined that a horse could turn a mill wheel 144 times in an hour (or 2.4 times a minute). The wheel was 12 feet (3.7 m) in radius; therefore, the horse traveled $2.4 \times 2\pi \times 12$ feet in one minute. Watt judged that the horse could pull with a force of 180 pounds-force (800 N). Watt defined and calculated the horsepower as 32,572 ft-lb/min, which was rounded to an even 33,000 ft-lb/min. Perhaps the irony is that the man who defined horsepower should give his name to units of electricity—watt, kilowatt, megawatt.[3]

The *Steam Horse* was constructed for colliery work by the Butterley Company in Derbyshire in 1813 following designs by William Brunton. The Napoleonic Wars from 1799 to 1815 had brought a great increase in the price of fodder for horses. Brunton was aware that the action of the horse up to that time had been the most successful means of hauling vehicles, and the question arose, why not utilize the action of the horse mechanically? The engine was duly built to put that idea in practice. It had a horizontal boiler and a single cylinder set on top with pistons connecting with levers that acted the part of a horse's legs. Also known as the *Mechanical Traveller*, it had a pair of mechanical legs with feet that gripped the rails at the rear of the engine to push it forward at about three miles an hour.[4]

On September 27, 1825, *Locomotion n°1*, built by George and Robert Stephenson, hauled the first train on the Stockton and Darlington Railway in northeast England. During this maiden trip, which was driven by George Stephenson himself, the train consisted of *Locomotion*, 11 wagons of coal, the carriage "Experiment," and a further 20 wagons of passengers, guests, and workmen. Reportedly, around 300 tickets had been sold but roughly twice as many people were believed to have been aboard. The train, which had an estimated weight of 80 tons and a length of 400 feet (122 m), reported reaching peak speeds of up to 38.6 kph (24 mph). It took around two hours to complete the first nine miles (14 km) of the journey to Darlington, but was slowed by a derailed wagon and a blocked feed pump valve, thus only achieving an average speed of eight mph (12.9 kph). It was the start of two types of motorized transport: of goods and of passengers.[5]

In the period 1825–9, Goldsworthy Gurney, a surgeon-inventor, designed and built a number of steam-powered road vehicles which were intended to commercialize a steam road transport business—the Gurney Steam Carriage

Company. His vehicles were built at his Regent's Park Manufactory works, and tested around the Park's barrack yard, and on frequent excursions to Hampstead, Highgate, Edgware, Barnet and Stanmore, at speeds of up to 20 mph (32 kph). They were, of course, modifications of existing horse-drawn carriages.

His enterprise was blocked by the horse lobby. According to Francis Maceroni in his 1836 book *A Few Facts Concerning Elementary Locomotion*:

> The many wealthy horse-coach proprietors, together with the narrow-minded country gentlemen and magistrates of the district, who erroneously conceived their interests threatened by the substitution of steam power for horse, formed one of the most disgraceful and mean conspiracies against a national undertaking that can be well remembered. By means of parliamentary intrigue, and false representations, these despicable persons obtained certain local turnpike bills to pass "the Honourable House" establishing tolls on steam carriages, which amounted to a virtual prohibition on their use.

A charge of £2 was levied on each steam carriage journey, while the toll for a horse drawn carriage was two shillings.

By this time, a number of pioneer railways had been built, some of these horse-drawn. The first passenger-carrying public railway was the Oystermouth Railway, authorized in 1807 and towed by horses. Between 1825 and 1833, despite its initial success, the Stockton and Darlington Railway operated with both horses and engines. When George Stephenson was building this railway, he decided on the gauge by measuring the axle width of 100 farm wagons and taking the average, the result being 4 ft. 8 in. He may have intended to allow local people to use the track to convey goods with their own wagons, for while coal wagons were hauled by steam locomotives from the start, passengers were carried in coaches drawn by horses until carriages hauled by steam locomotives were introduced. Once steam engines became more reliable, horses were replaced. For example, in 1830, engineer Peter Cooper built a locomotive called *Tom Thumb* to convince the new Baltimore and Ohio Railroad Company to use steam. On September 28, the locomotive had a one-to-one race with a draft-horse drawn stagecoach and lost due to mechanical failure. But the railroad company chose steam power all the same. The engine was slowly but surely replacing the horse.[6]

* * *

Please note that the word "ton" is dependent on context when it appears herein. When weight conversions are given, they are in metric tons (1,000 kilograms or 2,205 pounds) except for trucks in the United States, where the U.S. ton of 2,000 pounds is used. General usage of the word "ton" in the text, however, typically relies upon original sources that were not specific about the measurement. Particularly in a British context, these references may be to an Imperial ton (equal to 1,016 kilograms or 2,240 pounds).

ONE

Pioneers

In 1838, Robert Davidson of Aberdeen, Scotland, decided to scale up his small experimental electric engines to propel a vehicle. He obtained the backing of the directors of the Edinburgh and Glasgow Railway, whose line had been opened to passengers from Glasgow Queen Street railway station to Haymarket railway station in Edinburgh since February 21, 1842. Working with a young apprentice in the corner of a shed at the Haymarket, with access to the workshop, Davidson adapted two pairs of cast-off carriage wheels and axles for his engine but provided all the materials for the engines and batteries himself. It took 12 months to build a 16-foot-long (4m 80cm) prototype, each of its two axles carrying a cylinder upon which were fastened three iron bars with four electromagnets arranged in pairs on each side of the cylinders. The engines were "reluctance engines," the power source being zinc-iron batteries. Originally two batteries of about 20 cells each were placed at the ends of the carriage. The plates of iron and amalgamated zinc were 12 inches wide by 15 inches deep.

But as William Henley commented:

> … when first put in action, so powerful was the attractive force of the magnets that the frame-work was not strong enough to withstand the strain; it was drawn together, and, consequently, the first experiment failed. Money not being at hand to construct another carriage, Mr. Davidson was obliged to patch up the old one, and removed the magnets to such a distance from the iron to be attracted, that then at their nearest point he could introduce his hand into the space between them.[1]

The *Galvani*, named after the Italian pioneer of electrochemistry, was first tried out in the presence of several directors, on September 17, 1842.

> The ponderous machine, weighing between five and six tons, was instantly set in motion on the immersion of the metallic plates into the troughs containing a solution of sulphuric acid. One curious phenomenon connected with the motion of this new and ingenious instrument was the extent and brilliancy of the repeated electric flashes which accompanied the action of the machinery.[2]

In 1838, when Scotsman Robert Davidson tested his *Galvani* electric vehicle along the Edinburgh-Glasgow railway line, it was carrying a load of 6 tons. This full-scale working replica at the Grampian Transport Museum shows his ingenious pairing of electromagnets (Grampian Transport Museum).

Four days later, in front of a crowd of distinguished observers, Davidson's prototype electric truck ran at 4 mph (6.4 kph) while hauling a load of 6 tons over a distance of 1.5 miles (2.4 km).Despite enthusiastic reviews no backers were forthcoming and so Davidson packed up and headed for London. Here he again exhibited his various electromagnetic machines to great acclaim but no investors backed him. Vested interest in steam engines has often been given as the reason for the lack of uptake and this theory is fuelled by the story of the dismantling of *Galvani* by the railway company in Edinburgh while Davidson was in London. While this certainly happened and without his knowledge, it is likely that the loco was simply in the way and not considered a threat. Rechargeable batteries were not invented until 1859. Unfortunately, *Galvani* was destroyed before the inventor could get it back, by men unknown but suspected of being promoters of steam engines.[3]

Five years later, in 1851, Professor Charles Grafton Page, assisted by U.S. Congressional funds, made a trial run in America with a large electromagnetic locomotive of similar construction on a line between Washington and

Bladensburg in Maryland. The machine was powered by 100 Grove primary cells and is said to have developed 16 hp. From the start of the run, problems immediately arose. High voltage sparks broke through the electrical insulation of the electrical coils, resulting in short circuits. Many of the battery's fragile clay dividers cracked on starting up; others broke down subsequently. Page and his mechanic Ari Davis struggled to make repairs and keep the locomotive running. With some periods of steady running, eventually the distance of 5¼ miles (8.4 km) between these towns was covered in 39 minutes and a maximum speed of 19 mph (30 kph) was attained. Page prudently reversed direction there, for what was an arduous, calamity-laced return to the national capital. Soon after, the experiments were abandoned.[4]

Twenty-three years later, in Imperial Russia, in the years 1874–1876, Fyodor Apollonovich Pyrotsky, a friend of the famous electrical engineer Pavel Yablochov, began a series of experiments with electric traction with a horse-less wagon on an abandoned section of the Sestroretsk railway, near Saint Petersburg. Pyrotsky applied for a "privilege" or concession, while the results of the conducted experiments and works were published in 1877. The inventor had come to the conclusion, "the electric power transmitted to a distance can cause the wheels of the car to move along the rails." Pyrotsky presented these findings at a meeting of the Russian Technical Society, Panteleimonovskaya Street, St. Petersburg.[5]

It was thought in the mid–19th century that it would be possible to generate electricity more economically by the *consumption* of zinc in a primary battery than by burning coal under a boiler, and in America a company was established to exploit this supposition with a capital of $3 million. By this time the generation of electricity by steam-driven plant had passed the experimental stage and, with the development of the accumulator battery, traction had entered a new phase. In 1859, Gaston Planté of Meudon, France, announced that he had produced "a secondary battery of great power"—one that could be recharged. It was the first in the world. His early model had consisted of a spiral roll of two sheets of pure lead separated by a linen cloth, immersed in a glass jar of sulphuric acid solution. But the one he presented was a nine-cell lead-acid battery. Sooner or later this battery would be used for locomotion.

In 1896 Werner von Siemens and Johann Halske of Germany, having developed a dynamo machine, or electric motor, inspired by Pyrotsky, electrified a truck originally built for use in a coal mine and turned it into a passenger vehicle capable of pulling three small cars fitted with wooden benches, each car being capable of carrying six passengers for a ride along a 300-meter circular track. What was special about it was that the 150-volt direct current flowed through the two rails to the small locomotive via an insulated flat iron bar mounted between the rails. In 1897, Siemens presented the world's first fully operational electric train and streetcar at an industrial exhibition near

Lehrte Station in Berlin. During the four months of the exhibition, it carried 90,000 passengers around the circular track through the exhibition grounds at roughly the pace of a horse-drawn tram. This was so successful that Siemens & Halske received inquiries from all over the world about the investment and operating costs of goods-carrying electric railways.[6]

The invention of an electric vehicle not reliant on rails or cables was the achievement of a Frenchman. Until recently, the name Gustave Trouvé, Chevalier de la Légion d'Honneur, prolific Parisian electrical instrument inventor, was absent from any popular French encyclopedia. Yet, when at the end of the 19th century, Alexander Graham Bell, the world-famous inventor of the telephone, visited Paris, before leaving, he insisted on visiting Trouvé's workshops:

> I wanted to surprise you amongst your works that I so much admire. In addition, I want to take away to America, a complete collection of all your inventions, because for me they make up the highest expression of the perfection and the ingenuity of the electric science in France.[7]

Gustave Pierre Trouvé was born on January 2, 1839, at La Haye-Descartes, northeast of Poitiers. His father Jacques Trouvé was a gentleman farmer and with Gustave's mother Clarissa, brought up five children. From his earliest years, although Gustave did not show the greatest passion for math, he was very keen on mechanical objects. He never played with children of his age. From morning to night, armed with a knife, a hammer and several nails he amused himself by fashioning little chariots, telegraphs, rabbits and automatons fitted with wings moved by the wind. In 1846, the seven-year-old boy built a little fire-pump from a sardine tin. Then with little more than hairpins and bits of lead, this prodigy made a miniature working steam engine, using an old tinderbox for the generator. Four years later, between October and December 1850, Trouvé began his studies alongside his brother Jules at Chinon College. But as he wanted to specialize in math and mechanics, Gustave left his large family and his region to study at the Imperial School of Industrial Arts and Crafts at Angers. The marks obtained by the teenager (Control No. 264) for the first term of the 1854 school year are surprisingly lower than average, his strongest point being drawing.

By 1859, aged only 20, young Trouvé had obtained a job at one of the principal Paris clockmakers. During his spare time, he studied architecture, math and precision work. Seven years later, he set up his own establishment for the creation and manufacture of precision and scientific instruments, of which he would conceive and construct some 75 in all, particularly in the field of electricity. Among these was transportation, both ashore and afloat. Recently, Werner Siemens and Johann Halske of Berlin-Kreuzberg in Germany had developed an electric motor to power both the world's first elevator and streetcar. In 1878, examining the Siemens coil engine, French electrician Marcel Deprez improved the motor by placing the coil between the branches of a U-shaped magnet. But his motor still had a neutral moment.

Trouvé thought up a way to eliminate this weakness. He substituted an electro-magnet between the poles where the Siemens coil was placed. The current circulated in the wire of the electro-magnet and then passed, via the brushes of the switch, into the wire of the coil. In this way neutral was avoided.

The little motor built by Trouvé was only eight inches (20 cm) long and weighed in at only 71 lb. 4 oz. (3.3 kg). Simply by adding more coils in the magnetic field, Trouvé stepped up the power. His motor could run up to 18,000 revs per minute. In addition, as with all electric motors in general, it was reversible, so could be used as a generator of electricity as well a generator of power.

Having received Patent No. 136,560 (dated May 8, 1880), he began to consider how his little engine might be used for motive power; he thought that perhaps the most lightweight and stable vehicle to test it out on would be a pedal tricycle.[8]

From the mid–1870s, James Starley of the Sewing Machine Company of Coventry, England, had been building and improving tricycles—the Coventry Rotary and the Coventry Lever—for a world enamored by "wheeling." In the summer of 1881, Starley proudly delivered two of his stable "Salvo Tricycles" to Osborne House on the Isle of Wight, for possible use by Her Royal Majesty Queen Victoria and her daughters. The *Salvo* was renamed the *Royal Salvo* and before long there was not a crowned head who did not have a fleet of tricycles, both within and outside Europe. A firm called P. Rousset & Ingold became the general agents for France.

For Trouvé, the Salvo seemed the ideal mount. On April 16, 1881, he reported his trials along a straight road near his workshop in the Tissandiers' magazine *La Nature*:

> On a heavily built English tricycle, I fitted two of my little electric motors and 6 electric accumulators like the one in my polyscope. One of my friends climbed onto the tricycle, switched it on and accelerated it several times along the rue de Valois, certainly as rapidly as a good hackney cab. The experiment lasted an hour and a half. A speed of 12 km/h [7.4 mph] was recorded. The weight of the vehicle and of my friend amounted to 160 kg [352 lb.] and the force of the engines corresponded to 7 kilogrammètres [1¹⁄₁₀ hp]. Encouraged by these results, I immediately began to build a motor which was alone more powerful than the two others, even up to 10 kilogrammeters, so as to get even greater speeds, that is from 20 to 30 km/h [12 to 18 mph].

There were eye-witnesses: "One of Trouvé's friends has tried the new velocipede on the bitumen of the rue de Valois. He went up and down the road several times at the speed of a good carriage."[9]

His friend and supporter, journalist Abbé Moigno was also there:

I had just crossed the Palais Royal and arrived on the rue de Valois, when my attention was drawn by a man who was on a tricycle and was arriving at full speed. I would have left immediately if, upon the approach of the tricycle, I had not heard a few exclamations uttered by passers-by who said "Of course it is steam or electricity which propels it!" Upon hearing the word "electricity," I paid closer attention to the vehicle which was going by me at that precise moment and it was easy for me to notice that, the "soul" of the movement was indeed electricity, because I immediately recognized the small motor which had been presented and demonstrated by its inventor during a social gathering given by Vice-Admiral Mouchez in the Paris Observatory. However, I did not recognize M. Gustave Trouvé, the famous electrical engineer, as being the person who was on the tricycle, but I soon heard he was standing apart and that from a window in the Hotel de Hollande, he had followed all phases of the experiment. Let me tell you about it.

The tricycle had two steering wheels and a simple, large propelling wheel, the latter being, I believe of English manufacture, and appearing quite heavy. Placed beneath the axle joining the two small wheels were two small, Trouvé motors, each the size of a fist. These motors were communicating movement by means of two link chains each of which engaged its respective sprocket gear on either side of the big propelling wheel.

Behind the seat and sitting on the axle, a rough, newly fashioned wooden box contained six secondary batteries. These accumulators were quite similar to those of Mr. Gaston Planté and actuated the motors. To the left of the seat was a brake lever easily reached by the driver. On the lever was an electrical switch by which the driver could easily stop or start immediately...[10]

Although Gustave Trouvé proved to people that an electric vehicle was a reality, his prototype never had to transport goods hourly and daily. For that, better batteries were the key.

The inventor behind this was Camille Alphonse Faure of France. His key patent was taken out on October 20, 1880, No. 139,358: "Improvements to galvanic batteries and their application to electric locomotives" which he modified several times in January and October 1881. This was the birth of a new battery which would have such success and be heard about all over the world. Lead plates were coated with a paste of lead oxides, sulphuric acid and water, which was then cured by being gently warmed in a humid atmosphere. The curing process caused the paste to change to a mixture of lead sulphates which adhered to the lead plate. During charging the cured paste was converted into electrochemically active material (the "active mass") and gave a substantial increase in capacity compared with Planté's battery.

Thus, the innovation of storage cells (called "secondary") was made possible by the reversible chemical reactions of its elements permitting the cell to be recharged and used again and again. By 1883, no fewer than eleven concerns were engaged in the manufacture of Faure accumulators. These included from "La Force et La Lumière" of Paris; Faure Electric Accumulator Company of London; Force & Power Co of New York, USA; the French Metropolitan Electric Carriage Co.; EPS of London; India and Oriental Electric Power Storage Company—and even the Australasian Electric Light and Power Storage

In 1881 the world's first trackless electric vehicle, built by Gustave Trouvé, was briefly tested along the rue Valois, downtown Paris, France (Musée EDF Electropolis, Mulhouse).

Co. Following some litigation in the USA, the two American companies combined into the Electric Accumulator Co. of New York.

In the early Spring of 1882, La Force et La Lumière in Paris conducted the first experiment with an in-plant industrial use of battery transport. The large Duchesne-Fournet bleaching ground at Breuil-en-Auge, near Lisieux, wanted to mechanize the laying out and take-up of cloth, but the use of a small steam locomotive was precluded because of the smoke and cinders. Therefore their engineer Dupuy decided to kill two birds with one stone. He already had a lighting plant at the establishment and he decided to use this plant during the time that it was idle during the day for the operation of a small electric locomotive, weighing 2,500 lbs. (1,134 kg), driven by a Siemens dynamic run backwards as a motor, and carrying 635 kg (1,400 lbs.) of "Force and Lumière" batteries placed in baskets in a small tender. The locomotive ran up and down the bleaching meadow on small rails and drew in the cloth which had been exposed to the air for five to six days by attaching the motor to a small winch which drew in 10,000 m² at a time.[11]

In 1887, Michael Radliffe Ward, working for the Faure Accumulator

Company Ltd. with his London-based Ward Electric Car Company, developed a prototype electric truck for the Royal Mail Post Office, but chose to put his efforts into a battery-electric omnibus which was seen on the streets of London but never entered into regular service.

The Electric Storage Battery Company was founded in 1888 by W.W. Gibbs of Philadelphia. As vice president of the United Gas Improvement Company, a Philadelphia gas lighting firm, Gibbs recognized that electricity had great potential as a source for lighting, and as such, posed a threat to gas. Gibbs formed the Electric Storage Battery Company to create a dependable mechanism for storing power so electric lighting companies could provide services to their customers if and when it was necessary. Realizing that a better storage battery was a necessary first step, Gibbs purchased the ideas and patents of French inventor Clement Payen to transform good ideas about storage batteries (then widely referred to as "Pickled Amperes") into thoroughly reliable commercial products. With the development of the storage battery, or the "Chloride Accumulator," the Electric Storage Battery Company brought the electric lighting industry to a new level, as in electric locomotives, streetcars, passenger cars, and trucks, and for the nation's first automatic switching and signaling systems for railroads. In 1900, the Electric Storage Battery Company developed a product of greater capacity and less weight for electric taxicabs. This battery was the first to bear the name Exide, short for "Excellent Oxide."

Ignorant of such developments, most American businesses depended on the horse-drawn wagon—bakers, brewers, ice houses and coal distributors used large 5-ton wagons to deliver their products to local merchants. Local merchants and growing market-hungry department stores used small 1,000 lb. one-horse wagons to deliver merchandise to individual customers. People bought and sold locally. Horse-drawn carriages and carts might have continued carrying anything from postal letters to tons of raw minerals, had it not have been for a serious civic hygiene threat. Toward the end of the 19th century, the horse population in London was producing around 3,000 tons of dung per day, of which a substantial amount landed on the paving-stones. On dry days, the muck became dust that stuck to people's faces and clothes. On rainy days, streets were transformed in open sewers. Apart from pollution, thousands of iron horseshoes and wheels must have made a terrible racket, and traffic accidents were no less frequent than they are today. Moreover, being a horse in the city at the end of the 19th century was not an enviable

Opposite: **In 1882, the large Duchesne-Fournet bleaching ground near Lisieux, France, used this truck, powered by a Siemens electric motor and a stack of Force et Lumiere batteries, to lay and take up cloth using a small winch. This was the world's first electric truck (Musée EDF Electropolis, Mulhouse).**

fate. Pulling goods (sometimes with weights of over ten tons) on dirty and slippery cobble-stones was so exhausting that most animals dropped dead after just a few years of work. This was a commonplace but sad sight. New York removed on average 41 dead horses from the streets per day. Beatings and whippings were common.

There were a number of initiatives in the 19th century to try to improve the conditions of the city's horses, one of which was the Cart Horse Parade, established in Britain in 1885 with the aim of encouraging the owners of horses to take pride in their animals and to show to their peers and the public in a formal annual parade. The first Cart Horse Parades took place on Whit Monday in Battersea Park, London.[12]

By the turn of the century, the bottom had fallen out of the manure market. Whereas previously farmers had paid stable owners for the manure to use as fertilizer, by 1900 it was so plentiful that the stable owners had to pay the farmers to take it away. In summer, the farmers found it difficult to leave their crops to collect manure. City officials and residents began to pile the manure on vacant lots in U.S. cities, with some lots having manure mountains up to 64 ft. (20 m) high.

Manure storage often aroused fierce opposition from neighborhoods where dumps were located. Women from fashionable Beekman Place complained to New York's Board of Health about the 25 ft. (7m) high pile of manure kept on a vacant lot on East Forty-Sixth Street. The pile was the responsibility of Tammany-connected manure contractor Martin Kane who employed 100 horses to remove manure from stables holding 12,000–13,000 horses. Kane stored it, pending sales to the countryside, and if sales were slow or prices slow, his inventory grew. The woman complained of headaches and nausea.

Despite these pioneering prototypes, the civic health threat came to a head in what became known as the "Great Horse Manure Crisis of 1894." *The Times* of London predicted: "In 50 years, every street in London will be buried under nine feet of manure." In 1898, the first international inter-urban planning conference was held in New York, bringing together city leaders and problem solvers, with the problem of horse manure as its major theme. Although the conference was meant to run for ten days, they closed the doors after only three days as delegates could see no easy solution.

In answer to this, engineers had already begun to put together electric horseless carriages and trams—and wagons, so much faster and less mucky. In 1894, Henry G. Morris, a mechanical engineer, and Pedro G. Salom, an electro-chemical engineer of the Consolidated Electric Storage Company, both of Philadelphia, organized a firm called the Electric Carriage and Wagon Company. Both had backgrounds in battery streetcars and, as the battery streetcar business was fading, they teamed up to make battery road vehicles.

The two would produce most appropriate vehicles. Their first carriage they chose to call the *Electrobat*, stating it was a compound word, the term "bat" being derived from the Greek word "bainein" meaning "to go," hence a conveyance deriving its power from electricity. The first vehicle, converted from a delivery wagon of the day, with large rear wheels and smaller steerable front wheels, was considered a success. The weight of their vehicle was 4,250 lbs. (1,920 kg) with the chloride battery contributing 1,600 of the total, and giving energy to a 3 hp General Electric motor taken from a ship. Speed control was by voltage switching. Steering was by a suitable hand wheel with geared fifth wheel riding on ball-bearings, which engaged the front wheel axle.[13] When the two inventors took their electric wagon out for its first test run that summer, they had to receive a special permit from City Hall. Accompanied by a police officer tasked with conducting carriages away from the automobile (which was liable to frighten horses), the *Electrobat* made its way down busy, cobblestoned Broad Street. In an important *Times-Herald* contest of 1895, Morris and Salom's electric vehicle won a gold medal for superior craftsmanship in "absolute safety, elegance of design, cleanliness, simplicity of construction and control, economy of power, operation and cost, ease of handling, and absence of noise, odor, heat or vibration."

In 1895, having successfully tested their Electrobat, Henry G. Morris and Pedro G. Salom declared, "the most practical application for our vehicle is for service as *delivery wagons* and cab carriages..." (Musée EDF Electropolis, Mulhouse).

When interviewed by *Motorcycle Maker and Dealer*, the conscientious pioneers said, "the most practical application for our vehicle is for service as delivery wagons and cab carriages...." After their experimental delivery wagons had run several hundred miles over city streets and boulevards without mishap, Pedro G. Salom went on to develop a method to reduce the process of lead-plate formation from weeks to seconds. By September 1, 1895, the U.S. patents office overflowed with more than 500 applications for patents on vehicle motors alone. Between July and November of that year, no fewer than 300 types of motor vehicles were under construction—some destined to succeed and many to fail. Among those, the challenge of battery reliability raised its head. Various solutions were tried. In 1896, for example, to overcome range limitations and lack of charging infrastructure, a battery exchange (aka battery swap) service was proposed. Implemented by Hartford Electric Light Company, the service was initially available for electric trucks.

The first battery vehicle to run in England was built in London in 1889 and Mr. Frank Whinfield Crawter, manager of the Chloride Electrical Storage Company Ltd., makers of Exide batteries, drove it from Kentish Town to Oxford Street. To do this, Crawter had to obtain a special permit from Scotland Yard Police, because at that time 2 mph was the regulation speed in the UK for mechanically propelled vehicles. A man carrying a red flag had to walk in front of them. In 1894, Walter C. Bersey, a brilliant 20-year-old electrical engineer based in London, England, patented an "improvement in electrically operated common road vehicles" (UK #231,523) allowing horse-drawn vehicles to be adapted for electric propulsion. The rights to the Bersey system were held by the Universal Electric Carriage Syndicate Ltd. of Westminster, London. Two years later, with another electrician, Desmond Gerald Fitzgerald, Bersey patented "improvements in voltaic batteries" which used dry materials to avoid the problem of electrolyte sloshing. Instead of using an ordinary fluid electrolyte, a special "afluidic" or "dry" material was used, thus practically converting the cell into a dry battery. This avoided spilling, splashing and spraying of acid in the carriage. The strength was regulated by a single drive switch, giving any degree of speed required and also causing the vehicle to run either forward or backward. The accumulators were carried in a tray which slid into a well in the vehicle so that a fresh set could be substituted in two minutes. Electric carriage lamps used the same power supply.[14]

Bersey's "Electrically-propelled carriages," published by Morgan, Thompson, and Jamieson in 1898, was in fact a publicity brochure with testimonials and photos, such as this article, "An Electric Parcels Van," first published in *The Daily Telegraph* of March 3, 1894:

> Trial was made yesterday afternoon, during the busiest hours of the City, of an electric parcels van, designed by Mr. W.C. Bersey. The van took its place in the ordinary street traffic, accommodating its pace to a nicety, coming almost to a standstill in Newgate

Street block, and at other congested corners, availing itself of the clear run which Moorgate Street afforded, to increase its speed to a maximum permitted by police regulations. The steering was admirably managed, and the electrical van generally had the advantage of finding its way out of a tangle of buses, carts, cabs and conveyances of every description. With the van six people travelled with perfect confidence. It may be explained that the interior of the van is left free for goods; for the two motors, which are geared to the wheels, are placed beneath the driver's seat. The electricity is derived from 36 cells, which are carried under the body in a special box and so arranged so that they may be changed in two minutes when the accumulators are exhausted.... It is calculated that the costs of working such a van, which would have required two horses, is 2d per mile if electricity be used, and each charge gives about 30 miles of travelling...

Top: British electric engineer Walter C. Bersey had the vision to see the use of electric vehicles for the delivery of goods and mail (IET Library and Archives). *Bottom:* 1898: Walter Bersey's electric delivery truck, in the red-white-blue livery of Harrod's luxury department store in London, equipped with acetylene headlamps, parked outside the London Electrical Cab Company (IET Library and Archives).

Just under one year later, in February 1895, *The Railway Journal* reported:

> The first electrical van (the forerunner of electrical vehicles for ordinary roads), designed by Mr. Walter C. Bersey of Grosvenor House, Gore Road, South Hackney, has run about 1,000 miles in the City of London during the busiest hours of the day, and has proved a success both electrically and commercially.

Profiting from this reliability, Bersey was asked to supply electric trucks to a number of clients, such as Richard Burbidge, managing director of Harrods Ltd. luxury department store in London's fashionable Knightsbridge. To protect the goods during transit, this truck was fitted with a special patent design taken out by Bersey with Reginald Brougham whereby the batteries were suspended from the frame of the vehicle by links supported by springs, making for a smoother ride. Another Bersey was used as a Royal Mail van in the service of Her Majesty Queen Victoria's Post Office.

But for two years the London inventor and entrepreneur would put most of his energies into launching a 77-strong fleet of 3.5 hp Lundell-motor electric taxicabs in the capital, nicknamed "Hummingbirds" due to the humming noise they made. The cab enterprise lasted until August 1899. That year, Henry Moritz Leitner of Electric Undertakings drove his electric *Game Cart* fitted with "recuperative" control (regenerative braking) on the London to Brighton run, celebrating emancipation from the Red Flag Act; it had a maximum speed of 30 mph and a range of 60 miles and proved the reliability of electrics. Bersey was not alone.

During the next decade, several of the foremost vehicle engineers would approach the challenge of electric vehicle development in a scientific manner and develop commercially possible versions of both the pleasure car-type and commercial truck-type respectively.

Isaac Leopold Rice, a German-born Jewish American businessman and investor, was, like Walter Bersey, a man of vision. In September 1897, Rice assembled several battery electric vehicle companies, including Morris and Salom's Electric Carriage and Wagon Company, to found the Electric Vehicle Company, at 1684 Broadway, New York. Apart from launching a taxi-cab fleet that included service stations for quick change of battery sets and repair work, EVC also designed and built 50 standard trucks for heavy electric omnibuses and other vehicles. In 1898, Rice announced that he had placed orders for 4,200 electric vehicles with Albert Pope of the Columbia Electric Vehicle Co. in Hartford, Connecticut, and that before the end of the year he expected to have nearly one thousand vehicles in operation by the different subsidiary companies in New York, Boston, Philadelphia and Chicago, including delivery trucks. His recent acquisition of the plant of the New Haven Carriage Company, New Haven, Connecticut, would enable the Columbia Company to expedite this order. Although this made the EVC the largest motorcar manufacturer in the U.S., Rice's ambitious plan would eventually fail as though he could sell as many vehicles as he had produced, the purchasers encountered daily problems with battery maintenance and reliability.

Two electric delivery wagons built by the EVC went in regular use by Charles A. Stevens & Brothers, a silk house in Chicago. (Stevens had arrived in that city ten years before with bolts of fine silks, at first establishing an extensive silk house but gradually extending the scope of the business until he transformed it into a prestigious store featuring ready-to-wear clothing.) EVC claimed that its 44 storage batteries weighed only 13 lbs. (6 kg) each. Stevens' wagons were so successful that four more wagons soon went into service. Removal of a small control lever at the seat, normally used for reverse, prevented the theft of vehicles.[15]

Among the first to see weaknesses of electric trucks was John Henry Munson of La Porte, Indiana. In 1898, Munson, on applying for a patent, stated:

> At present electric-motor vehicles are provided with storage batteries which after being full charged are capable of furnishing sufficient electricity to run the vehicle for from three to five hours, after which lapse of time it is necessary to visit a power-station and have the batteries recharged in order to continue the trip or journey. On account of this dependence upon power-storage stations electric-motor vehicles cannot be used in making long country tours, and the use thereof has been restricted to cities, and even in cities it is often inconvenient to reach the power-stations, and, further, the cost of maintaining the ordinary electric vehicle is great. The specific object of this invention is to provide a combined electric and vapor vehicle, the electric motor thereof being employed to propel the vehicle and the engine to be employed to drive said motor as a dynamo for the purpose of replenishing the batteries on the vehicle at times when the vehicle is still, as when in the barn or waiting in the road.

In short, his U.S. Patent 653199A concerned a hybrid-electric vehicle. On April 25, 1898, Munson demonstrated his invention. It was operated either as a generator or a motor, according to the speed of the engine. The armature or revolving part of the electrical machine was the flywheel of the engine. The engine and electric machine were slow speed units ranging from 250 to 500 revolutions per minute. Adjacent to the machine was a two-speed gearbox with a friction type clutch activated by a lever in front of the driver to provide a slow speed when needed and a high speed for good roads. A secondary shaft from this transmission provided direct drive by spur gears to the differential gear on the rear axle. Munson's brochure features two buggies but also a 12–15 hp delivery wagon, weighing 3,000 to 3,500 pounds (1300 to 1500 kg) with hauling capacity of 3,000 pounds. One of these, lettered *The Fair*, was used Ernst J. Lehmann for his popular Chicago Discount Department Store.

Over in Maidstone, Kent, southeast England, William Arthur Stevens had built his first petrol-electric vehicle using designs patented by Percival Harry Frost-Smith. A petrol engine was connected to an electrical generator and the current produced passed to a traction motor that drove the rear wheels. Stevens also patented a system for converting conventional petrol buses run by Thomas Tilling for either battery-electric or petrol-electric propulsion. The Tilling-Stevens system was also used for trucks and fire engines.

In Spain, in 1898, Field Marshall Emilio de la Cuadra founded a company called General Española de Coches Automóviles, based in Barcelona. He teamed up with Carlos Vellino, a Swiss battery-maker also residing in that city, in order to start an electric vehicle production. Their "empresa hispano-suiza" planned to offer four types of vehicles such as a two-seat car, a van, and a five-ton truck. At the same time, de la Cuadra was the representative of German Benz vehicles in Spain. So, the hybrid solution was to combine Vellino's batteries with Benz engines. The first registered order was a bus for Barcelona's Hotel Oriente on Las Ramblas to transport its guests to the Estación de Francia railway station. For the 20-passenger luxurious vehicle, Vellino's lighter weight batteries would power twin electric motors of 15 kW each, with a total power of 43 hp, enough for the vehicle to reach 20 kph and overcome slopes up to 12 percent. Electricity would also power external and internal lighting. A 15 hp generator set would recharge the batteries during its journey. In August 1900, the press was summoned to make the official presentation of the bus outside the company's facilities, where a demonstration would be made along the Victoria highway. The vehicle started, left the factory, traveled a few meters then stopped, to the despair of its builders. Efforts to get it going again proved unsuccessful. The bus had to be towed back to the factory workshops by a horse. Vellino disappeared, leaving his colleague, a 22-year-old Swiss engineer named Marc Birkigt, to sort things out using more conventional batteries. This was also unsuccessful, so in the end the Hispano-Suiza Company went over to designing and building 100 percent gas engines for automobiles and airplanes. It would be another 40 years before the company even planned an electric truck.

In 1899, Hippolyte Vladimirovich Romanov, related to the Imperial family, built and demonstrated the first domestic electric car called the *Ekomobil* along the streets of Saint Petersburg, Russia. During the next 15 years Romanov designed and built a range of electric vehicles, including an omnibus capable of carrying 17 people at a speed of 20 kph over a distance of 60 km, and a patent for a single-rail electric overhead railway. He also tested four electric trucks. The Saint Petersburg City Council authorized Romanov to developed a plant to build his range. He boldly anticipated that within three years he could produce 400 doubles and 300 four-seaters. Unable to obtain state financing from the Russian Duma with its vested interests in horse traffic, in 1917 Romanov fled to New York, where he later invented things such as an anti-gas respirator, reinforced concrete sheeting and packaging.[16]

During this period some silent electric vehicles, including trucks, had to be equipped with small bells to announce their approach. The clip-clop of horses' hooves had been reassuring.

B. Altman, R.H. Macy's, Gimbels', Tiffany, Abraham and Straus, and Gorham in New York and Houghton & Dutton in Boston were among the first companies to purchase electric commercial vehicles. Since 1865, Benjamin Altman as chief of a luxury department story in midtown Manhattan had employed horse-drawn delivery wagons but began to experiment with electric trucks in 1898 as a cost-cutting measure. The first were built by Frederick R. Wood & Sons, of New York, using a Westinghouse motor, and running gear from the Riker Electric Motor Company of Brooklyn. This transmission system was built on a framework of tubular steel where the batteries were arranged in crates so that the number of crates used was varied according to weight and capacity of the vehicle. It was claimed that distances from 25 to 30 miles (40 to 50 km) at a 9 mph rate could be obtained on one charge of batteries.[17] Before long, Woods Motor Vehicle Company could present more than 30 styles in its electric lineup, including the private broughams, theater and road wagons, cabriolet and landau models. One of the earliest, if not the first automobile display advertisement, to run in the *Chicago Tribune* newspaper, was placed by this company. Appearing in the Thursday, Septem-ber 21, 1899, *Tribune*, the simple, illustrated announcement suggested readers drop Woods a postcard with their name and address, so that a representative could call on them with one of their vehicles to demonstrate, or, at least mail readers a catalog upon request. Prompt deliveries of their vehicles were promised in 30 to 90 days. One of their clients was the U.S. Army, for assignments in general transportation. Brigadier General Adolphus Greely, Chief Signal Officer of the U.S. Army, purchased three Woods electric automobiles for use by his officers. The inventory listing included a notation that vehicles were so equipped that a mule could be hitched to it in case the automobile did not run. Fischer Equipment Company of Chicago also delivered two heavy electric delivery wagons to the Corps. These wagons, with range of 30 miles (48 km) at an average speed of 12 mph (20 kph), were also fitted with attachments so horses could be used—if necessary.[18]

That year, Andrew Riker established a new plant for the Riker Electric Company at Elizabeth, New Jersey, to produce a full line of electric commercial delivery trucks. Riker's first big electric truck was proclaimed as the world's largest, measuring all of 14 ft long × 6 ft wide (4 m × 1.6 m). When loaded, the truck carried 6 tons, the batteries accounting for 1½ tons. Two 10 hp electric motors, geared directly to the rear wheelers, achieved 5 mph (8 kph) when fully loaded. An electric cab in Boston demonstrated its capabilities by pulling a 17-ton load for nearly one mile.

The Columbia Automobile Company introduced an electric emergency wagon, built to accommodate a crew of four or five men. It was equipped

In 1900, Andrew L. Riker of Elizabethport, New Jersey, built a series of electric vehicles. Here Riker stands behind his wagon watching progress (American Historical Truck Society).

with fire extinguishers, extension ladder, stretcher, lanterns and a complete kit of linemen's tools and apparatus. The vehicle weighed 4,500 lbs. (2040 kg) and had a range of 18 miles (30 km) at a speed of 10 mph (16 kph).

In November 1900, the first National Auto Show of the Automobile Club of America was held at Madison Square Garden in New York City. This included the first annual automobile parade, held in downtown Manhattan, filmed by Edison's kinetoscope camera showing nearly every driver wearing a top hat. The most prominent display of commercial vehicles was by Riker, which displayed, in addition to a "golf break," an electric street-railway repair wagon, a 20-passenger bus, a patrol wagon and a delivery truck. A special ramp was built at the show to demonstrate the hill-climbing prowess of the different "horseless horses." Five electric delivery wagons also staged a quick-stop contest; driving 100 ft., the drivers stopped as quickly as possible. Stopping distances varied from 6 to 23 feet (2 to 7 m), and their times varied from 5.8 to 8.6 seconds. Reports of this event published in *The New York Journal* and its rival *The New York Herald* were delivered by fleets of electric trucks.

In this first year of the 20th century, Altman's had a fleet of 12 trucks making twice-daily trips from midtown Manhattan to Harlem. Each one was fitted with two series-wound motors, each of 2 kW, and the motors were geared to the rear wheels, three speeds ahead and two astern. The maximum speed was 9 mph (15 kph) and range was 30 miles (50 km) on good roads. The MV7 type 44-cell battery was supplied by the Electric Storage Battery Company. The vehicle was finished in a very superior manner, having electric side lights and combination voltmeter and ammeter. Commodious quarters for the storage of the Altman fleet and up-to-date charging facilities were provided. In the basement of the imposing five-story structure on West Eighteenth Street, called the "stable," the engine and boilers generated electricity for both the department store and the fleet. By 1901 the total number of electric vehicles owned by the firm was 12, but the building of an additional number was contemplated. The total equipment consisted of 121 new delivery wagons and 14 trucks. Several of these were gasoline-powered. An operator and a deliveryman were assigned to each vehicle and no difficulty was experienced in training the men. This fleet reliably remained in Altman's service for over twenty-five years.

Altman's use of electric trucks particularly interested Thomas A. Edison, who asked permission to experiment with one of them as part of his ongoing mission to develop a new type of storage battery that could extend its radius of travel. Since 1889, the inventor from Menlo Park had been looking for a way to make batteries lighter, more reliable, and at least three times more powerful so that they could become the basis of a successful electric car. He created the Primary Battery Division of the Edison Manufacturing Company to produce these batteries. Edison and his team of assistants conducted tests of all sorts of metals and other materials, looking for those that would work best in batteries. Everything that had been published on the subject of non-acid batteries was reviewed then abstracted, including all applicable French, German, British and American patents going back to the start of the nineteenth century.[19]

In June 1899, Edison ordered stocks of zinc, copper and copper oxide for his West Orange laboratory and for the next 13 months the laboratory notebooks were filled with experiments in the CuO-KOH-Zn system. The tests numbered in the thousands and lasted until he finally declared his battery finished. The battery consisted of a cathode made of nickel and an anode made of iron, bathed in a potassium hydroxide alkaline solution. True to character, Edison announced the new battery with great fanfare and made bold claims about its performance. He claimed his nickel-iron design to be far superior to batteries using lead plates and acid.

Manufacturers and users of electric vehicles, which now included many urban delivery and transport trucks, began buying the Edison battery, including companies such as Detroit Electric and Baker Electric. Edison also had several patents: U.S. Patent 678,722/1901, U.S. Patent 692,507/1902, and German patent No 157,290/1901.

Then stories about battery failures started coming out. Many of the batteries began to leak, and others lost much of their power too quickly. The new nickel-graphite conductors were failing. Engineers who tested the batteries found that while lightweight, the new alkaline battery did not significantly out-perform an ordinary lead-acid battery.

Edison shut down the factory immediately, and between 1905 and 1908, the whole battery was redesigned. Edison came up with a new design, and although the new battery used more expensive materials, it had better performance and more power. Edison found that layering nickel hydrate and pure nickel flake gave the best performance. The flake was obtained by dipping copper cylinders in a copper bath, leaving a coating of copper. The process was repeated until each cylinder was coated with 125 layers of copper alternating with 125 layers of nickel. By 1910, battery production was again underway at a new factory near the West Orange, New Jersey, laboratory, where 3,000 storage cells could be manufactured during each 10-hour day. In 1911, Thomas Edison negotiated with J.P. Morgan, Jr., for the promotion of his battery in Great Britain. In 1913, U.S. Edison set up Edison Accumulators Ltd. (Telegraphic address: "Edibatt") in London to import and sell vehicles and batteries, employing an electrical engineer, Raymond Mitchell, to oversee their promotion and installation. During the inaugural luncheon at the new premises in December 1913, Lord Montagu and others spoke hopefully of the future of the electric delivery van and heavy lorry on show with their Edison steel battery, if and when ample supplies of current all over the country became obtainable at one penny per unit. Among their first orders were a fleet used by Islington Town Council for road-sprinkling, and others for the Pullars Dye Works, Osram electric lamps and Johnnie Walker whiskey.

A colleague of Thomas A. Edison, German-born Sigmund Bergmann, had already established a successful business in New York City selling Edison batteries, electrical lighting, telephone equipment and typewriters when in 1906, he decided to return to Berlin and set up a similar company, the Deutsche Edison Akkumulatoren Company (DEAC), then also Bergmann-Elektriztatswerk for making trucks. By 1912, Bergmann was offering a 2-ton truck with 24 hp motor and a 4-ton truck with 32 hp motor. During the First World War, the Berlin concern built army trucks: 3.5-ton with 38 hp and 4.5-ton with 40 hp. Some of these were used by the Luftwaffe.

Meanwhile, the electric truck business had continued to grow. In 1898, Consolidated Ice of New York asked for bids to convert 1,000 horse-driven wagons to power-driven vehicles. The following year, the U.S. Post Office Department began experimenting with powered vehicles. Testing a Winton electric automobile for mail collection in July 1899 in Buffalo, New York, it only took an hour-and-a-half to collect mail from 40 boxes, less than half the time it took the horse-powered wagon. During the next 100 years, it would often be the postal services, at home and abroad, that would lead with electric delivery trucks. In 1900, New York City and Los Angeles newspapers began using electric trucks for newspaper distribution.

In December 1899, B. Dreher & Sons of Cleveland, Ohio, used a Woods Motor Vehicle truck for delivering pianos around Chicago. Alexander H. Revell, also of that city, who had been operating twenty double horse teams for furniture delivery, went over to trucks. E.A. Hunt of Syracuse, New York, replaced his two teams of horses and two wagons with the Vehicle Equipment Company's truck to collect and deliver laundry.

Since time immemorial, the milkman's horse-drawn delivery wagon would pull up to the curb and the milkman would use the traditional 40-quart dip can and ladle to dispense his wares and collect three cents per quart. While horses were being be replaced by electric trucks, milk churns were being replaced by bottles, as invented by Dr. Hervey D. Thatcher, a 48-year-old druggist in Potsdam, New York.

In 1884, Thatcher proposed the use of his bottles to three milk dealers in nearby Ogdensburg, the largest city in the area. One of these, Mr. Wilcox, loaded a few bottles in his wagon on August 6, 1884, and set off for the city. They rested on a bed of straw and were capped with makeshift wooden plugs carved by Batchelder. As a result, the bottles jostled and spilled most of the milk before Wilcox completed the 2½ mile (4 km) journey. Wilcox had to return to his farm that day and start all over with traditional can and ladle. Indignant, he sat down that night and wrote Dr. Thatcher that his bottle system was a failure and would never amount to anything. Soon after, Thatcher replaced his wooden plugs with glass stoppers and the Thatcher Glass Manufacturing Company purchased an Owens automatic bottle machine for its Elmira plant and never looked back, manufacturing millions of milk bottles which were initially transported by electric trucks.[20]

Milton Snavely Hershey was an American confectioner and philanthropist. He founded the Hershey Chocolate Company and the "company town" of Hershey, Pennsylvania. Excited by the potential of milk chocolate, which at that time was a luxury product, Hershey was determined to develop a formula for milk chocolate and market and sell it to the American public. Through trial and error, he created his own formula. The first Hershey bar was produced in November of 1900. That year, Hershey purchased a Riker Electric, built in Elizabethtown, New Jersey. According to the company, the vehicle was purchased to attract attention and make people think that the chocolate company was modern and up-to-date. The arrival of the machine was announced in the Lancaster *New Era* on February 13, 1900:

The Hershey Chocolate Company will have the distinction of having introduced the automobile into Lancaster, and for business purposes, too. One was received here this morning from the Riker Electric Vehicle Company, and it will be put in shape for operating tomorrow, and be used in the delivery service. It will haul a load of about 2,000 pounds [900 kg] and has a storage battery with sufficient power to carry the machine 30 miles [50 km].

After running around Lancaster for a few days—and nights, because the young clerks liked to drive it after hours—it set off on a tour of the cities of Pennsylvania, visiting Allentown, Bethlehem, Scranton, Wilkes-Barre, Pottsville, and other centers. With it was a crew of salesmen with order books in hand, under F.W. Delori. The "operator" was R.C. Orndorff of Baltimore. Reporters in the various cities through which the truck passed noted that it had won a $1,500 prize at New York's recent Madison Square Garden Automobile Show, that it cost $2,000 (some said $2,500), weighed 3,500 pounds (1,588 kg), had four storage batteries (each weighing 300 lbs./136 kg), and was equipped with electric lights, an electric bell, a brass "steering apparatus," and brakes. Its top speed was 9 mph (15 kph).[21]

From May to October 1901, a Columbia Mark XI electric delivery wagon built by the Electric Vehicle Company of New York transported mail between the Buffalo Post Office and a temporary postal station at the nearby Pan-American Exhibition. It could carry 1,000 lbs. (450 kg) besides the driver and letter carrier and was able to travel 40 miles (60 km) on one charge.

During one weekend in October 1901, electric vehicle races took place between local builders Woods Motor Vehicle Company and Hewitt-Lindstrom Motor Company at the Washington Park Race Track, as part of the Chicago Auto Show. Charles Lindstrom was an inventor and held many patents on mechanisms to be used in cars. Among those listed by the U.S. Patent office are brakes for electric motors, an electric carriage, a supporting frame for motors of electric carriages and a controller switch. Perhaps the most interesting is the work he did on the "perches" of the vehicles, which permit the wheels to adapt to the inequalities of the road (what we today call suspension). In the long race of the meet, first and second prizes were taken by Hewitt-Lindstrom lightweight runabouts with a winning time of 15 minutes and 4 seconds. The special two-mile Ladies' Race was won by M.A. Ryan, with Charles Lindstrom's 13-year-old daughter Jeanette Lindstrom wearing a straw hat with flowers, coming in second, both in the Hewitt-Lindstrom vehicles with a time of 6 minutes and 43 seconds. In a special one-mile race of electric vehicles of standard type, Alfred F. Leopold came in first; Bruce Clark second, both in Woods vehicles, in a time of just over 3 minutes. But most relevant to our history, there was a two-mile *postal truck* competition in the novel form of a mail-collecting contest between three electrics. Eight mailboxes were placed at various distances around the course, with a blank card within.

Each driver had a key, and during the course of five miles was supposed to open a box each time he passed, write his initials on the card and lock the box, making 40 stops in all. The Woods owned by the Siegel & Cooper department store (the largest and most opulent store the world had ever seen, sprawling out over 18 acres of selling space), won in 44 min 20.4 seconds.

In spite of taking part in these races, by 1902, the Hewitt-Lindstrom company had dissolved for unknown reasons.[22]

In October 1901, the U.S. Postal Department contracted with the Republic Motor Vehicle Company for five electric vehicles, with operators, to collect mail from boxes in Minneapolis and to carry mail between the Minneapolis Post Office and its stations for a trial period of seventeen months. Some rural mail carriers, who supplied their own vehicles, also used electric models. According to an article in the May 9, 1909, issue of the *New York Times*, a rural carrier in Manchester, New Hampshire, used his Waverley electric automobile to deliver mail during the warmer months of the year beginning in 1905.

In 1901, Robert Lloyd founded the Vehicle Electric Company in Brooklyn, New York, together with Lucas T. Gibbs, with the declared purpose to manufacture chassis of an electric car for which the American coachbuilders had to provide the bodywork. When the plan was about to be realized, the coachbuilders were no longer interested so the company decided to start its own production. Among their first clients was Tiffany & Company, the luxury jewelry store. By 1903, the Rainier Company, acting as sole agents for Vehicle Electric Company, proclaimed them as "The Largest Builders of Electric Vehicles in the World." Among their clients were: the Anheuser-Busch brewery with 24 trucks; Christian Schmidt & Sons brewery with 15 trucks; Jas A Hearn & Sons, 17 trucks; and Adams Express Co., 20 trucks. In 1905, the Vehicle Electric Company burned down, but the following year, it was bought by General Electric and became General Vehicle or GV. A new factory was built in Long Island City which began to turn out electric trucks. From 1907, the GV design was standardized with all parts interchangeable. Payloads ranged from 750 lbs. to five tons. By 1910, it had sold more than 1,600 units. American Express purchased 58 GV trucks in 1912. According to an advertisement, 1,091 GV trucks had been sold in one city alone. In another ad, published in *The Motor Age* on January 2, 1913, GV stated that of their trucks, leading retailers used 488, express companies 300, brewers 522, manufacturers and wholesalers thousands more. Their trucks were in use from Portland, Maine, to San Diego, California, and from Toronto, Canada, to Dallas, Texas, while Rio de Janeiro and Havana had 13. The biggest fleet of 250 trucks was owned by the Adams Express Company for a freight and cargo transport business in Rochester, Brooklyn, Indianapolis, and Philadelphia.

GV were part of a trend. After a slow start around 1895, total electric vehicle sales in America reached the $30 million mark in 1913. Of the 30,000 electric vehicles sold, some 20,000 were cars or "pleasure vehicles," and the rest for commercial use. Businesses using these wagons or trucks were not mavericks but expert bean counters, some of whom are around to this day. Just 41 of these business establishments owned 1,759 electric vehicles at the time, and four had fleet sizes of 100 or more. Needless to say, they had invested in the vehicles after careful trials. The American Express Company, for instance, had placed orders for more than 80 electric chassis after trialing 20-odd vehicles.

Electrics were known to be durable, as this comment shows: "95% of all the commercial electric vehicles installed during the past eight years are successfully operating, while several installations show over 15 years of actual service. Even the US government have more than 75 electric trucks."[23]

In 1902, in New York City, Macy's flagship store moved uptown to Herald Square at 34th Street and Broadway, so far north of the other main dry goods emporia that it had to offer a steam wagonette to transport customers from 14th Street to 34th Street. Soon after, Macy's converted to 15 electric trucks which had always done their day's work by 6:00 p.m. whereas horse-drawn rigs had not returned until 10:00 or 11:00 p.m.

In New York City, piano delivery was much easier by electric truck because, in addition to moving the instrument from warehouse to customer, the battery could power a winch to lift the piano into the apartment or house. Similarly, central stations fitted electric trucks with a lighting tower, a flying bridge from which the driver could both operate the vehicle and adjust the street lamp lights. These specialized vehicles served limited markets.

In 1903, some 700 trucks were built in the USA, most of them electric. An article in the March 4, 1904, issue of the *Dry Goods Reporter* quoted the manager of Marshall Field's shipping department: "We use only electric machines as the odor of gasoline, in our opinion, injures the goods."[24]

Wells Fargo Express, the oldest bank in the West, also invested in an electric fleet for its Pony Express.

Often, those who had taken the initiative of transferring over to electric trucks were already dynamic entrepreneurs. Adolphus Green, William Moore and John G. Zeller merged to form the American Biscuit and Manufacturing Company in 1890 after acquiring 40 different bakeries. This resulted in the National Biscuit Company (NABISCO), a company with 114 bakeries across the USA. The word "biscuit" is a traditional term for what are now termed "cookies" and "crackers" in American English. To preserve the crackers' crispness, the marketer packaged them in airtight, waxed paper-lined packages. For delivery, NABISCO chose electric trucks.

Over in Great Britain, electric vehicle makers had a good choice of battery makers: Faure-Sellon-Volckmar, Fulmen, BGS Modified Fulmen, Faure-

King, Rosenthal "National" cell, and Lee-Coll (lead and zinc with cadmium). In 1902, Arthur Brunel Chatwood B.Sc. of Chatwood-Milner Ltd. safe and lock manufacturers in Liverpool, Lancashire, a member of the Institution of Civil Engineers, had been asked to design some electric trucks for a firm of steel-merchants—electric instead of steam. The region in which Chatwood lived was full of cotton mills and he believed that there was a large field in the south of Lancashire for heavy 5-ton load electric lorries. We do not know whether this e-truck ever went into service. In 1908, Chatwood went out to Hyderabad as astronomer to the Nizam's government, building and organizing the observatory there.[25] In 1904, the Great Western Railway shipped over a Riker car chassis, fitted it with their own bodywork and then operated it out of Paddington Station, claiming it as the first commercial electric truck to operate in the United Kingdom.

Thomas Parker, electrical engineer of Wolverhampton, England, set up a battery-manufacturing business financed by Paul Bedford Elwell, whose family had a factory there that made nails and horse shoes. In 1893, an American branch of Elwell-Parker was founded in Cleveland, Ohio. Searching for electric motors for his lift-trucks, industrialist Alexander Brown came across Elwell-Parker and purchased the rights to manufacture the motors in his factory. Elwell-Parker of Cleveland, Ohio, soon built up a fine reputation for some of the most reliable electric vehicles, including a 6-ton street truck built in 1903 that at the time was the largest battery-powered vehicle ever produced, a distinction it held until 1942. Looking for ways to diversify the company's product lines and to improve business, E-P transferred a 30-year-old draftsman named Morris S. Towson to the 23-person shop on St. Clair Street. In 1906, Towson innovated a battery-powered baggage transport known as the "electric porter." The first model was essentially an ordinary hand truck with batteries and an Elwell-Parker motor installed below the deck. It was easy to start and move but difficult to stop, and soon Towson added other features such as an operator platform and a mechanical brake. Efficiency at sites such as Pennsylvania Railroad's Jersey City Terminal quadrupled overnight. The electric porter proved a major success and was soon being exported to railroads and ports (where they were called electric stevedores) around the world. By 1910, Morris Towson noticed that some industrial shops had begun using Elwell-Parker's baggage trucks for interplant haulage. As time went on, newer trucks designed by Elwell-Parker revolutionized storage methods in the country, manufacturing platform and pallet lift-trucks that raised and lowered cargo at various heights (beginning of the modern-day forklift). Elwell-Parker trucks could be seen handling paper rolls, heavy cargo and various other products.

In 1906, when American retail magnate Harry Gordon Selfridge traveled to London on vacation with his wife Rose, he noticed that although the city was a cultural and commercial leader, its stores could not rival Marshall Field's in Chicago or the great galleries of Parisian department stores. Recognizing a gap in the market, Selfridge, who had become bored with retirement, decided to invest £400,000 in a new department store of his own, locating it in what was then the unfashionable western end of London's Oxford Street but which was opposite an entrance to the Bond Street tube station. From the start, Selfridges & Co. boasted a large fleet of delivery vans. At first, they were horse-drawn vehicles but, inspired by the examples of Marshall Field back in Chicago, they were later replaced by imported Walker Electric Trucks. The company livery, the letter "S" in a laurel crown, was emblazed on the outside of every van, and they soon became a common sight all over London. Customers liked the fact that they could order big bulky items of furniture and arrange for them to be delivered to their homes, with the added advantage that their neighbors might see that they shop at the new Selfridges store. Delivery trucks were also used by Carter Paterson, a British road haulage firm, closely associated with the railway industry and by London breweries such as Whitbread & Co. Ltd. and Meux's Brewery Co. Ltd. (founded in 1761).

From 1905, hat manufacturer Henry H. Roelfs & Co. used a delivery truck made by the Vehicle Equipment Company and stored it in the company's horse stables. Its energy came from 15 plate, 44 cell Exide batteries, washed out once a week. For recharging, in the floor of the stable Roelfs sank an ordinary range boiler in which a door was cut and through which the charging wires ran, connecting directly with the factory dynamo room. An electric bell attachment gave notice to the engineer when to turn the current on and off when recharging began and when complete.

During this time, engineers such as Henry Ford, Charles Brady King, Alexander Winton and Ransom Eli Olds had been working on their gasoline automobiles—noisy, belching fumes, not entirely reliable but quick to refuel. At first electric truck manufacturers did not see this as a threat.

On May 20-21, 1903, at a commercial vehicle contest and test trials involving 11 vehicles, six were steam-powered, four gasoline-engine and only one electric. Nineteen hundred four was the first year truck registrations were counted separately from automobile registrations. Trucks totaled 700, and most were electric, with steam a close second. In 1905, nine electric and seven gasoline commercial cars were displayed at the New York Automobile Show.

Others continued to combine the two propulsion systems. In 1903, Lars G. Nilson of the Fischer Motor Vehicle Company of Hoboken, New Jersey, invented an "electrogasolene"/petrol-electric system whereby a three-cylinder gas engine was linked to an EMF dynamo to power both a bus (two electric motors) and a truck (one motor) also incorporating regenerative braking. The London General Omnibus Company ordered a total of 10 Fischer hybrids, but the London Metropolitan Police refused to license the bus. In October 1903, the LGOC asked to have it taken back and to be refunded the cost.[26]

Some engineers were particularly innovative. In 1904, Melvin Church of Grand Rapids, Michigan, and Karsten Knudson of Chicago, Illinois, built and patented a truck with a 2 hp gyroscopic electric motor on each wheel. This allowed all four wheels to steer and allowed for the elimination of a differential. The original motors designed in 1904 were located within the hollow wheels. The truck used storage batteries capable of lasting a 40-mile radius of the town before a charge. The unique propulsion utilized a streetcar type controller consisting of five points of speed (three forward and two reverse). Church and Knudson set up the Holson Motor Patent Company and exhibited their prototype at the Coliseum Automobile Show in Chicago in 1905. There they demonstrated their Holson truck's ability to turn in exceptionally narrow spaces. A number of these trucks went into service. Melvin Church continued to innovate: a gas-electric "combination" truck solved range limitations, as used by the Grabowsky Power Wagon Co., in Detroit, Michigan.

Among those closely involved with Edison's batteries was John M. Lansden, Jr., son of a highly respected attorney. From 1901, Lansden, his brother David S. Lansden and their associate William M. Little of Alabama had been running the Birmingham Electric Manufacturing Company, producing electric elevators, light and power plants, signal and wiring systems, electric cranes, hoists and pumping plants, when they started to experiment with electric vehicles, one a car and the other a wagon. In a letter to Edison, dated 1903, Lansden writes:

> I have both machines well under way, and propose to complete them, [and] send the up to you.... When may I get the batteries for the two machines? I believe that these two cars, when fully developed will meet the usual requirements in a commercial field, without difficulty, barring the rubber tire question. My ultimate object has been for the past few years, to turn out a common-sense machine in every respect, and with your valued opinions and suggests, and interest in my efforts, I am anxiously awaiting the results of any test or trial you may give them, when completed.[27]

Edison replied:

> If the vehicles turn out well, I can probably introduce you to people who will furnish capital to go ahead in a modest way.... If you want a loan of $1000 for six months on the vehicles, you can have it. I am anxious that a practical vehicle shall be put on the market.

The loan was accepted and in August, Edison was advising Lansden that for a good motor he should deal directly either with Alexander James Churchward of Chicago, Illinois, assignor to General Electric in New York, who among his many inventions had patented a synchronous AC motor and also a current regulator for DC motors. But on August 4 Lansden wrote to Edison:

> We have not yet been able to hear from Mr. Churchward regarding the two motors for our vehicles. We have now reached the stage of our work when we need them.... We have not taken the matter of motors up with the Westinghouse people,... Our machines are well underway and we will be ready for the batteries in two or three weeks. We have two Elwell-Parker motors which would fit for our temporary service if there is any delay on the other motor.

In 1901, the Westinghouse Electric & Manufacturing Company of Pittsburgh, Pennsylvania, had purchased the patents of bankrupt Hub Motors Company of Chicago, as taken out by Fred J. Newman and Joseph Ledwinka, for one 10 hp electric motor placed in each wheel. According to their catalog:

> From the very inception of the electric vehicle, Westinghouse Electrical & Manufacturing company assisted in its successful development by securing the service of experts to design and manufacture suitable electrical equipment such as motors, controllers, cut-switches, charging receptacles and plugs for use in electric vehicles. They have developed a complete line of motors ranging from that required for the smallest runabout to that for a ten-ton truck. Two windings are provided for each size frame—one for the 80-volt and one for the 60 volt classification to be used with lead-acid and Edison batteries respectively. The motor frame is made of cast steel and its cylindrical in form with one end open and the other end partly closed. The brush holders, of the radial sliding box type, are made of high-grade graphite. Braided copper shunts protect the brush springs. The armature is built up on a cast-iron spider.... A corps of experts devote their time to the design, manufacture and sale of electric vehicle equipment, and experienced engineers are always read to assist prospective manufacturers in selecting the proper equipment.[28]

Edison advised Landsen:

> Don't wait for Churchward. Use Westinghouse Motors and hurry vehicle forward. We can put batteries in here and place our Laboratory Machine shop at your disposal to make changes after wrecking trials.

> On September 25, Lansden delivered a progress report:

> Despite delays, we have received the Westinghouse motors and we are using Goodyear tires, endless solid tires on the express wagon and their flat tread detachable pneumatic on the passenger car. I am now counting on shipment in the middle of October. We can promise you two very successful machines from every standpoint.

In later November, the Lansden vehicles were shipped from Birmingham, Alabama, the thousand miles to New Jersey and in 1904, a corporation with the name The Lansden Company was formed, its namesake inventor having taken up residence nearby. Following a trial where one truck made a run from Washington to New York, production began. Whenever the Lansden Co. found its supply running low, Edison's plant ceased manufacturing all other products to concentrate instead on churning out more batteries. In 1906,

Lansden obtained a patent for a reduced friction wheel and three years later for more resilient suspension for trucks. In 1908, Edison even took a controlling interest in the company. Lansden vehicles were also put to use as ambulances, buses and brewery wagons. A few of the company's more high-profile customers were Wells Fargo, Bellevue Hospital, the New York Public Library System, and rival department stores Macy's and Gimbel Brothers. During the 1911 Chicago Auto Show at the Coliseum in Chicago, Lansden exhibited Adams Express Company's creation: "*Adam*, the oldest living power wagon with the nerve to make the run from Washington to New York made in 1904, worked every day since, will be at the Madison Square Garden Show, Jan. 16 to 23rd as the guest of the Lansden Company, Newark, N.J. Edison Battery."

Edison might have desired a monopoly. For a time, his American rivals were the Exide *Ironside* and the Philadelphia Storage Battery Company which began making batteries for electric vehicles in 1906. Eventually, Philco moved away to supply batteries to the infant radio industry.

After a few years of formidable productivity and sales, Edison's Lansden Company ran into rough times. This is evidenced by the company's end of

The banner on the side of this Lansden truck explains it all (U.S. Dept. of the Interior, National Park Service, Thomas Edison National Historical Park).

the year profit and loss account for 1910: "Orders received May 21st: none. Bank Balance: $227.96." Under this, Edison penciled in the word "Rotten." This is backed up by correspondence between W.E. Eldridge of the Electric Wagon Company in Boston and Edison.[29] It begins with a letter written on October 11, 1911, by Eldridge:

> The facts are these: On March 15th 1911 I entered into an arrangement with the Lansden Company to act as selling agent. Notwithstanding that "demonstrations" of commercial vehicles prove nothing and are a waste of time and money, Mr. Morgan insisted that two "demonstrators" be ordered and refused to make the arrangement otherwise. Accordingly two wagons were ordered—a 1-ton and a 2-ton. Mr. Morgan stated that he had a 1-ton on hand "practically new" which he desired me to take. When it came I found that it must have been run many thousand miles. The tires were half worn out, the body old, rough and hastily painted over. Mr. Morgan had simply unloaded some dead stock at an exorbitant price. Meanwhile I had engaged a capable manager for the agency, hired an office and a man to operate the "demonstrator." Advertising in the papers was started and a few trucks sold. In the first flush of enthusiasm I did not ship back Mr. Morgan's "gold brick" as I should have, but tried to make shift with it. I soon found that the wagon was doing more harm than good. Soon rumors began to come along that the Lansden Company would get out new and better models. Realising that it was useless to try and get business with models about to become obsolete, I cancelled the order for the 2-ton wagon, and put the 1-ton on storage. On July 14th I made the request that the Lansden Company take this 1-ton off my hands. On July 21st I asked

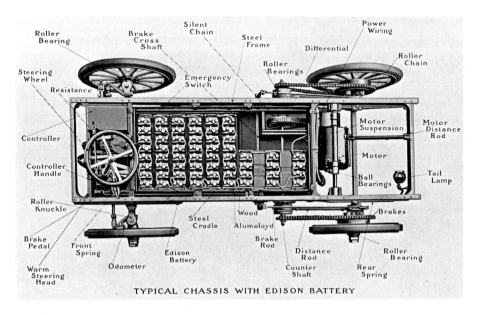

TYPICAL CHASSIS WITH EDISON BATTERY

This cutaway diagram shows the layout of a Lansden truck, complete with Edison batteries (U.S. Dept. of the Interior, National Park Service, Thomas Edison National Historical Park).

SOME PROMINENT USERS *of* THE LANSDEN ELECTRIC

Abraham & Straus
Adams Express Co.
Aitken, Son & Co.
American Meter Co.
The Arlington Co.
Armour & Co.
Atlantic Ice & Coal Corporation
Bayonne Hospital
Bellevue Hospital
H. W. Boettger Silk Finishing Co.
Boston Rubber Shoe Co.
Carew Manufacturing Co.
Columbia Storage Warehouses
Commonwealth Edison Co.
Cornelius Hotel
D. L. & W. Railroad Co.
The Albert Dickinson Co.
Eagle Printing Ink Co.
Edison Chemical Works
Edison Electric Illuminating Co. of Brooklyn
Edison Phonograph Works
Edison Storage Battery Co.
Thomas A. Edison
George Ehret
Empire State Dairy Co.
New York Edison Co.
Chas. Eneu Johnson & Co.
Fairfield Dairy Co.
Forbes & Wallace
Robert Gair Co.
Gimbel Bros.
Globe Storage & Carpet Cleaning Co.
Hamburg-American Line
Harrisburg Light, Heat & Power Co.
Hartmann Brewing Co.
James A. Hearn & Son
The Higbee Co.
A. G. Hyde & Son
International Provision Co.
Jersey Biscuit Co.
Jewish Daily News Co.
Lalance & Grosjean Mfg. Co.
John C. Letts Grocery Co.
Lewandos French Dyeing & Cleaning Co.

August Luchow
R. H. Macy & Co.
Henry Maillard
Mandel Bros.
Manhattan Electrical Supply Co.
Massachusetts Homeopathic Hospital
Metropolitan Opera Co.
The Jacob Metzger Co.
Mishawaka Woolen Mfg. Co.
Eugene E. Nice
Northwestern Supply Co.
F. J. Newcomb Mfg. Co.
New York Dock Co.
New York Hospital
New York Public Library
New York & Springfield Despatch
New York Telephone Co.
New York Transportation Co.
Olds, Wortman & King
Olson Cartage Co.
Olympus Hotel
T. K. Orton
Otis Elevator Co.
D. Pender Grocery Co.
Presbyterian Hospital
Public Service Corporation
Sauquoit Silk Mfg. Co.
J. H. Small & Sons
Hotel Seattle
F. G. Smith Piano Co.
Springfield Waste Co.
Standard Varnish Works
Steinway & Sons
Hotel Stewart
The Surbrug Co.
Thompson & Norris Co.
United States Express Co.
A. A. Vantine & Co.
Virginia Railway & Power Co.
Wilkinson, Gaddis & Co.
Williams Printing Co.
Winchester Repeating Arms Co.
Witman Bros.
Henry R. Worthington
Wells-Fargo & Co. Express

AMERICAN LITHOGRAPHIC CO., N. Y.

This list gives an idea of the range of clients who used Lansden trucks (U.S. Dept. of the Interior, National Park Service, Thomas Edison National Historical Park).

for a reply to this letter and I have still not received one. Mr. Doty has suggested that I sell the wagon at a price which would cover my investment in it. Mr. Doty knows it cannot be done. My Lansden experience has cost me about $1,300 spent for expenses plus $1,500 paid on account of the truck. Credit is due to me for commissions on sales to the Boston Rubber Shoe Co., the Lowell Electric Light Co. and the Mass. Homeopathic Hospital. No proper account has ever been rendered. My means are limited and this is a serious matter with me; I entered into the arrangement in good faith and I have been abominably treated. I have every confidence that you will promptly see to it that what is right shall be done. Very truly yours."

On this letter, as was typical, Edison penciled a reply:

Buchanan. Investigate this, I want to do the square thing by him but want to know what is the square thing.

Robert A. Buchanan of Lansden reported back:

I believe that Mr. Eldridge was not used properly in the matter in as much as he was told that the won had run but 500 miles and probably had gone 25,000 miles. The chains, sprockets and tires were born badly and the body was poorly constructed, but I have been informed that Mr. Eldridge had the machine he was buying and was apparently satisfied. This however is not reliable information. Mr. Eldridge used this particular wagon to make a demonstration to the Lowell Electric Light Co. on the strength of which he made a sale; also, a wagon practically in the same condition as the one Mr. Eldridge had bought. This is the wagon we had to take back.

On October 28, 1911, Edison replied to Eldridge that if he would return the truck and give full release of all claims, he was willing for the Lansden Company to send him a check for $1,500 on receipt of the wagon at Newark and would cancel his agency contract. Eldridge declined to accept Edison's offer, saying it was not enough. By this time, Eldridge had started his own company, "Couple-Gear" Motor Trucks in Grand Rapids, which could be used on both electric and gasoline trucks, front wheel drive and steer, four-wheel drive and steer. Motors contained in the wheels had a single reduction of 25 to one.

Another letter, found in the same archive box, is equally damning. Dated November 25, 1911, it was sent from Mr. H. Prescott Beach of the popular downtown New York department store, James A. Hearn & Son:

During the almost total tie-up of our business in the holiday season of 1910 when seven or eight of our City vehicles and our two Orange-Montclair and Newark vehicles were being towed in every business day running 25, 26 and 27 miles with batteries listed to do 85 miles, I complained daily to the Lansden Company and many times directly to the Edison Battery Company without receiving assistance. Your batteries at that time were unprotected and no one from the battery company or the Lansden Company (although knowing of our trouble and constantly investigating) suggested that they be protected. Your batteries at that time, were put up in wooden trays, fastened with nails driven from underneath, the points of which rested on the metal cells. It was found that part of the current of the battery was actually being taken in the wooden trays through these nails, the trays being sufficiently charged to give a reading on the meter.

For two weeks a representative of the Lansden Company rode on our Orange-Montclair car to see where and what the troubles were, every single day of which the car was towed. We were informed that this type of vehicle had been originally tested and approved at the Edison Company's works. Your Lansden Company sold us in the Summer of 1910, fifteen chassis and two heavy trucks (Numbers 150 and 151), probably the most inefficient, improperly constructed vehicles being operated in this vicinity today. You yourself sold me that the copper leads of the battery to motor were only one-sixth of what they should be to get benefit of the battery's power. You say nothing of your promises to make good on this point, though you surely have not forgotten. Your own people admitted that the trucks were so inefficient and badly constructed that the Lansden Company ought to have taken them back at the start and refunded the purchase price.

To which Edison penciled in:

Find out what it will cost to put these chassis in good order.

This was done, evidenced by a receipt dated April 1, 1912, from the Lansden Company:

For one half our loss on rebuilding J.A Hearn & Son's Old Lansden Truck No 151 as agreed: $183, then in August 1912 to half the cost of "making good" on 15 old Hearn chassis as agreed: $3840.

Edison, however, refused to give up, determined to produce the reliable electric truck, no matter what it took. Years before, his project to produce an efficient light bulb had involved the fabrication and testing of hundreds of different metal filaments, including platinum, before he arrived at the bamboo lamp. He took the same approach for the electric truck as is evidenced in a report written by J. Chesler on January 9, 1913, entitled "Battery Storage Delivery Wagon Endurance Tests":

In the Spring of 1912, Mr. Edison travelled all over the district (of Newark) within a radius of ten miles of the Works, looking for very rough roads to test the wagon on. After much difficulty a circuit of sixteen miles was mapped out. This road was as rough as could be found, and covered all road conditions, from deep mud and sand to boulders varying in size from two to eight inches. The operator was instructed to follow the mapped course, and never to reduce speed unless to avoid an accident. At various times, an inspector would start in another machine and follow the operator up to see that he kept to the roughest parts of the road. A timekeeper was also put on the job and he kept a schedule of the number of runs made per day and length of time for each run. After each run the vehicle was thoroughly inspected and a report made on any nuts or bolts that had loosened or any parts broken or out of adjustment. We found broken bolts, lost bolts and nuts, fractured frames, axles and loose wheels. It must be remembered that these tests were made on very rough roads with iron-tired wheels in front and rubber-tired in back or driving wheels. Under ordinary conditions on fair roads with front wheels rubber tired the vehicle would probably stand up for a very much longer time. Mr. Edison figures that after a test of one thousand miles with full load of 2,500 lbs [1130 kg] of iron over the test course, he has given the vehicle more abuses and put it to the straining point a great deal oftener than it would get over ten thousand miles in ordinary commercial service. The motor which has driven the vehicle over 7,000 miles [1130 km] still has its first set of brushes and these are only half worn; the battery equipment now consists of eighteen A-8 cells and gives us forty miles on a charge with full load; The vehicle will go up Eagle Rock Hill which is one mile long and averages eighteen per cent grade at the rate of five miles per hour with full load. I believe it is Mr. Edison's intention to build the complete vehicle, unless some manufacturer is willing to take the proposition up, in that case we will sell the whole electrical equipment, that is, motor, controller and battery.[30]

In 1913, Lansden showed a full line of its machines, including an ambulance, a 1,000-pound express wagon, a 1-ton covered express wagon, a 1.5-ton express wagon, a 2-ton express wagon and a special 1-ton emergency wagon built for the Consolidated Gas Company, which was arranged with a special tool tray under the floor.

At precisely this time, Edison and his friend and great admirer, Henry Ford of Detroit, were working on a prototype electric automobile, even though Ford's best-selling gasoline-engined Model T, on the market since 1909, was equipped with a flywheel to avoid using batteries. The Edison-Ford's motor was to be provided by none other than Thomas Churchward. Ford was said to have bought an electricity-generating plant in Niagara Falls, as well as a site off Woodward Avenue specifically for the production of the Edison-Ford. It was reported that the car would sell for somewhere between $500 and $750 and have a range of 100 miles (160 km). The Achilles heel of the project was, ironically, Edison's nickel-iron battery, the very high internal resistance incapable of powering a higher speed longer-range car under many circumstances. Remarkably, four years before, Maud, a Bailey electric automobile equipped with Edison batteries and driven by Captain George W. Langdon, had completed a thousand-mile endurance run from New England to New Hampshire. At any rate, thinking they knew best, Ford engineers decided to replace the Edison-Ford with heavier Exide Ironside batteries behind their employer's back, and when he found out, he was furious. The program quickly fell to the wayside with other projects demanding Ford's time. According to *The Ford Century*, Ford had invested $1.5 million in the electric-car project and nearly bought 100,000 batteries from Edison before the project fell apart.

During this period, Newark, New Jersey, did not, of course, have exclusivity on electric truck development. In 1905, the Canadian Government, realizing that the possibilities of the Dominion with regard to agricultural pursuits were not so widely known in Great Britain as they deserved, decided to send a motor van through the kingdom carrying specimens of Canadian produce, visiting nearly every town and village in the country. Their petrol-electric Advertising Wagon was built by the Commercial Motor Vehicle Company of Windsor, Ontario. The wagon was painted in brilliant vermilion,

Thomas A. Edison contemplates his nickel-iron battery, developed in the West Orange, New Jersey, laboratory, on which he placed great hopes for the future of electric vehicles and trucks (U.S. Dept. of the Interior, National Park Service, Thomas Edison National Historical Park).

with gilt lettering: written on the front end of the wagon was "Canada. The Granary of the Empire."[31]

In 1906, the Pennsylvania Railroad introduced battery-powered platform trucks for moving luggage at their Altoona, Pennsylvania, train station. The controls were placed so that the operator had to walk out in front. So popular was the idea of pedestrian-powered trucks that their use rapidly extended to other lines of industry. For example, Anheuser-Busch Brewery's fleet totaled 25 trucks.

In 1904, the Alden Sampson Manufacturing Company of Pittsfield, Massachusetts, entered the motor trade, and three years later they had come up with what they called a Road Train. This six-wheeled petrol-electric unit could supply energy to up to four separate 17 ft. long (5 m) self-propelling units, giving a total length of 70 ft. (2 m). Both central wheels on the generator unit were driven by electro-motors. Interest was shown by American manufacturers and miners in those districts far removed from railways. The Commercial Truck Company of Philadelphia, Pennsylvania, also produced large electric trucks. Their half-ton and one-ton wagons were each fitted with a single motor to the rear axle by means of the Morse-Williams driving gear. For heavier loads of two to five tons, a separate motor was used for each wheel giving a four-wheel drive.[32]

Not all businesses were managed well. Apart from his record-breaking racing career, Camille Jenatzy also tried to enter the petrol-electric market. In the UK, Messrs H.M. Hobson Ltd. exhibited a 30 hp heavy lorry fitted with the Jenatzy patent suspension, but it did not prove successful. Dr. Edward Ernest Lehwess of the Electric Van Wagon and Omnibus Company presented a range of electric trucks—a lightweight, a 1-tonner and a 5-tonner reputed to run 35 miles (56 km) on a single charge. Batteries would be supplied by the Gould Storage Battery Corporation of Depew, New York State. Two years later, Charles Gould successfully sued Dr. Lehwess for failure to pay for the batteries.

The U.S. Postal Service was trying out various approaches. In 1909, electric mail trucks were put in service in New York City and Boston. During the 1911 Christmas season, New York's electric vehicles operated night and day, with batteries and drivers changing every eight hours. There were hundreds of car companies nationwide, and mail contractors often used cars of local manufacture. For example, in the mid–1910s, an electric automobile made by the Argo Electric Vehicle Company of Saginaw, Michigan, was used by the Saginaw Post Office. In 1916, an electric mail truck built by the Walker Vehicle Company of Chicago was used in Chicago. Parcel Post service, which began in 1913, increased the need for motor vehicles because more and heavier packages began entering the mail-stream. *Harper's Weekly* opined, "under the most ordinary conditions, one motor vehicle can do the work of three horse-drawn wagons."[33]

William B. Tremaine of The Aeolian Company of New York, manufacturer of the highly popular Pianola (a pneumatic player piano) announced that, after four years of testing, the firm would use motor vehicles exclusively for delivery. Eight Studebaker electrics and three Sauer gasoline trucks were ordered.

As the Studebaker Brothers of South Bend, Indiana, were one of the world's largest producers of quality horse-drawn carriages, it was inevitable that they should become interested in the newly invented horseless carriage. In 1902, Studebaker began to manufacture their own twin-motor electric vehicles, twenty of which were sold that year. A unique feature of the Studebaker electric freight wagons was the location of the battery under the center of the frame. Its battery compartment was built integral with the frame. In 1909, the H.C. Piercy Company, which handled deliveries for 80 New York merchants, ordered 25 electric delivery trucks from Studebaker to replace 300 horses and 200 wagons. They had a range of 35 miles (56 km) with top speed of 9 mph (15 kph). The showpiece of the new transport rationality was the "largest modern electric garage" of the New York department store Gimbel Brothers. It was built in 1910 on West Twenty-Fourth Street, west of Tenth Avenue, one of the most densely populated city quarters in the USA. Three years later, it housed 83 electric trucks. A postcard showed an injured elephant that was named either "Maude" or "Millie." She is seen with a bandaged left front leg and the text on the card tells how the Studebaker Electric Truck was being used as an ambulance to take her to a vet.[34] Another Studebaker electric was designed to haul automobiles, carriages, or wagons. The body platform was built on a slight incline with a tail gate or ramp section on the end. A special electric hoist under the driver's seat pulled the car aboard.

By 1910, the Los Angeles Creamery at San Pedro Street proclaimed itself as the largest and best creamery in the world. Its boiler and engine house was a large, one-story concrete building adjoining the main plant, and was provided with two 200-horsepower Sterling high pressure water tubular boilers, with two Hamilton tandem compound condensing Corliss engines, each connecting to two 50-ton Baker Ice machines. Each engine also drove a 75-kilowatt generator, which in turn furnished the electricity for the motors to drive all the different machinery. Either one of the power units was capable of cooling brine to refrigerate the daily output of 1,000 pounds of milk, or 12,000 gallons (46,000 liters). The company and the directors were milking over 2,500 cows and expected to increase the number to 4,000. In March 1912, the innovative George E. Platt, president of the Los Angeles Creamery, was found guilty of adulterating the "cream" his company sold. The pricey product was proven to be ordinary milk mixed with the condensed variety. Platt appealed his conviction, claiming he had the right to regulate his inventory, but he lost the appeal and was fined $25.

Another of George Platt's projects was to see whether electric vehicles could be operated more cheaply than horse wagons in milk delivery. As no machines were on the market having the center drive feature and the company had a well-equipped motor shop, it decided to build a truck to suit its own needs. The truck had a frame furnished by Parish and Bingham of Cleveland, a GE 10-26 23 hp motor and an Exide MV Ironclad battery. The Electruck, as Platt called it, was designed by A.W. Harrison, the firm's electrical engineer, and built in its shops under the supervision of Eustace B. Moore, Superintendent. Two Electrucks, with a 3,000 lb. payload and capable of speeds of 12 mph, faster than horses, went into operation from May 1914. A third was added the following year, then a further ten, with a number of refinements and improvements in design, were added to the fleet. During the early 1920s, the name Electruck was associated with the Los Angeles Creamery and Auto Company.

Charles A. Ward of New York City was head of his family's baking company, made up of the Mackey Company, the Ward Corby Company, the Ward Bread Company and the Ohio Baking Company of Cleveland. In 1911, Ward also decided to replace his horse-drawn delivery vehicles with electric trucks, thus doing away with the unsanitary stable previously part of or adjacent to the bakery. For this, he recruited Harold Hayden Eames, formerly with the Pope electric auto concern. Ward, who chose the Edison battery/Westinghouse motor for his 1,000 lb. (450 kg) truck guaranteed to run 45 miles (70 km) on a single battery charge, was pleasantly surprised when it made more than 78 miles (126 km) on its official test through the congested streets and over the steep hills of Pittsburgh.

In the advertisements they took out for their Electric Vehicle Motor in such publications as *The Saturday Evening Post*, *The Cosmopolitan*, *Colliers*, *The Motor*, *The Horseless Age*, etc., Westinghouse claimed sales in 45 American cities, referring people to their "Circular 1059." Among Ward's clients was the Tebelmann Baking Company who had "YurFavorite Cake" painted on the side and "Why bake at home!" along the top of its trucks.

The year 1906 onwards signaled a period of tremendous growth for electric cars and trucks. In Cleveland, Ohio, Walter Baker's Motor Vehicle Company was a very successful business. In 1906 alone Baker made 800 electric automobiles, making them the largest electric vehicle maker in the world at the time. They bragged in advertisements that their new factory was "the largest in the world." In 1907, Baker also introduced a range of trucks with capacity of up to five tons. Spokane Toilet Supply Company also had a Baker Electric truck and it probably never delivered toilets. It primarily moved towels, aprons and other toilet accessories.

Another manufacturer of electric trucks was Walker, whose success was thanks to their innovative Walker Balance Gear. The story of Walker trucks goes back to the 1860s with James Monroe Walker, attorney and president of the Chicago Burlington & Quincy Railroad, from 1870 to 1875. Walker amassed considerable power in Chicago throughout his years there, having control at various times of the Union Stock Yards, the Kansas City Stock Yards, and the Wilmington Coal Company. Close to the railway tracks over which Walker presided was a small Illinois village called Clarendon Hills. Falling in love with the spot, Walker purchased the land south of those

In 1911 Ward's fleet of bread delivery trucks used an Edison-Westinghouse power-plant with a 50-mile range. Drivers wear an elegant "Tip-Top" uniform (U.S. Dept. of the Interior, National Park Service, Thomas Edison National Historical Park).

tracks. Indeed, one of the famed curved streets in the village is named after him.

In 1907, George R. Walker, 39 years old, of Clarendon Hills, a relative of James, was granted a patent for a driving mechanism for automobiles. It was a way of mounting the electrical transmission in the four wheels of a truck. In particular it referred to a mechanism of that character in which a speed-reducing gear mechanism was arranged within the wheel and directly driven from the armature shaft of a motor supported by the axle concentric with the wheel. The company which built the prototype truck was then called the Automobile Maintenance Company, already in existence for three years. Its address was 53rd Street, Ohio at the Illinois Central railroad tracks in the Hyde Park neighborhood. But by 1909, following successful sales of the first batch of 3,000 lb. (1,360 kg) payload trucks, the company changed its name to Automobile Maintenance and Manufacturing Company and moved to 213–219 Green Street, Chicago, a three-story building providing a total 30,000 square feet of floor space, enabling them to increase their facilities to build electric trucks in quantities. For their second 1,500 lb. (680 kg) payload truck, to reduce the cost and make the drive system even simpler, George Walker came up with

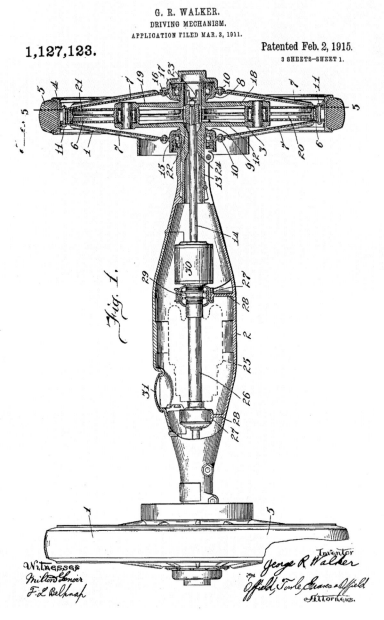

G. R. WALKER.
DRIVING MECHANISM.
APPLICATION FILED MAR. 3, 1911.

1,127,123.

Patented Feb. 2, 1915.
3 SHEETS—SHEET 1.

Fig. 1.

In 1915, George R. Walker of Clarendon Hills, Illinois, came up with an ingenious system for one DC motor mounted between the rear wheels using internal gear drive. With a speed of between 12 and 14 mph, smaller battery, and lighter weight, the "Walker Balanced Wheel" electric truck enabled the company named after him to build and sell whole fleets, distinguished by their closed wheel spats.

This rare photograph shows a Walker truck lowering a load onto another Walker truck (U.S. Dept. of the Interior, National Park Service, Thomas Edison National Historical Park).

one DC motor mounted between the rear wheels using internal gear drive. With a speed of between 12 and 14 mph (20 and 22 kph), smaller battery, and lighter weight, the "Walker Balance Wheel" electric truck enabled the company to build and sell whole fleets to Commonwealth Edison, Marshall Field & Co., Pirie, Scott & Co., Chas A Stevens & Bros, all satisfied clients, not to mention sales in Detroit, Michigan, Rochester, New York, Brooklyn and San Francisco.[35]

In 1911, George Walker filed for another improved patent where the transmission unit was positioned near the vehicle wheel, or between the differential gear unit and the wheel. This was granted in 1915. By that time, the recently renamed Walker Vehicle Company had acquired the Chicago Electric Motor Car Company, with Commonwealth Edison's Vice President William A. Fox named as president, and G.A. Freeman, also from Commonwealth Edison, as vice president. The wooden-bodied, solid-tired model range consisting of 750-pound to 3½-ton vehicles used Edison alkaline batteries. Edison knew a good thing when he saw it.[36] Among the clients, the Dwinell-Wright Company in Boston employed a Walker Electric Truck from 1914 through 1960 to move freight—primarily green coffee beans—from the docks to their South Boston warehouse.[37] When, in 1919, George Walker applied for a third

The Philadelphia Electric Company used this extended Walker truck to transport a tree trunk, perhaps destined for a telegraph pole or even the mast of a ship. Their slogan was, "If it isn't electric, it isn't modern" (American Truck Historical Society).

patent, obtaining US1455943A in 1923, he was still described as Assignor to the Walker Vehicle Company of Chicago, Illinois, itself owned by the Anderson Electric Car Company of Detroit since 1916.

An electric cargo three-wheeler was developed by William G. Wagenhals of Detroit. Wagenhals, a railway engineer by profession, had not only designed a three-rail system for the New York Central, but also invented the first really working electric headlight for automobiles in the Motor City. Some 200 Wagenhals three-wheeler horseless trucks, with their 800 lb. (360 kg) capacity, were built between 1910 and 1914, when the firm switched to gasoline engines.

From 1912, the Curtis Publishing Company of Philadelphia used a fleet of 22 Commercial Truck Company Model A 10 trucks not only to deliver *The Saturday Evening Post, Ladies' Home Journal, The American Home, Holiday, Jack & Jill* and *Country Gentleman* to the post office and area newsstands, according to the seller's representative, but also to haul paper, coal, and waste. The majority of these trucks were built using red oak, while the flatbed was originally constructed from two ¼" steel plates secured using over 500 ⁷⁄₁₆" bolts. The Curtis fleet continued in service for the next fifty years.

By then, electric vehicle builders had become well aware that they were losing out to the more reliable gasoline-engined vehicles. To combat this, the Electric Vehicle Association of America was created in September 1910. The following year, the first National Truck Show in Madison Square Garden featured 286 exhibitors, including 27 gasoline, and only seven electric. Two years later the Boston Truck Show featured 48 gas trucks and only six electric. By 1915, the Ninth Edition of the Electric Vehicle Association's book of *Electric Automobile Charging Stations and Route Maps* was published, a map indicating recharging points extending to the north as far afield as Pittsfield, Massachusetts, to as far south as Atlantic City and Philadelphia, to the west as far as Easton and to the east as far as Port Jefferson. But were they too late?

Two

Outside the USA

Across the Pond, in Paris, while Gustave Trouvé, the pure inventor, was creating other machines such as luminous electric fountains and light radiators for skin diseases, a small electric vehicle industry had been growing up in France's capital.

In 1895, science-fiction writer Jules Verne published his *Voyages Extraordinaires* including the story "L'Île à hélice" ("The Self-propelled Island"). It relates the adventures of a French string quartet in Milliard City, a city on a massive ship in the Pacific Ocean, inhabited entirely by millionaires.

> The island is oval shaped; it is divided into two sections separated by the third avenue, three kilometers long. It is made of steel, and consists of 275,000 boxes. It has two ports, one on the port side and the other on the starboard side, each time with engines for the propellers, powered by nearby plants and supplying the electricity required for the propellers, because "electricity is the soul of the universe" (p. 57). It is produced by factories that consume oil that ships bring into each of the two ports. *Trucks like the rowboats are electric*, as well as the moving sidewalks of the main arteries.

In 1898 and 1899, Count Chasseloup-Laubat of the Automobile Club de France and the dynamic Georges Forestier organized a Concours des Véhicules Industriels (Industrial Vehicle Trials) for heavy motor vehicles around Versailles where steam, gas, and electric trucks competed over three routes: 26, 29 and 41 miles (40, 45 and 64 km). Among the competitors were the Mildé et Mondos electric delivery truck, which broke down; the Compagnie des Electromobiles, Jenatzy and the Compagnie des Voitures Electriques Kriéger.

On January 17, 1899, Camille Jenatzy, out to break a speed record, took his adapted dogcart powered by one 80 cell Fulmen lead acid battery and established a new record of 41.42 mph (66.7 kph). His second challenger, *Le Jamais Contente*, was a torpedo-shaped vehicle with no resemblance to a horse-drawn carriage, which was timed at 65.792 mph (105.882 kph). While Jenatzy was a racing driver, Louis Kriéger was a brilliant technician. He had started work as an engineer for the French Northern Railway Company. In 1895, he participated in the Paris-Bordeaux-Paris motor race with Charles Jeantaud, supplying him with batteries with a very modest energy density of 20 W-h/kg, along the route. Kriéger then built his first electric vehicle by converting a horse-drawn hackney cab used by the Compagnie l'Abeille in Paris. In 1897, he created the System Kriéger electric car company and the following year a Kriéger won the electric fiacre contest.

In 1898, Postal Vinay built a 22 ton electric heavy vehicle for the sugar beet refiner Begin Say, who could produce electricity at their Paris factory in the 13th arrondissement of Paris, and planned to replace their horse-drawn fleet; its front wheels were activated by a servo-motor. The following year, Jenatzy electric trucks were making deliveries for Les Grand Magasins du Louvre, a big department store.

Observing this, the Brigade des Sapeurs-Pompiers de Paris (Paris Fire Brigade), a French Army unit, asked a question: Could an electric vehicle that was no longer horse-drawn be used to fight fires? After observing an auto contest organized by *Le Petit Journal* in 1894, the Fire Brigade staff decided to experiment. At the time, gas automobiles were considered unreliable, so

1899: Over in Paris, Les Grands Magasins du Louvre department store was the first to use electric trucks for deliveries around France's capital city. The chain transmission was developed by Belgian engineer Camille Jenatzy, complete with wooden brake shoe, with a metal strap for emergency stopping. Note that it did not have a number plate, as these did not come until September 1901 (Collection J-N Raymond).

Captain Engineer Cordier and a Brigade team focused on electric traction by accumulators. At the Regiment's own workshops, they built the first electric prototype, able to carry six men, fire-extinguishing equipment, hand ladders and life-saving equipment. At first, the pump remained steam-powered. Commissioned in 1899, at first it was used to respond immediately to any call when the nature of the fire was not indicated or when the information given suggested a fire of little importance. Further innovations followed. While Major Engineer Vuilquin installed an electric ladder made by Gugumus Brothers with a working height of 19 m which could be raised in two minutes and 20 seconds, an electric pump was designed and built by Adjutant Morvan. This meant that the machine, weighing three tons (3,000 kg) including crew and water, could travel to the scene of the fire and also operate the pump electrically, extinguishing 95 percent of the fires it attended four minutes faster than a steam fire engine. The hoses were then connected to the city fire hydrants for more water if needed for a large fire. In August 1900, the Paris Fire Brigade electric truck, having been tested over six months, was proudly demonstrated at the International Fire Brigade Congress at Vincennes. It attracted a great deal of attention. Also on board was a cable car-

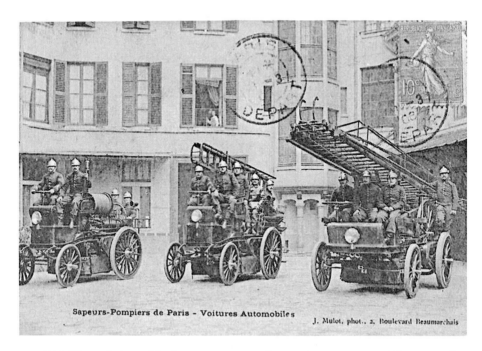

Sapeurs-Pompiers de Paris - Voitures Automobiles

J. Mulot, phot., 2, Boulevard Beaumarchais

1900: The workshop of the Sapeurs-Pompiers de Paris (Paris Fire Brigade) pioneered these first electric fire engines, equipped with both electric pumps and ladders (Havard Collection).

rying ten incandescent lamps which had proved of invaluable service for both cellar fires and night work. Its batteries, as supplied by BGS (Bouquet, Garcin and Schivre) of Neuilly, gave a range of 35 miles (60 km) at an average speed of 12 mph (20 kph). From 1902, two electrically propelled chemical fire engines went into service in Hanover, Germany, clocking a total of 2,000 miles (3,200 km) each year for the next three years.

One of the first examples of the use of electric trucks to carry out menial services in a city was an electric-powered street washer developed in 1901 by vehicle manufacturer Bouquet, Garcin & Schivre (BGS) for use in the streets of Neuilly-sur-Seine, where their plant was producing electric automobiles, single-seater chariots and a minibus using their exceptional 20–22 Ah battery.

From 1897, the French Post Office, as directed by the forward-thinking Under-Secretary of State for Posts and Telegraphs, Léon Mougeot,[1] had been looking for a way to replace horse-drawn mail vans with mechanical transport, trying out Serpollet steam railcars to collect letters from post boxes on the line between Creil and Beauvais. Charles Jeantaud at the rue de Ponthieu in Paris exhibited one of his parallelogram steering electromobiles with motor by Zenobe Gramme and battery by Camille Faure, called *L'auto-poste*, at the Paris Motor Show but it created little interest.[2] Businessman Duboys, who ran the fleet of horse-drawn tilburys in the service of the Paris Post Office, proposed using automobiles. In November 1900, Duboys was authorized to make his trials, but at his own risks and dangers. From February 21, 1901, to May 11, 1902, Duboys experimented with two types of propulsion, one electric and the other gasoline. Fifteen vehicles were built, 14 of them carrying telegrams. Twelve Kriéger electric vans with a payload of 1,300 lb. (600 kg) and a range of 40 miles (65 km), as fitted out by well-known saddle makers and coachbuilders Million-Guiet et Cie. of Levallois-Perret, began to circulate and to service the city's railway stations such as Montparnasse, Lyon, Austerlitz and Nord.

Le Petit Journal published a paragraph entitled "Postmen in Automobiles":

> One should hand it to Monsieur Mougeot, Under-Secretary of State for Posts and Telegraphs that he is taking such pains to improve the services he is directing. Profiting from scientific progress, he is at present organising a service of postmen travelling by bicycle or automobile. The experiment has taken place. Monsieur Mougeot was involved and is very pleased. The service has occurred without problems and in conditions of such rapidity that on certain points, one gains on almost half the time of that taken previously. The advantage for the public consists in that they can post their letters in the box one quarter of an hour or twenty minutes later than before and this is a very important advantage for those who are in business.

But the Post still needed convincing. With determined campaigning by the new Under-Secretary of State for Posts and Telegraphs, Alexandre Bérard, supported by Deputy Marcel Sembat, subsidies were found to resume conversion to automobiles. Enter Charles Mildé. In 1878, Mildé and his father had presented an ingenious electric bell and clock at the Paris Universal Exposition and were awarded a silver medal. They earned another silver medal at the 1881 Paris International Electrical Exhibition. In 1882, Mildé Jr. created Charles Mildé, Fils et Cie, in the rue Laugier, Paris 17ème, manufacturing and installing electrical equipment. In 1897, Mildé installed a 3 hp electric engine on a horseless carriage. It weighed over a ton, with a range of 30 mi (50 km) for a speed of 10 mph (15 kph). Mildé took part in various competitions, including one organized by the newborn French Automobile Club. In May 1900, Mildé published a catalogue presenting the range of his electric vehicles, including an omnibus, a break, a delivery truck with a gallery and a slatted-side lorry. The truck measured 10.8 ft. long × 6 ft wide (3.3 m × 1.85 m), with four wood-spoked pneumatic-tired wheels. Its 485 lb. (220 kg) motor was powered by a 1,650 lb. (750 kg) battery located between the two axles. Rear-loadable up to a volume of 1.5 cubic meter and an increased payload capacity of 1,400 lbs. (650 kg), the Mildé truck had a top speed of 7.5 mph (12.5 kph) and a range over 37 mi (60 km). Price: 1,800 francs, not including extras such as a replacement battery and tool box.

Just over three miles (4.5 km) from Mildé's new workshops in the rue Desrenaudes was the French Postes et Telegraphes Service, located at the Hôtel des Postes, rue Jean-Jacques Rousseau, Paris. The Société des Messageries des Postes de France, a concessionaire of the State Sub-secretariat of Posts and Telegraphs, ordered fifteen electric trucks from Mildé to carry mail between sorting centers and railway stations. They also ordered several Peugeot gasoline cars. The Mildés proved more reliable than the sputtering internal combustion engine which had to be hand-cranked every time it stopped, so the order was placed for another fifteen. Following charging up from midnight to 4 a.m., the fleet was ready to run from 5 a.m. and the trucks were used for continuous 17-hour periods with only one recharge, enabling them to cover 45 miles (70 km) at speeds no faster than 12 mph (20 kph). Mildé's electric van had a U-shaped chassis, with batteries at the front of the vehicle, under the feet of the driver so they could be changed and replaced by recharged batteries in five minutes. The electric motor formed the differential through two inductors mounted in the same frame. There were eight speeds, two recovery positions, two electric brake positions and three reverse gears, to allow the driver to accurately find the speed of the vehicle ahead without constantly turning off the power. The batteries were exchanged at the Hôtel des Postes, rue Gutenberg, almost at the corner of the rue du Louvre where passersby could see the batteries being exchanged and the vans repaired, if necessary. By 1920, when it was completely replaced by gasoline vans, the Paris e-fleet had totaled more than 190,000 miles (300,000

1903: For 15 years, a fleet of these Mildé electric trucks daily delivered letters and parcels around Paris. Charging from midnight to 4 a.m., the fleet was ready to run from 5 a.m. and the trucks were used for continuous 17-hour periods with only one recharge, enabling them to cover 70 kilometers at speeds no faster than 20 kph (Collection J-C Bastian).

km) "de bons et loyaux services" (good and loyal services) around the capital city.

An idea of what was involved with battery maintenance can be gained from J. Laffargue's "The Practical Manual for the Driver-Electrician" published in Paris by Bernard Tignol:

ACCUMULATOR MAINTENANCE: When recharging, never go beyond the intensity regime indicated by the manufacturer. To avoid this, look out for an abundant emission of gas which appears when the batteries are sufficiently recharged, the liquid also taking on a milky appearance. Automatic limiters have been designed which switch off the charge. There are also charge state indicators. One of the most annoying aspects of battery operation is the production of lead sulphate which covers the plates preventing them from working. When this happens use hydrogen, plunging them in a slightly acidic bath or mixture of bicarbonate of soda and water. Batteries should be cleaned every 2 to 3 months. Unscrew the bolts and take out all the plates, plunging them in pure water and cleaning them. Then put them back carefully so they do not touch each other. Also clean out any accumulated deposits from the bottom of the vase. Replace the sulphuric acid. When an element does not function, this may be due to peroxide or material produced by oxidisation.... If the plate appears whitish for the negative or sandy for the positive, brush it clean ...

Other European cities saw the advantage: in Munich, Germany, a postal delivery electric tricycle was used on a route of 4 mi (6.4 km) with 27 mail boxes which all had to be emptied 15 times a day. Therefore, the vehicle with a weight of 950 lb. (430 kg) would have an efficiency ratio of only 30 percent. But the batteries could not cope with continually accelerating from standstill: their life span was only a quarter of what had been promised, so an economical operation did not seem possible. When, however, the three-wheeler was transferred to "Stadtverbindungsdienst" (bulk mail transport service) in 1903, where the stopping-and-starting operations were not necessary, it was perfectly satisfactory.[3]

In 1902, the British Royal Mail trialed a postal truck in Battersea, southwest London. It was built in Camden Town, northwest London, by Carl Oppermann of the Grosvenor Garage, but his batteries were not up to a full delivery round. Similar trials took place in Milan, Italy, in 1904, then Vienna and Hanover in 1905. Several electric postal delivery trucks were built by ABM of Cologne and Namag in Bremen, all with the Kriéger front-wheel-drive.

Louis Kriéger of Paris, like his American counterpart, John Henry Munson of La Porte, Indiana, saw the range advantage of the hybrid-electric. Since 1895, Kriéger's large factory in the suburb of Puteaux had built and sold some 240 pure electric vehicles built by 300 workers, including such patented innovations as regenerative braking. Among these was a "Petro-electric Omnibus" for the Omnibus General Company, Paris: a generator was placed at the front of the chassis consisting of a 24-valve Richard Brasier engine coupled to the dynamo behind. The electrical energy distributed to the engines driving the drive wheels thus eliminated the gear shift and the differential. To prove his point, in 1900 Kriéger motored from Paris to Laroche (Yonne), 93 mi (152 km), without recharging; the following year he motored from Paris to Chatellerault, 190 mi (307 km) again without recharging at the average speed of 11 mph (17.5 kph). At the 1904 Paris Auto Show, French President Loubet made Kriéger a Chevalier de la Légion d'Honneur. The following year, Kriéger took part in the Industrial Vehicle Contest, where he exhibited an electric truck that powered an onboard searchlight.

Over in northern Italy, in 1905, the Società Italiana Automobili Kriéger, based in Corso Regina Margherita, Turin, planned to make electric vehicles including "camions elettrici" or trucks based on the French hybrid-electric system, which were lighter and had increased range. Selling shares enabled it to rename as STAE (Società Torinese Automobili Elettrici). In the following years, however, the emergence of combustion engine vehicles would put the producers of electric cars in serious difficulty and, between 1912 and 1913, also complicated by the long strikes of those two years, the STAE folded. Its local rival, the Fabbrica Italiana Automobili Torino (FIAT) went from strength to strength.

1910: An electric refuse truck BOM No. 7 in the streets of Paris (Collection J-N Raymond).

Across the Atlantic, in Canada, Frederick Featherstonhaugh, a successful patent attorney, lived in Mimico, west of Toronto, where he had one of the first electrified homes. One of his professional clients was William Still, an English-born electrical engineer who had developed a lighter, more efficient storage battery, who visited Featherstonhaugh to arrange for a patent. They discovered a mutual interest in the emerging motorcar. Still had been working on the idea for several years, and Featherstonhaugh was keen on owning a horseless carriage. With the engineering completed, the search for a company to build the new machine brought them to John Dixon's carriage works at Bay and Temperance streets in Toronto. Dixon had a reputation for high-quality products, and he was commissioned to build a vehicle that would accept Still's electric drive system. In 1893, Featherstonhaugh's car was so successful it inspired a group of Toronto businessmen to form the Canadian Motor Syndicate (CMS), Canada's original commercial automobile enterprise. The Canadian Motor Syndicate lasted only until 1899. Still then collaborated in another venture, the Still Motor Company, which built electrically powered three-and four-wheeled passenger and commercial vehicles. In 1900, the Royal Canadian Mail commissioned the first of a fleet of electric parcel delivery trucks from Still Motors.[4]

Mr. E.M. Trowern Secretary of the Retail Merchants Association Toronto, Canada, has recently returned from Detroit and Cleveland where he has inspected motor delivery wagons and drays in use in those cities. He presented a report which is favourable to the adoption of the electric motor delivery system. It is stated that the recent developments indicate that the delivery of parcels and even heavier goods by electric motor vehicles is probable in Toronto ["Electric Motor Delivery Vehicles," *The Electrician*, March 31, 1905].

In 1902, the Manchester Motor Transport Company in northern England was formed to undertake the collection by Still electric motor wagons of parcels and goods, including agricultural and diary produce in and around Manchester. *The Electrician* said on March 21, 1902, "It is probable that there is a wide and remunerative field for motor car businesses of this description, and we expect to see many more such undertakings arise in the near future."

In Austria, at the International Automobile Exhibition in Vienna, the Gnenossenshaft Cooperative exhibited an e-truck driven by two motors. Oesterreichische Electromobilwerke exhibited a beer wagon designed to carry a load of five tons, driven by two 5 hp battery weighing 1.2 tons (1,200 kg) with 400 amp/h capacity. When fully charged and loaded, this wagon could make a run of 37 mi (60 km). The wagon and battery together weighed 3.5 tons (3,500 kg). In neighboring Germany, the company Motorfahrzeug und Motorenfabrik Berlin-Marienfelde (MMB) had embarked on the production of electric vehicles in 1899. Owned by shareholders and supervisory-board members of Daimler-Motoren-Gesellschaft (DMG), MMB was taken over by DMG in 1902. It later became the Berlin plant of Daimler AG. It produced electric vehicles under license from Columbia Automobiles in the USA. In addition to passenger cars, MMB manufactured light-duty trucks, buses and fire-fighting vehicles with electric drives. Department stores used electrically powered vans for their deliveries, while hotels transported guests in electrically powered omnibuses. In 1901, MMB's range included commercial vehicles with 770 lb. (350 kg) payload, baggage vans with 1-ton (1,000 kg) payload, and mail cars with up to a 1.3-ton (1,300 kg) payload.

In 1898, Ferdinand Porsche joined the Vienna-based factory Hof-Wagen- and Automobilfabrik Jakob Lohner & Company, which produced coaches for Emperor Franz Joseph I of Austria, as well as for the monarchs of the UK, Sweden, and Romania. Jakob Lohner had recently begun construction of automobiles at a firm directed by Ludwig Lohner in the trans–Danubian suburb of Floridsdorf. Their first automobile design was the Egger-Lohner vehicle (also referred to as the *C.2 Phaeton*), first unveiled in Vienna, Austria, on June 26, 1898. Porsche had engraved the code "P1," standing for Porsche, number one, signifying Porsche's first design, onto all the key components. It was driven by two electric motors within the front wheel hubs, powered by batteries. This drive train construction was easily expanded to four-wheel drive, by mounting two more electric motors to the rear wheels, and a four-motor example was ordered by Englishman E. W. Hart in 1900. In December that year, the car was displayed at the Paris World Exhibition under the name *Toujours-Contente*. Even though this one-off vehicle had been commissioned for the purposes of racing and record-breaking, its 4,000 lbs. (1,800 kg) of lead-acid batteries presented a severe shortcoming. Though it showed wonderful speed when it was allowed to sprint, the weight of the batteries rendered it slow to climb hills. It also suffered from limited range due to limited battery life. Ingeniously, working with a team at Daimler-Motoren-Gesellschaft's Marienfelde plant, Porsche combined Lohner's electric technology with Austro-Daimler's gas technology into the Mercedes-Electrique or Elektro-Daimler or Daimler-Mixte. The system's problem-free, permanent readiness for use made the Mixte drive system an attractive solution for fire departments, which until then had turned out to the scene of a fire with horse and cart and bicycles. Over 300 Lohner-Porsche chassis were sold up to 1906, either front- or rear-wheel including beer transport trucks, garbage and other municipal trucks, with up to 4-ton (4,000 kg) payload. A single battery charge gave the trucks a range of up to 43.5 miles (70 km) with a top speed of 10 to 12 mph (18 to 20 kph). In 1908, the Berlin Fire Brigade acquired four Mixte trucks and employed them to great effect. The London Fire Brigade also ran an electrically driven escape van from their headquarters in Southwark, southeast London.

Across the German border in Switzerland, from 1904, Joseph Albert Triblehorn of Feldbach, a village near Rapperswil, located on the north bank of Lake Zurich, built electric trucks, autos and boats. In 1909, Zurich baker Hermann Buchmann bought a Tribelhorn delivery van second-hand at the Printemps department store in Paris: he would use it in the districts of Zürichberg and Friesenberg for the next 35 years.

In 1910, Berlin's fleet of new electric mail delivery vans were built by Norddeutsche Automobil Motoren-Gesellschaft of Bremen. A first batch of three was submitted for trial in 1909. But whereas the trial vans were used simply for transporting sealed mail bags, the permanent vehicles possessed windows so that, to a certain extent, sorting could be done en route. The Bremen firm contracted to maintain batteries, tiring and bodies on the basis of a given sum per kilometer; the Berlin Electric Works supplied the current. The next challenge would be to grapple with the suburban parcels post, still towed by horses.[5]

Around 1908, Schuckert engineers Ernst Valentin and Franz Starkopf designed a commercial vehicle powered by two rear-wheel hub motors. In addition to the normal steering wheel, there were additional left and right steering wheels on the outside of the truck, which could be operated by the driver beside the vehicle. The design was used for both a truck and a bus, its chassis manufactured by the Siemens-Schuckert plant on Motardstraße in Berlin-Siemensstadt and the motors by Siemens & Halske. S-S also produced several electric delivery tricycles for the Bavarian postal authorities. These were equipped with both a foot and an electric brake. Because of their greater speed, they were used for "Eilsendüngen" (express delivery). In 1909 a Siemens-Schuckert delivery truck was acquired from the British agents F.A. Wilkinson & Partners for use by Peter Robinson Ltd., a fashionable drapery store in nearby Oxford Circus, London. In 1911, the Berlin factory temporarily halted manufacture of its 4 hp motor, then having scaled up, resumed two years later to manufacture a large number of 40 hp trucks with 3-ton payload and 50 hp with 4.5-ton payloads. Post-war preference for gas trucks sent the e-trucks to the scrapyard. Later, Schuckert became part of Siemens.

However, those electric vehicle manufacturers such as Kriéger in Paris and Baker in Cleveland who had invested in electrically powered vehicles were forced to accept that their battery-motors would be replaced by the more convenient gasoline-tank engine. In 1909 Kriéger stopped making electric cars.

In 1894, René Panhard and Emile Levassor, coachbuilders of D'Ivry, Paris, built the world's first gasoline-engined lorry, soon followed by Gottlieb Daimler. Grievances against electricity, the charging station, weight of the

This Berlin-built Siemens-Schuckert *Elektromobil* Type P, photographed in 1910, was used for electric telegraph maintenance (Siemens AG).

batteries, and unavailable replacement batteries, pushed the technicians at the Paris Fire Brigade to opt for the hybrid gas-electric engine which, having made enormous technological progress, offered more flexibility of employment. Gasoline engines built by De Dion Bouton and Delahaye Farcot were adapted. The first ground-breaking diesel-engined trucks from the then still separate companies Daimler and Benz would come out a little later in 1923.

Over in the USA, several innovations happened which would push electric trucks to the back of the garage. On January 10, 1901, Captain Anthony F. Lucas, who had been patiently drilling for oil at a depth of 1,139 ft. (347 m) at Spindletop, near Beaumont, Texas, struck lucky. The Spindletop gusher blew oil over 150 feet (50 m) in the air at a rate of 100,000 barrels (16,000 cubic meters or 4,200,000 gallons) per day. It took nine days before the well was brought under control. In time, Gulf Oil and Texaco, now part of the Chevron Corporation, would be formed to develop production at the Lucas Geyser.

In 1910, Edison Records was manufacturing a new range of Phonographs and Ediphone dictating machines which, like Edison Portland Cement, needed transporting and delivery, so what better than electric trucks using the Master's steel-alkaline storage batteries (U.S. Dept. of the Interior, National Park Service, Thomas Edison National Historical Park).

In the days before refrigerators, huge blocks of ice would be delivered by firms such as the Standard Plate Ice Company and Consolidated Ice, using Edison batteries (U.S. Dept. of the Interior, National Park Service, Thomas Edison National Historical Park).

In 1908, Henry Ford began mass-producing his Model T gasoline-powered automobile. Twenty years later he would watch the 15 millionth Model T Ford roll off the assembly line at his factory in Highland Park, Michigan. During that time, companies adapted the Model T for truck use. One thing which had deterred the electric truck owner from going gasoline stemmed from a common health problem caused by cars at the time: motorists' broken arms. As a driver hand cranked the gas engine, the crank often swung back violently, injuring the driver's arm. Efforts to eliminate dangerous engine cranking led to the development of battery-started vehicles. The 1912 Cadillac became the first battery-started car with an internal combustion engine, produced under cooperative development between the Electric Storage Battery Company and Charles F. Kettering. Once it became easy to start an internal combustion engine, recharging an electric became somewhat tedious. Last but not least, America's burgeoning road culture made speed and convenience at long distances the decisive criteria for customers' choices.

In 1913, Kroger replaced their horse and wagon teams with 75 Ford Model T trucks. Many of these were used for home deliveries. As a chain store, Kroger also needed trucks to supply its own stores. Later it developed its own bakers and meat processing plants and had fleets making direct deliveries to stores from these plants, as well as from its warehouses. In addition to excellent luxury cars, Packard Motor Company built gasoline trucks. By 1911, Packard gasoline trucks used by Wanamaker's store in Philadelphia were traveling 110 miles per tank. A Packard truck carrying a 3-ton load drove from New York City to San Francisco between July 8 and August 24, 1912. The same year, Packard had service depots in 104 cities. Also during this time, the Pierce-Arrow Motor Car Company, an American luxury automobile manufacturer based in Buffalo, New York, began to manufacture their 5-ton commercial truck. By 1916, at least 19 different body builders were producing stock model bodies that fit the Ford Model T chassis. Disenchanted by the electric truck, Henry Ford went one step further. In July 1917, he brought out the Model TT which retained the Model T cab and engine. When first produced, the Model TT was sold as a chassis with the buyer supplying a body. Three TTs were built in 1917, and 41,105 in 1918.

The first national truck show was held at Madison Square Garden in 1911. Displayed were 27 gasoline trucks, seven electric trucks and 18 motorcycles. By 1912, it had become conventional wisdom that the future lay in gasoline-powered engines rather than heavy, sluggish electrics, and the limited production of electric cars stopped. When the production of electrics was discontinued in 1912, a total of 1,841 Studebaker electrics had been produced and sold. An official announcement from the newly re-incorporated Studebaker Corporation stated: "The production of electric automobiles at South Bend has ended…. It has been conducted for nine years without much success, and ultimately the superiority of the gasoline car (is) apparent."

In June 1913, members of the International Brotherhood of Teamsters, Chauffeurs, Warehousemen and Helpers of America completed the first transcontinental delivery by electric motor truck. It took them 90 days to travel from Philadelphia to San Francisco. The same year, a battery-electric coupé traveled from Dumfries to London, a distance of 362 miles (583 km). In that year the Incorporated Municipal Electrical Association held their Annual Convention in London, and a parade of vehicles was arranged at Kingston-on-Thames. One of these vehicles was an Edison Arrols-Johnston coupé, which at the time of the convention was held at the Arrol-Johnston Works, and it was decided to bring it to London by road instead of by train. Mr. Maurice E. Fox, chief engineer to Edison Accumulators Ltd., was in charge of the vehicle and W.E. Warrilow, then on the editorial staff of *The Electrician*, traveled as observer. The run was successfully carried out in two and a half days, including resting for one night and a number of stops for battery charging. The battery was a 60-cell A4-type Edison of 150 Ah capacity, 36 cells placed under the bonnet and 24 cells under the rear seat. This vehicle operated in London for a number of years and then spent the last five of a useful life of 15 years as a milk-delivery float in Southport.

In 1914, a government-owned and -operated motor vehicle service began in Washington, D.C., and was gradually introduced to other cities. The department used gasoline-powered vehicles, in part because electric vehicles lacked sufficient speed and power. In 1915, William H. Haycock, superintendent of mails in Washington, D.C., told the Electric Vehicle Association:

> If machines of the electric type can be built with sufficient speed and hill-climbing qualities to meet the requirements of the collection service they would undoubtedly be found to be particularly desirable ... the fact that electric machines are so much more simple of operation and can be easily driven by carriers, without the extra cost of chauffeurs ... is a decided advantage in their favor.[6]

Although electric vehicles held on in the commercial market longer than in the passenger market, production gradually shifted to gasoline-powered models. In 1914, in New York—the state with the most registered vehicles—electric vehicles accounted for about 6 percent of passenger cars and 29 percent of commercial vehicles. By 1917, however, nearly all of the commercial vehicles manufactured in the U.S. were gasoline models.

During World War I, the French, British, German and Russian governments subsidized gas trucks instead of electric. The "Liberty Truck" was designed by the Motor Transport section of the Quartermaster Corps in cooperation with the members of the Society of Automotive Engineers. Production of the 3–5-ton truck began in 1917, and the first models appeared ten weeks after the design was standardized. Of the almost 9,500 Class B Liberty trucks produced by 15 manufacturers, more than 7,500 were sent overseas. The Liberty's four-speed transmission coupled with its 52-hp gasoline engine gave the truck a top speed of about 15 miles per hour (24 kph).

The electric truck-building industry continued to put up a brave fight against the gasoline menace, particularly with the latter's ease of refueling. The Hartford Electric Light Company (HELCO) was located on Pearl Street in Hartford, Connecticut. Between 1911 and 1924, HELCO attempted a battery exchange and maintenance system. Initially faith in the imminent solution of the battery problem ran high, but expectations were never fulfilled. By 1916, at least 200 vehicles were enrolled in battery service programs in ten cities nationwide. By 1924, Willis Thayer, long-time manager of battery exchange at Hartford Electric, had become president of the Electric Transportation Company, an independent provider of battery service for electric vehicles.

In 1914, GV (slogan: "General Vehicle, Greatest Value") claimed that 25

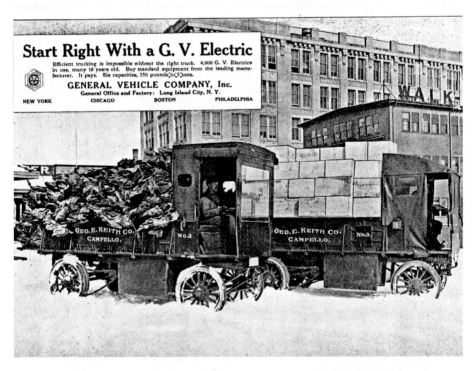

By 1910, the General Vehicle Company of Long Island City had sold more than 1,600 electric trucks. Leading retailers used 488 trucks, express companies 300, brewers 522, manufacturers and wholesalers thousands more. These were in use from Portland, Maine, to San Diego, California, to Toronto, Canada, to Dallas, Texas, while Rio de Janeiro and Havana had 13 (private collection).

firms already operated a total of 941 trucks and that there would soon be 4,000 GV electric trucks in service. The U.S. War Department in Manila used 40 GVs, while eight Navy yards used them. The following ad appeared in *Traffic World*:

The superiority of the Electric for city work is already appreciated by the more experienced users of motor vehicles. In numbers the Electric is just beginning to make itself felt, but in proving certain economic laws it has already made history. You can call "white" "black" for a while but when it comes to a show-down somebody loses.

Experienced motor truck users have ceased to buy motor trucks on price alone. You can buy a pleasure car by-product for half what you pay for a good Electric, but it will last one-third as long and in most cases it will be out of commission so often that the necessary reserve equipment will eat up any possible saving. That's not exaggerating— just talk to the older users.

Honestly now, did you ever seriously set out to learn *why an Electric truck is different from a gasoline truck for city work?* Another question: How big a premium in operating costs are you willing to pay for your prejudice or indifference to efficient delivery in the city?

Would you be interested in learning what G.V. users say about G.V. efficiency? Then write today for Bulletin 104.

But even GV was becoming aware of the superiority of the gas-truck indeed before long it was charged with manufacturing materials needed for war supplies such as the French-designed Gnome rotary airplane engine. In 1915, GV merged with the gas-truck department of the Peerless Motor Company. The production ran until 1920. The U.S. Army purchased a number of Peerless trucks. They were well liked by the Army. When World War I broke out, England purchased 12,000 Peerless Truck chassis and used them in the war, supplying the armies in Europe.

Another who fought on to the bitter end was Edison's former colleague, John M. Lansden, Jr. Somewhere between 1906 and 1912, he left his namesake company, having been hired by the General Motors Truck Company for his years of electric truck designing, manufacturing and marketing expertise. In 1914, Pierre S. du Pont, the dynamite and smokeless powder manufacturer in

DuPont de Nemours Powder Company preferred the electric truck to the internal combustion engine with its fumes to transport its volatile explosives (American Truck Historical Society).

Wilmington, Delaware, had bought stock in General Motors. One reason was to use electric trucks for the safer transportation of his volatile explosives.

Indeed, in a booklet prepared by Arthur La Motte, manager of the Technical Section of the DuPont Company, we realize why they needed to avoid the internal combustion engine with its fumes and vibration:

> In handling by truck or wagon, the principal points to be considered are that the body of the vehicle should be clean and that any exposed metal should be covered with boards or canvas or similar material. Where explosives are not transported in a closed body, the stock should be covered by tarpaulin. In hauling through cities, avoid congested streets and unnecessary stops.

Between 1912 and 1917, the General Motors Truck Company sold nine electric trucks ranging from 1,000 lbs. to 12,000 lbs. (450 kg to 5443 kg) capacity, built by Rapid and Reliance Trucks. A 1912 GMC Electric catalogue states that every GMC Electric was built under the direction of John M. Lansden and of the 600–700 units built in seven years, all were still in service. The catalogue also stated that Lansden and his associates were not hampered by expense and were given a clean slate in the perfection and new higher standard of electric truck construction. A total of 173 electric trucks were produced by GMC in 1912, accounting for 39.8 percent of all the trucks GMC produced that year, and 509 more were produced between 1913 and 1917. By 1914, GMC Electrics accounted for 22.6 percent of production, 10.3 percent in 1915, and 3.2 percent by 1916. Only one GMC Electric was built in 1917.

In 1913, Walter Baker's firm was overtaken in sales by Detroit Electric and in 1914 merged with fellow Cleveland automaker Rauch and Lang to become Baker, Rauch & Lang. The last Baker cars were made in 1916, but electric industrial trucks continued for a few more years. Sales gradually declined as owners realized the inconvenience of frequent recharging and of slow hill-climbing speeds. The Baker Motor Vehicle Company addressed those problems by constructing several recharging stations in the major stations. Its largest opened in 1910 at East 71st Street and Euclid Avenue, near Cleveland's wealthy east side. Baker, a visionary, hoped to have recharging stations at every major intersection, an idea scoffed at although eventually realized by the gasoline automobile producers and the oil companies.

According to "The Future of the Electric Commercial Car" published in *Motor Field* in April 1914: "The American electric truck is now used in 43 of the 48 states and in 9 foreign countries. Canada has nearly 200, the Philippines have approximately 75, while Cuba, Mexico, Brazil, England, France, Germany, South Africa, Australia, and Japan a limited number."

Despite this, the writing was on the wall. Looking at the lifespan of electric truck makers, by noting their years of cessation, the pattern becomes evident, although two or three would survive beyond the war: Argo 1912–

1914, Atlantic, Bailey 1908–1916, Baker (5 models) 1899–1917, Borland of Chicago 1903–1914, Champion 1912, Commercial Truck Co. of Philadelphia 1909–1928, Detroit Electric 1910–1916, Fritschle 1907–1917, GMC Electrics 1912–1924, General Motors Truck Company, 1912–1916, General Vehicle 1906–1918, Jatco, Lansden, M1P, Toledo 1912, Urban 1912–1917, Walker 1907–1937, Ward 1911–1935, Waverley 1898–1917, Electra Battery Co. 1913–1915.

In 1908, 85 percent of German cities with more than 25,000 residents and 55 percent of the smaller towns used some form of horse-drawn street-sweeping machines—a great potential for e-truck builders. The very low speed of these vehicles kept gas competition at bay, as controlling the combustion engine at these speeds was problematic. Kriéger-style tractors were known as "Elektrsiches Pferd" (electric horses). On the outbreak of World War I, Berlin owned 42 electric street sprinkling cars called "Strassenbesprengung." The German fire-engine fleet had increased to 400 in 90 cities, 148 of them electric.

In 1913 Sanford J. Bernheimer (Levi) of Saint Louis, Missouri, took out U.S. Patent 1119225A for "a certain new and useful improvement in that class of motor trucks known commercially as industrial or baggage trucks, the principal object of my present invention being to provide a motor truck of the kind stated having means for simultaneously actuating the braking-mechanism to off and on position and closing and opening the electrical circuit to the source of electrical energy or motive power of the truck." In 1914, Bernheimer linked up with Orenstein-Arthur-Koppel of Pasadena to set up the Electro Mobile Company and make a range of trucks—Types E, C and A—which went into general use in industrial plants in Saint Louis and in neighboring cities.

Another hybrid was developed by Percy K. Hexter, formerly secretary of the New York Liverymen's Association and owner of Hexter's stables, one located in Harlem and a second at Broadway and 84th Street. In 1908 he founded the Hexter Taxameter Cab Company, which had a fleet of 50 Sultan taxicabs. Hexter designed a heavy motor truck that utilized a gasoline engine mated to a General Electric-sourced electric transmission and controller. Two motors were employed, each driving a rear wheel independently through a side chain and sprockets. In order to keep the weight down, Hexter used a double-speed reduction, the first step using a short silent chain running to a countershaft which carried a sprocket that drove a second, larger sprocket on the rear wheel for its second reduction. The Hexter truck was built in 1914 by the Roland Gas-Electric Corporation in New York City in two versions (1.5 and 3.5 tons). The Hexter truck was short-lived and its inventor returned to selling gas trucks.

In 1914, according to an AFA survey, Germany had a total of 1,689 electric vehicles, 554 of them trucks and 270 for commercial and mail use. At that time 220 electric vehicles were in use at the Reichspost (including Bavaria and Württemberg), 113 in Berlin (71 three-wheelers and 47 for parcel delivery) and 30 in Leipzig. Vienna had 30 electric mail trucks. France had 318 battery electric vehicles of which 190 were trucks, while England had 288, 62 of them trucks.[7]

In October 1914, an exhaustive test was made of the reliability of four Edison Accumulator BEVs, one of them a van and another an ambulance. They made a 60-day run with an average 50–60 miles (80–95 km) daily, including a steep climb up a hill near Worcester. The tour took in Reading, Oxford, Cheltenham, Gloucester, Worcester, Birmingham, Wolverhampton, Burton-on-Trent, Stroke-on-Trent, Derby, Chesterfield, Sheffield, Leeds, Bradford, Harrogate, York, Hull, Lincoln, Nottingham, Kettering, Bedford and St. Albans. Some days were spent in and around Birmingham in view of the annual conference of the Municipal Electrical Association being held in that city. The vehicles were in Hull when war broke out on August 4, 1914. As "electrics" they were immune from impressments. Other companies lost their gas or horse vehicles. For example, Messrs J. Lyons and Co. Ltd. lost most of their fleet. To fill some of the gaps, the whole London stock of Edison Accumulator vehicles was commandeered within half an hour on the day after war was declared, three of these four touring vehicles included. From this moment the one pressing requirement was to get them back to London as quickly as possible.[8]

The 70-year-old Thomas Edison had still not lost faith in the battery alternative. In 1915, Edison Accumulator Ltd. issued a 32-page catalogue entitled "Edison Accumulator Commercial Electrics," printed in elegant sepia and gold coloring and with the title "To Electrify, is to Simplify":

> Until the advent of the Edison all-steel accumulator, some six years ago (1909) the Electric had fought a losing game with petrol. Much progress has been recorded since that time and there are now in American over 20,000 commercial electrics in very successful service ... although the English industry in Electrics is still in its early youth, yet a number of important firms including Messrs Liberty, Harrods, Lyons (Steam Bakeries), the Stratford Cooperative Society and Pullars Dye Works of Perth, Scotland, have Edison Accumulator vehicles in daily service. All Edison Accumulators are fitted with an Ampère Hour Metre; For use in factories and at railways, the Edison Accumulator Industrial Truck should last from 15 to 25 years. Type F 1-ton, *Buckwater* Truck 30 cwt. has been supplied to railway companies and industrial firms.

Liberty's of London had tested their first Edison Accumulator truck beginning in June 1913, then in May 1914 ordered another two. Other satisfied clients were E. C. Robson and Sons, Sunderland; Osram electric lamps; Jo Lyons & Co. Ltd. Bakers; the United Co-operative Baking Society and Glasgow and Whiteley's, a large retail company.

During the war there was a shortage of horses as most of them had been requisitioned for the war effort. Eight million horses and countless mules and donkeys died during the combat. They were used to transport ammunition and supplies to the front and many died, not only from the horrors of shellfire but also in terrible weather and appalling conditions. During some periods of the war, 1,000 horses per day were arriving in Europe as remounts for British troops, to replace horses lost. Gasoline was in equally short supply. This proved a boon for electric vehicle manufacturers, provided they could obtain the raw materials. Electric refuse trucks during World War I had a high loading line and lack of protection against their contents being blown about the roads. According to *The Motor, Marine and Aircraft Red Book* published by Technical Publishing Company in 1917, Edison Accumulators had equipped some 24 40-cwt trucks, often for refuse collection. The cleansing superintendents in the towns and boroughs in Birmingham, Glasgow, Wallasey, Blackpool, Enfield, Leyton, Sheffield and Nottingham cooperated with the manufacturers to improve the design.

When any existing technology is seriously threatened by a new technology, instead of being replaced, after a little shuffling, it frequently adjusts its role to take up its place alongside. This was to become the case for electric trucks during the inter-war years.

THREE

Inter-War Years

Although barred from the front-line battlefields, electric trucks had been silently working behind the scenes—through deployment in ammunition transportation, on the harbor piers, and in the navy depots beside the factory-based industrial truck. Such mini-trucks could ease congestion in the harbors, so the U.S. federal government bought 1,500 of them during the war.[1] A large gasoline car manufacturer had a fleet of 49 small electric tractors in operation in 1917. Each drove about 6,000 yards (6 km) per day. Electric mini-trucks—truck cranes, tractors, forklift trucks, platform cars for railroad platforms—did not replace horses, but manpower (on average ten men per truck), which the electric truck lobby saw as patriotic during the war as it freed up more men for service.

In 1919, about 5,000 electric industrial trucks were produced by 12 manufacturers, while estimates of the total fleet ranged from 6,000 to 15,000, most of them built during the war. Most used an exchange charging system. Between 1919 and 1940 the industrial truck in the USA would experience an explosive growth; in 1932 the fleet size increased to 12–15,000 units. At the time, the industrial trucks accounted for 44 percent and the electric street trucks for 23.5 percent of the total electric truck fleet energy consumption of 100 million kWh.

During World War I, the greater part of the German Post Office's e-fleet was lost and mail delivery took place again by horse traction. In 1924, the post office in Berlin put 360 2-ton delivery trucks back into action. Nationally the PO possessed 1,632 e-trucks, four times the number of gasoline trucks, and an unknown number of three-wheelers. By the mid–1930s, the Berlin mail delivery fleet consisted of 1,300 vehicles, of which 724 units were electric. Other fleets were found in seven other major German cities, making up a fleet of 2,400 vehicles.

But some just did not manage to make ends meet. In 1915, Tribelhorn of Switzerland took orders for only three trucks, three buses, one ambulance for Zurich and four doctor cars. Tribelhorn ventured into big trucks with a 5-ton payload. Most were also given an additional mechanical "mountain gearbox" with a smaller gear. Its switching was extremely ticklish—load, incline and speed had to be estimated accurately. Switching gears and controllers in the correct order was practically important at the same time, always with a view of the ammeter, so that the 200-amp fuse did not melt. Each Tribelhorn vehicle received exactly the battery that best suited its intended use, including three-wheeled electric vehicles. In 1920, 30 such tricycles were delivered to the Swiss postal service, but for five months in 1921, there was not a single new sale, and the following year the company declared bankruptcy.[2]

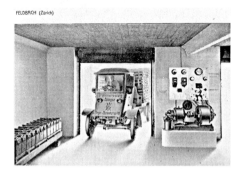

Above, left: **A truck built in the early 1920s by Tribelhorn of Feldbach, Switzerland, enters its charging station (Uetiker Museum).** *Above, right:* **The Tribelhorn range of trucks at the SBB in Lucerne, Switzerland (Uetiker Museum).** *Right:* **Tribelhorn also produced an electric three-wheeler delivery truck. In 1920, thirty such tricycles were delivered to the Swiss postal service (Uetiker Museum).**

The gas-powered truck had become the standard. Ford continued with his Model TT. Starting in 1924, the truck was available with a factory-produced body. By 1926, the price had dropped to $325. By 1928, Ford had sold 1.3 million Model TTs before replacing the truck with the more capable Model AA with a 1.5-ton chassis.

The Clark *Tructractor* prototype had been assembled in 1917 in Buchanan, Michigan, by employees of the Clark Equipment Company. Originally configured with a flat bed or cargo box, manually loaded and unloaded, this seated counterbalanced vehicle was used to haul materials between Clark's various axle, drill and wheel departments. What made the *Tructractor* unique was that it was the world's first internal combustion-engined industrial truck. Visitors to the plant, impressed, asked Clark to build units for their warehouses and factories. In 1918, eight *Tructractors* were built and in 1919 more than 75 were manufactured. Production would continue until 1970.

In 1918, when the war ended, thousands of gas-engine military trucks were sold off second-hand and put into peacetime service. But there were some who fully understood that once their limitations were accepted, electric trucks were very reliable. In 1919, Montgomery Ward of Chicago financed a special electric house-to-house delivery truck featuring a hinged dashboard that swung away for easy access and exit. Ward's drop-frame electric anticipated the low cab-forward movement. In September 1921, at the New York Electrical Show, among the 90 booths, an electric truck display formed one of the features. Among the manufacturers taking space were the Commercial Truck Company, the Lansden Company, the Walker Vehicle Company (now owned by Commonwealth Edison), the Ward Motor Vehicle Company, the Steinmetz Electric Motor Corporation, Walter Motor Truck Company, and the Baker R. L. Corporation.

R.C. Williams & Co. Inc. of New York, established in 1811, was one of America's first truly global companies, the original "supermarket to the world." This company was constantly innovating. It was among the first to distribute food in cans, and was a pioneer in packaging, marketing, merchandising and retailing. They were also trend spotters, who predicted—to their enormous profit—that coffee would become king in the American home and Prohibition would be short-lived. They created one of the first international brands, *Royal Scarlet*, which they then franchised across a series of retail store locations. Beginning in 1909, with a fleet of 25 electric trucks by 1922, they no longer had any need for horses. By 1920, New York City had a 4,000-strong fleet of electric parcel delivery trucks.

Around this time, Ward of New York decided to call the trucks by the name Electruck, the name already used by the Los Angeles Creamery, and indeed there is reference to a court case between the two companies. Whether in or out of Court, Ward must have won because in 1926 the Electruck Corporation of New York City, with capital of $1,000,000 to make motor trucks, purchased a five-story building at 534–540 West 46th Street. Ralph D. Ward was president of the company. Equally, Walter S. Ward and Benjamin H. Britt patented a device (U.S. 1,602,521) whereby a hand-crank system could raise and lower the battery for flushing and charging. That year Electruck

Price # 4325.00

One Ton *Electruck* Side-Door Panel Body and Vestibule Front

The word "Electruck" was originally invented in 1914 by the Los Angeles Creamery at San Pedro Street, Los Angeles, then taken over by the Ward Company in New York City in 1926 for their e-trucks. Soon after, Commercial Truck Co of Philadelphia acquired the Electruck Corporation including machinery, parts, drawings, patents, etc., surviving the Depression and continuing to build Electrucks until 1937. During the 1950s and 1960s, T.H Lewis of Watford, London, England, built thousands of Electrucks for Express Dairies. The name has resurfaced some 50 years later used by TransPower in Escondido, California.

proudly produced a brochure entitled "The World's Finest Electric Delivery Vehicle." Their 75,000 square foot plant included a paint shop (color copy and design submitted by the purchaser) and service station. The brochure claimed:

> Over 900 of our trucks, Models 43, 39 and 27, are being operated and maintained under our direct supervision in cities of the east and Middle West. Many years of research have been spent in an effort to attain that perfection in the construction of an electric vehicle which would withstand all the tests.

Their slogan was GROW, an acronym for "Go Right on Working." Soon after, the Commercial Truck Company of Philadelphia acquired the Electruck Corporation including machinery, parts, drawings, patents, etc., surviving the Depression and continuing to build *Electrucks* until 1937.

Horn & Hardart used 18 of these trucks to deliver hot prepared food to their chain of 33 Automat cafeterias around Manhattan to be taken away by busy New Yorkers (American Historical Truck Society).

One company which relied on electric trucks was Horn & Hardart of New York City, operator of the Automat Cafeterias which sold pre-packaged automat favorites. Using the advertising slogan "Less Work for Mother," the company had popularized the notion of easily served "take-out" food as an equivalent to home-cooked meals. H&H used 18 trucks from 2.5 to 5-ton capacity to distribute food prepared in the company's commissary to their 33 restaurants in Manhattan in time to meet the meal-hour rush of hungry thousands.

In 1926, Ashton B. Collins, Sr., 40-year-old commercial manager of the Alabama Power Company, created "Reddy Kilowatt," a stick figure whose body and limbs are made of stylized lightning bolts and whose bulbous head has a light bulb for a nose and wall outlets for ears. Reddy Kilowatt made his first published appearance on March 14, 1926, in an advertisement in *The Birmingham News* and soon became the long-time symbol for electric companies. His logo was still seen on the side of Battronic electric trucks 70 years later.

By 1927, Borden Brothers of Columbus, Ohio, innovators of condensed milk, had 88 trucks, although they had practically none just five years before. The American Railway Express Company, a national package delivery service,

For half a century, Reddy Kilowatt was the symbol for electric companies (public domain).

also had a big fleet of short-haul trucks. With a fleet of 18 electrics already employed in the delivery of ice cream, the Jersey Ice Cream Company of Chicago ordered three more 5-ton trucks.

Properly maintained, e-trucks had become known for their longevity and short-haul reliability. For example, one delivery service had been operating a truck purchased 20 years before (1908) which had totaled about 80,000 miles (130,000 km) with its owner estimating that the truck was good for at least five more years' service. One of four trucks which Chicago's largest department store had purchased in 1910 was still running as part of a fleet of 296 vehicles 15 years later. Three other Chicago department stores had installed electric vehicles in 1911, totaling 13 electrics. By 1928, 97 electrics were operated by these three companies. Another fleet in New York of 30 electrics included a vehicle in service since 1912 that had run up some 100,000 miles (160,000 km) and carried a total of 128,160,000 lbs. (58,132,000 kg) of goods. In harbors such as Boston, Walker trucks were being used to transport ice from an icehouse to preserve the catches of fishing boats.

Then there was the continuing success story of the industrial truck. In 1868, Linus Yale, Jr., and Henry R. Towne had formed the Yale Lock Manufacturing Company, later to become Yale & Towne Manufacturing Co., in Stamford, Connecticut. For use in their plant, in 1919, Yale and Towne approached the C.W. Hunt Company of Staten Island, New York, already known for their rope, coal-handling equipment, cranes, and complete industrial railways. Hunt made them the world's first battery-powered lift platform truck. Making further improvements, Yale soon launched a range of high-lift platform trucks, tow tractors and one of the first lifting trucks with tilting forks, manufactured at their Tacony Street plant in Philadelphia. These were followed by an electric truck with rising forks and elevated mast. For export, Fenwick of Paris, established by Noël Fenwick in the 1870s, imported the Yale & Towne units from 1918. Then in 1927, following the devaluation of the French franc to the U.S. dollar, Fenwick obtained the license to manufacture Yale's forklift trucks.

With the acquisition of Steubing Cowan Company in 1931, Yale & Towne added hand-manipulated trucks to their range. During the 1930s, Yale grew internationally with manufacturing in England, the acquisition of BKS forklift trucks in Germany and the sale of lift trucks in Japan. Two years later, it acquired the Walker Vehicle Company, manufacturers of electric trucks and electric automobiles. Walker had continued to innovate. In 1926, John G. Carroll, assignor to Walker Vehicle Company of Chicago, had obtained two patents, one for an axle for vehicles (U.S. 1,570,941) and the other for brake construction (U.S. 1,570,942), and in 1931 Carl J. Blakeslee filed for a wheel patent for the Walker Vehicle Company. In 1938, Yale & Towne introduced the first electric sit-down forklift truck. Yale went on to develop innovations such as power steering, center-control trucks, caster steering and the use of high heat-resistant Class-H silicon insulation in electric motors, still considered among the industry's finest.

In 1922, perhaps in competition with Yale & Towne, Baker presented a truck with a duplex compensating suspension for use in plants and warehouses. America's entrance into World War I had saved the Baker R & L Company from impending failure. The company's war work included the manufacture of electric bomb handlers and lift trucks. Recognizing the potential of the electric lift truck field, the Baker R & L Company ceased its production of the Baker R & L electric and the Owen Magnetic cars in mid–1919. It reorganized later that year as the Baker Raulang Company, manufacturing electric lift trucks at the Baker plant and assembling the truck bodies at the Rauch and Lang plant. The latter plant also continued its production of automobile bodies for other companies.

In 1918, the Municipal Electricity Department in Christchurch, New Zealand, had bought a half-ton Walker for delivery services. In 1947 the MED took the Walker truck out of service after it had completed 320,000 miles (515,000 km).

In 1920 in Great Britain, the Royal Mail purchased a modest fleet of thirteen electric trucks for transporting mail between the Birmingham sorting office and the Birmingham New Street Railway Station. They proved so successful that such carts were soon plying their trade on railway station platforms across the country.

During the 19th century, Messrs Ransomes, Sims & Jefferies Ltd. of Ipswich, Suffolk, had been a major manufacturer of agricultural machinery, often steam-powered. Deciding to build an e-truck, in 1912 they approached a Belgian-born electrical engineer, Paul Alphonse Hubert Mossay. From 1902 to 1906, Mossay had designed the first induction motors built by the British Thomson-Houston Company in Rugby, going on to innovate larger induction motors for the British Westinghouse Electric and Manufacturing Company in Manchester. He had then spent four years as chief engineer at Hansa Lloyd Works in Bremen, Germany, designing their engines and battery-driven vehicles. Returning to his native Belgium, Mossay was responsible for the design and manufacture of gasoline-engined pleasure and commercial vehicles at the Germain Workshops in Monceau-sur-Sambre. Back in London, he had started up his own consulting company when Ransomes, Sims & Jeffries asked him to design a truck.

Apart from getting the iron-chloride batteries to provide enough energy, the Belgian engineer did not use gearboxes, realizing that they simply wasted power. Instead he used two IMV 9 type 40-cell batteries of 290 ah capacity and two compound motors. These could be connected in various series/parallel arrangements via what looked like a gear lever. This gave a good starting torque and a decent, for the time, nine mph running speed. He was also aware of regeneration and gear position two was selected when going downhill. A further challenge was that he used motors connected to the front wheels, but this could only be achieved with 50-cwt trucks. Larger 3.5-ton trucks needed larger 8.5 hp motors, so he redesigned the truck with motors mounted halfway along the chassis, driving the rear wheels via chains. Satisfied, R, S & J called their first prototype truck the Orwell after the River Orwell where their plant was situated. Although several of these went into service, one of them supplying a parcel service for the Midlands Railway, during World War I, Ransomes built 350 Royal Aircraft Factory F.E.2 fighter planes for the Royal Flying Corps. With the Armistice, men who returned after service in the armed forces, some of them broken in body and mind, did not find the "Land Fit for Heroes" that they had been promised. For many of them there was no work. In 1921, Ransomes had to close three departments and 1,500 men lost their jobs, the rest of the workforce being put on short time. The women who had taken work in engineering works, including Ransomes, found themselves cast aside. Ransomes had to diversify and in late 1918, they presented their 3.5-ton *Orwell* electric tipping wagon with a semi-enclosed cab and a 2-ton electric chassis. Although the batteries used were Ironclad-Exide IMV8s as provided by Batteries Ltd., whose supplier, first for whole nickel-iron NIFE

In 1913, Belgian electric engineer Paul Mossay designed this electric truck for Ransomes, Sims & Jefferies Ltd. of Ipswich, England, which they named the Orwell after the local river. It would give service to a large number of well-known industrial concerns, railways such as the Great Western Railway Company at Paddington Station, and government departments. It was also exported all over the British Empire, such as to the New Zealand Express Co. in Christchurch (Ransomes, Sims, and Jefferies ltd. Ipswich).

batteries and then for the components to make them in Redditch, was the Swedish battery company Svenska Ackumulator AB Jungner; Waldmar Jungner had developed a battery couple very similar to that of Edison.

Based on the *Orwell*, Mossay developed a prototype electric bus, chain-driven with double wheels at the rear, eventually sold to George Hargreaves & Co. of Accrington as a 40-seater front-entrance staff transport at their colliery. The ingenious Belgian also designed a mobile crane with a small steering caster at the front and another at the rear, linked together. He provided two pairs of wheels across the middle, each pair driven by an electric motor. Turning the steering wheel around to full lock energized the motors in opposite directions—the front and rear wheels were completely sideways, so the crane simply turned around and around. Mossay also built a prototype electric motorcycle and sidecar in which the batteries were fitted under the seat of the sidecar. Even though the vehicle, with a top speed of 16 mph, was registered for road use (registration DX-1834) and ran at a third of the cost of gasoline, it never went into the manufacturing stage, but was used by Mossay to commute to the plant. In 1923 Mossay took out a patent for a charging apparatus for annealing ovens and furnaces. Up to 1948, Paul Mossay remained inventive, patenting, among other things, pneumatic tools, a system of cooling dynamo-electric machines, improved pole caps for electric alternators and synchronous motors, a multiphase AC transformer and a flame-proof electric motor. His telegraph address was appropriately "Asynchrone."[3]

By 1925, Ransomes were doing a good business in refuse tip wagons, works trucks and runabout cranes. Their 1-ton truck was in service with a large number of well-known industrial concerns, railways such as the Great Western Railway Company at Paddington Station, and government departments. They were also exported all over the British Empire, such as to the New Zealand Express Company in Christchurch.[4]

Like Ransomes, through the Victorian era, Richard Garrett and Sons Ltd. of Leiston, Suffolk, had been building large numbers of steam engines exported worldwide. From 1916, alongside their steam-powered machinery, they presented a 3.5-ton electric refuse truck based on a brewer's type body, with curb control to assist in house-to-house collection of refuse, for which its 35-mile (55 km) range was largely adequate.

Harrods Ltd. of Knightsbridge, London, continued to cater to royalty, the aristocracy and the wealthy of the United Kingdom. Twenty years before, they had run a red, white and blue-striped delivery van, built by Walter Bersey of London. Wanting to replace their fleet of 100 gasoline trucks, in 1913, Sir Woodman Burbidge Bt., the store's CEO, visited the USA to check out several electric delivery truck manufacturers. He returned home to order several electrics ranging in size from 10 cwt to two tons, including 12 ft 9 in (4 m) Walker Trucks.

But, as revealed in a copy of a report archived at the Thomas Edison Historical Park, on their first trials these trucks did not appear to be traveling at the speed stated by the manufacturer. Maurice E. Fox, electrical engineer for the Edison Accumulators Ltd. in London and Paris, stated:

At the beginning of 1913 Harrods purchased four Walker Electric Trucks, equipped with Edison Storage Batteries. Monnot had previously demonstrated an Edison battery-equipped truck of another make, and the results achieved decided Messrs Harrods in purchasing electric trucks and having them Edison battery equipped. I was instructed to superintend the installation of the battery when the trucks arrived in London. In March, rumors began to circulate that they were not satisfactory, their speed being much slower than that specified by Walker in their catalogue. I knew the battery was in good condition so the fault must lie with the electrical equipment of the vehicle. I examined the motor of one of the trucks carefully but found no name plate or any designation as to the type and size of motor. After further investigation I advised Mr. Howes, the Harrods engineer, that the evidence gathered led him to believe that the motors supplied were designed for a higher voltage than were suitable for the Edison Battery sixty-cell equipments. In other words, that a lead battery motor, eighty volt had been installed in error. I also requested that I be allowed to take one of the trucks for test, to see if I could further confirm this belief, but Mr. Howes stated that he needed the vehicles and before doing anything further, would acquaint the manufacturer with his difficulties.[5]

In May, William Howes told Fox that Walker had not been able to give an explanation for the arrangement and they were considering the substitution of a lead battery for the Edison to see if the vehicles would run better. Fox continues:

We do not wish to see our battery maligned, especially upon its initial appearance on the English market. I persuaded Howes to let me have a Harrods truck and to test it. I found that Walker had supplied lead-acid equipment and that the voltage of the Edison 60 cell was lower and the cars refused to deliver their required speed. Harrods also complained that the battery boxes were not made low enough to accommodate the Edison battery, so that in order to fill the cells with distilled water, it is necessary to disconnect the trays and pull them sideways. As they are very tightly wedged together, this treatment is causing the trays to disintegrate. Again the ampere-hour meters are of the simple model, instead of the differential shunt type usually installed nowadays so that they are of little use in charging the vehicles. It is merely necessary to add a sufficient number of Edison cells × 4 to give the required voltage. Or to remove the 80-volt motor and replace with a 60-volt motor. These extra cells or motor must be shipped over by Walker.

Some field shunts were shipped on April 14th to Messrs Frazer brothers, the Walker Company's agents in New York and when these are installed, the speed will be increased. The Walker Company has ordered new field coils from the Westinghouse Company which will be shipped from Chicago in about twenty days and which will give even greater speed. As to the question of filling the cells with distilled water, a special filler such as this company uses with Edison batteries has been sent to the customer. The Walker people are fully alive to the necessity of having these first vehicles equipped with Edison batteries in London entirely satisfactory and they believe they will be then equipped with the new field coils which are being sent. The Walker people are exceedingly friendly and are at all times doing all they can to encourage purchasers of their vehicles to use Edison batteries. The Walker Company believe that their portion of the vehicle as shipped is up to specifications but they are very glad to do everything they can to make the wagons satisfactory. They personally believe that the very heavy bodies put on them (nearly double the weight of the bodies ordinarily used with this model) contributed to the trouble.

Once these problems had been ironed out, by 1917 the Harrods fleet had grown to 60 white-topped vehicles, each one numbered, plus half a dozen electric industrial trucks for working in the storehouse, all of American manufacture: Walker, Anderson, Lansden and General Motors. Mostly of 10 cwt capacity, the entire 3.5-ton fleet used 72-volt nickel-iron Edison batteries which Harrods bought, charged and maintained themselves. After their 66 to 80-volt batteries had been recharged, the vehicles, with their olive green livery, could operate for around four hours when fully laden at speeds of 25 mph (40 kph) with a driving range of around 50 miles (80 km). Seventy-five percent of Harrods' deliveries were foodstuffs. The services were grouped under three headings: local and town, i.e., in the vicinity of the firm's stores; suburban, up to a radius of 10 to 15 miles (15 to 25 km); and country, for distances of 15 miles (25 km) and upwards. With Harrods' male personnel having enlisted to fight on the Western Front, these journeys were often made by female chauffeurs.

From 1919, Harrod's Ltd. of Knightsbridge ran a fleet of Walker Trucks in dark olive green and white livery. Here they are lined up in Hans Crescent beside the store (Harrods Company Archive, London).

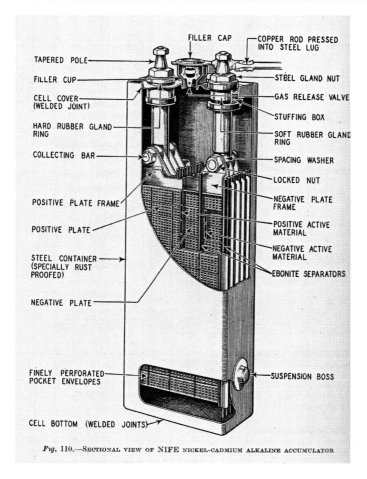

FILLER CAP

COPPER ROD PRESSED
INTO STEEL LUG

TAPERED POLE

FILLER CUP

CELL COVER
(WELDED JOINT)

HARD RUBBER GLAND
RING

COLLECTING BAR

POSITIVE PLATE FRAME

POSITIVE PLATE

STEEL CONTAINER
(SPECIALLY RUST
PROOFED)

NEGATIVE PLATE

FINELY PERFORATED
POCKET ENVELOPES

CELL BOTTOM (WELDED JOINTS)

STEEL GLAND NUT

GAS RELEASE VALVE

STUFFING BOX

SOFT RUBBER GLAND
RING

SPACING WASHER

LOCKED NUT

NEGATIVE PLATE
FRAME

POSITIVE ACTIVE
MATERIAL

NEGATIVE ACTIVE
MATERIAL

EBONITE SEPARATORS

SUSPENSION BOSS

Fig. 110.—SECTIONAL VIEW OF NIFE NICKEL-CADMIUM ALKALINE ACCUMULATOR

Cutaway drawing of the inside of a nickel-iron battery (author's collection).

Motor vehicle imports were prohibited during World War I and British manufacturers were unable to produce battery vehicles in anything like the numbers needed. This resulted in Harrods' fleet growing much less quickly than the managers would have liked. The vans were housed in a garage in the main Harrods building, immediately above their private power station. The firm generated the whole of the energy needed for lighting, power supplies and battery recharging throughout its huge stores, its powerhouse being situated in the basement beneath the electric vehicle garage. The plant comprised six high-speed steam sets directly coupled to DC generators, while a 55kW motor generator supplied by J.H. Holmes & Co. was used for battery charging. While charging, the trucks were lined up, end-on, at a loading platform which occupied two sides of the garage. Thirty trucks could be charged

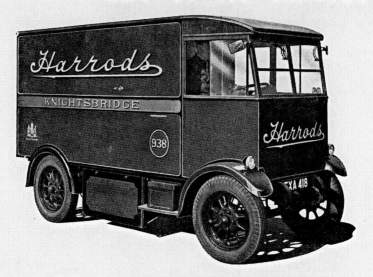

Again, those four words of wisdom . . .

GET IT AT HARRODS

Remember, if you live at a distance from Town, that Harrods many-sided Service is as near as your telephone or your nearest letter-box and Harrods Motors deliver free, promptly and regularly, in thirteen hundred districts, covering nearly three thousand square miles a day.

A copy of this Book and of Harrods weekly Food News will be posted to any friend of yours likely to be interested if you'll kindly send name and address.

HARRODS LTD   *SLOane 1234*   **KNIGHTSBRIDGE SW1**

When their Walker truck fleet began to age, between 1937 and 1939, Harrods engineers redesigned and rebuilt a new fleet as shown in this advertisement. Improved batteries gave them an extended range of 60 miles per charge. In total, some 60 vans were built, staying in service until the 1960s (Harrods Company Archive, London).

at a time, taking between four to five hours, and it was planned that additional accommodation would be provided as needed. An average of 8,000 deliveries were made each day by electric vans, a delivery sometimes being made up of a single packet, but more often of a number of items. Christmas saw the number of deliveries increase by some 25 percent, but this was well within the capacity of the electrics. By 1917, the vans had covered more than 900,000 miles (1,400,000 km). Tires lasted, on average, for about 12,000 miles (20,000 km). Six industrial Edison-Elwell-Parker type pallet trucks were used in the general stores.[6]

A decade later, from 1937 to 1939, Harrods built their own electric vans. They were assembled at the rate of one per fortnight, the very first designated Model *EVM1*. Electrical equipment was provided by Bruce Peebles & Co. Ltd. of Edinburgh (motor) and Chloride 36IMF (batteries). There was a substantial element of U.S. Walker components, but all the other work including chassis and bodywork they carried out at their own workshops, the Engineering and Coachbuilding Works at Barnes, beside the River Thames. Improved batteries gave them an extended range of 60 miles (100 km) per charge. In total some sixty vans were built, staying in service until the 1960s.

During the 1930s, the British biscuit (cookie) manufacturer Huntley & Palmer Ltd. of Reading came up with the novel idea of packaging their biscuits in tins shaped like vehicles, calling the brand "Mechanical Biscuits." These included a locomotive, a steamship, a steam wagon, a streetcar, an airship and an electric truck, in the manufacturer's dark blue livery. Inside was a delicious assortment of ginger nut and Tribrek breakfast biscuits, considered an excellent gift for children.[7]

In October 1928, a truck was ingeniously converted into an electric traveling bakery by Walker, Hunter & Co. Ltd. of Port Down Iron Works, Falkirk, Scotland, specialists in bakery equipment. The vehicle was a Tilling-Stevens petrol-electric, and via a change-over switching system, use was made of the current generated by the petrol engine to operate the 10kW electric baking oven, an electric dough cutter and an electric baking plate—or all three simultaneously.

Captain C.F. Roberts MC, transport manager for the bakers Hovis Ltd. of High Wycombe, Buckinghamshire, was running a fleet of electric vans including a Garrett 6-tonner, a Walker tractor and five Walker 5-tonners with 44-cell batteries. Charging was carried out by either the Lancashire Dynamo & Crypto Company or by Macfarlane Engineering Ltd.

From 1916, in the great port of Liverpool, northwest England, electric platform trucks were in regular service on the Mersey Dock Estate for the well-known steamship owners Messrs Elder Dempster & Co. Ltd.'s berth, West Toxteth Dock. It was situated above a London, Midland & Scottish goods railway station. A fleet of Walker trucks was used to transport cargoes,

During the 19th century, Richard Garrett and Sons Ltd. of Leiston, Suffolk, had been building large numbers of steam engines exported worldwide. From 1916, alongside their stream-powered machinery, they presented a 3½-ton electric refuse truck based on a brewer's type body (National Motor Museum, Beaulieu).

such as African and Honduran mahogany logs, weighing from 1 to 8 tons, from one part of the dock sheds to another. Sir Owen Cosby Philipps, head of Elder, Dempster & Co. Ltd. Cosby and the Royal Mail Steam Packet Company, also acquired a controlling interest in more than twenty other companies, including the Union-Castle Line and the Pacific Steam Navigation Company. Acquisitions continued, culminating in the purchase of the White Star Line in 1927. All of these used electric trucks.[8]

The GV *Giant* articulated 10-tonner was the largest British-built battery-electric vehicle (BEV). Made in 1924 for the Manchester Corporation, it had a platform 16 by 7 feet (4.9 by 2.1 meters) and an overall length of 38 ft. (11.6 meters). It was used for carrying cable drums of up to seven tons. It had an innovative front-opening door. Another council also using large trucks was the town of Leicester. They bought a chain-drive 3.5-ton refuse collector from Clayton of Lincoln, a firm well known in the steam wagon and traction-engine field, who also made battery-electric trucks.

During this period, the Commercial Motor Vehicle Users Association helped development by providing classes for electrics in their annual parades, a number of them in the town of Nottingham. During the later years, veteran electrics that had run more than 100,000 miles and were more than ten years old were winning prizes and proving the long life of this class of vehicle, to the consternation of some gasoline enthusiasts. At the 1926 parade, in the electric section, Carter Paterson and Co. Ltd. had three GeVeCo-built vehicles, one of which had run over 35,000 miles (55,000 km). Next to this was a Walker owned by the Chloride Electrical Storage Co. Ltd. Hackney Borough Council had an Orwell and two Garretts. One was equipped as a water cart and another with a special double-container body for house refuse, this having lugs at the side for lifting purposes. Hurls Ltd., in addition to their other teams, had one composed of a Walker and two Edisons, all these having run considerably over 40,000 miles (65,000 km), but this record was easily beaten by the Edison belonging to London Wholesale Dairies Ltd. which had covered more than 109,000 miles (175,000 km). Finished in striking blue and situated next to this was a Walker belonging to the Metropolitan Electric Supply Co. Ltd. The team entered by Cadbury Bros. Ltd. consisted of 50-cwt Tilling-

The Tilling-Stevens system, innovated by William Arthur Stevens of Maidstone, Kent, for coach and truck fleet builder-manager Thomas Tilling, enabled trucks like this one to run either by battery-electric or petrol-electric transmission (National Motor Museum, Beaulieu).

Stevens hybrids, the oldest of which had over 40,000 miles (65,000 km) to its credit. In the Electric Vehicle Section, the winner gained the special plaque presented by the Electric Vehicle Committee of Great Britain Ltd. (a section of the British Electrical Development Association). First place was taken by the Willesden District Council with their Orwell tipping wagon. Second was London Wholesale Dairies Ltd. Edison. Third, fourth and fifth places went to the Metropolitan Borough of Hackney, for their Orwell and two Garretts. Sixth was Meux's Brewery Co. Ltd.'s GeVeCo while seventh, eighth and ninth were Hovis Ltd. Walker and two Edison trucks. And the tenth place was awarded to Carter Paterson and Co. Ltd.'s GeVeCO.

Another example of longevity was an electric brougham, built by Kriéger of Paris, delivered to the UK in 1907 and purchased in 1912 by a Mr. Scott of London. It was still in running order in 1932. When last seen it had covered some 130,000 miles (210,000 km). It had two motors and was rated at six horsepower. The controller gave six forward gears and one reverse, while there were two brakes, one electric, giving regenerative control, and one hand brake. The average running speed was 15 to 20 mph (25 to 30 kph) and the vehicle would travel 45 to 50 miles (70 to 80 km) on one charge. The battery was a 48K13 D.P. Kathanode, having a capacity of 168 Ah at the five-hour rate.

Walker Electric Trucks went from strength to strength. A 1922 advertisement bore the slogan: "Watch out for those disc wheel electric trucks!"

In 1925, Marshall Field & Co. of Chicago were operating 276 Walkers, their livery also a deep green color with the Marshall Field coat of arms on each side of the body of the largest fleet of electrics in the world. The chassis was a Model 10 Walker with a wooden body by the Champion Auto Equipment Company. Also using the Walker Model 10 chassis and the 3.5 horsepower rear-mounted Westinghouse motor with Edison A6 batteries, the Elysee Delivery DeLuxe Corporation of Hagerstown built some very smart-looking town delivery vehicles, which went into service in the fleets of New York's Bonwit Teller & Co., Arnold Constable & Co. and specialty retailer Stewart & Co. department stores for delivery to the suburbs, well within the Walker 10's 40-mile range. No wonder that Walkers were shipped all over the world. More than 200 Walkers were in use in Christchurch, New Zealand. In Winnipeg, Canada, T Eaton Company received delivery of Walker Chassis No. 9597, then turned to a local company, Chalmers Auto, Truck and Body Works, to create a custom design in its traditional blue, red and white livery. It was in service for the next 20 years.

The Knickerbocker Ice Company of New York, formerly using horses for their delivery of ice packs, began with one Walker truck in 1923 and increased to 78 by 1928. The bodies were built of the finest oak and cypress in the company's own body shop in Brooklyn; the chassis, wheels and running

WESTINGHOUSE VEHICLE MOTOR FOR LIGHT SERVICE, SUCH AS PLEASURE CARS,
LIGHT DELIVERY WAGONS, ETC.

Westinghouse Electric & Manufacturing Company, East Pittsburgh, Pennsylvania, produced a very reliable motor for the truck industry (Westinghouse Electric Corporation Photographs, Detre Library & Archives, Heinz History Center).

gear were painted red and the body bright yellow, with black letters shaded in vermilion and white. These electric ice trucks could carry 34 cakes, weighing 300 pounds each, enabling driver salesmen to finish their routes in three hours less daily time than they could when using horses.[9]

According to Arthur Williams, Vice President in charge of Commercial Relations, New York Edison Co., in an address of welcome to a conference of electric truck executives given on March 6, 1928, in New York, $5 million worth of electric trucks had been purchased by users throughout the U.S. during the previous year.

Electric trucks soon replaced steam power for mining: Bucyrus Foundry & Manufacturing Co, an American surface and underground mining equipment company, was founded by Daniel Parmelee Eells in 1880. In 1924, a Bucyrus 50-B revolving electric shovel mounted on caterpillar crawlers and equipped with a ¾-cubic-yard bucket was installed at the Wabigon mine, and a Bucyrus 80-B revolving, electric, caterpillar-traction shovel at the Richmond mine, in Palmer, Michigan.

When riveted construction was replaced by electric welding, in 1926, two Bucyrus 120-B revolving, electric, caterpillar-traction shovels with four-cubic-yard buckets were placed in operation at the Susquehanna mine, Hibbing, Minnesota. These three shovels were the first of their type and size using direct-current motors to be employed in the Lake Superior district.

Since then shovels of this type have come into general use on the Mesabi Range, most of them being equipped with four- to five-cubic-yard dippers. The electric 120-B shovel utilized separate DC motors for its various motions and employed the Ward-Leonard system of control. This system, used on all Bucyrus shovels until recent times, replicated the precise control of the former steam shovels and provided maximum torque at stall speed. AC power was supplied to the shovel via a trailing cable that drove a 275-horsepower motor-generator set. This in turn provided DC power to the hoist, crowd and swing motors, propeller-driven from the main hoist motor through a train of gears, shafts and clutches.

About 330 of the 120-Bs were sold around the world over a period lasting almost three decades. In 1924 the first installation of standard-gauge electric locomotives in open-pit ore mining in the U.S. was made at the Wabigon mine in Buhl, Minnesota. The equipment included one Marion 300-E and one Bucyrus model 50-B, both equipped with direct-current motors operated by motor-generator sets; the model 300-E had full Ward-Leonard control, whereas the 50-B had partly rheostatic control. In 1928–29, a similar installation was made at the Mesabi Chief mine in Keewatin, Minnesota, using one Bucyrus 225-B 90-foot-boom, 8-cubic-yard-dipper, full-revolving shovel, and two Bucyrus 120-B 32-foot (10 m) boom, four-cubic-yard shovels, all full-revolving type with caterpillar traction and equipped with direct-current motors and Ward-Leonard control. General Electric 60-ton eight-wheel locomotives were used. The rolling stock comprised 16 air-dump side-pivot, drop-door cars of 30 cubic yards capacity. A Bucyrus heavy-type spreader was employed on the dumps for spreading the spoil and a Nordberg track shifter was used for throwing tracks and for general utility work. By 1931, Bucyrus-Erie 120-B, four-cubic-yard electric shovels were used at Jerome, replacing the old Marion 300, eight-cubic-yard, coal-fired steam shovel.

In December 1927, the Survey Committee of the Society of Electrical Development Inc. in New York published a booklet, prepared by Harold J. Payne, entitled "Profitable Application of Electric Industrial Trucks and Tractors." Among those manufacturers mentioned: Automatic Transportation Co. of Buffalo for its elevating platform truck models; Baker Raulang; Crescent (electric pallet trucks) Electric pallet truck brochure 1915; Mercury Manufacturing; Yale and Towne, and Elwell-Parker. This was proof that this type of electric truck was increasingly popular.

Developments in France

Over in France, following the 1918 Armistice, the price of gasoline was high so some continued to invest in electric transport. Swiss chemical engi-

145698 - Truck Type Switchboard

The truck-type switchboard with interchangeable units of all steel construction is rapidly becoming standard equipment among operating companies.

The Westinghouse track-type rheostat switchboard with interchangeable units of all-steel construction enabled regular simultaneous recharging of a fleet of electric trucks (Westinghouse Electric Corporation Photographs, Detre Library & Archives, Heinz History Center).

neer Victor Hérold had founded "La Société Industrielle des Accumulateurs Alcalins" (S.I.A.A), based on the nickel-iron technology developed separately by Edison and Jungner. Made in Romainville, near Paris, these first batteries were used to power luggage carousels at Paris railway stations and to light locomotives of the Paris-Lyon-Marseille (PLM) Company at Lyon station. World War I prevented production from starting. In 1918, S.I.A.A. production started under the product name "La Société des Accumulateurs Fixes et de Traction" (S.A.F.T), which manufactured and distributed nickel-based batteries for industrial applications and storehouse trolleys.

In 1922, the Union of Electricity Trade Unions, representing electrical equipment manufacturers and electricity producers, decided, under the impetus of the public authorities, to organize trials with a triple objective: to identify the manufacturers of electric vehicles; to stimulate activity and progress in the construction of these vehicles; and to make the public aware of the current state of affairs in France. For this purpose, from September 25 to October 10, 1923, the first Test Drives of Electric Vehicles with Accumulators, as well as an Exhibition of Electric Vehicles with Accumulators, were organized. The idea of the Union was to have an official commission check, under indisputable conditions, the consumption and speed of vehicles. Four organizations were involved: the Technical Committee of the Automobile Club de France which supervised the automobile aspect; the Central Electricity Laboratory which supervised the electrical aspect, in particular the calibration of the measuring instruments; the Ministry of War which participated in the development of the regulations and which was responsible for monitoring the tests; and finally, the National Office for Scientific, Industrial and Inventions Research, newly created in 1922. The trials were provided with the latter's facilities at Meudon-Bellevue, former chateau of the Marquise de Pompadour, situated on the steep Montmartre Hill above Paris. Two sheds were installed in the grounds of the National Office of Research and Inventions for the battery-powered vehicles taking part in the competition. Initially, the vehicles were divided into five categories according to the payload from less than 500 kg up to more than five tons. Each competitor was limited to three vehicles. In 1923, there were three Berliet vehicles (500 kg, 700 kg and five ton), three Kriéger cars (300 to 500 kg), and a 5.6-ton Crochat truck with regenerative braking. A film was even made during the inauguration of the contest by Mr. Reibel, Minister of Regions. By 1924, the classification had grown to seven categories and a dozen manufacturers participated in these tests: Berliet, Kriéger, Crochat, Renault, Laporte-Bergmann (Toulouse), SCEMT (Grenoble), Electrix De Dion et Bouton, Satmé and A.E.M. Batteries.

Starting from the Patents Office at Bellevue, every day for a fortnight the electric fleet motored around Paris and its suburbs, climbing hills at places such as le Pecq, Chesnay, Rocquencourt, la rue Raynouard, rue Lepic, and the rue Norvins, each circuit finishing with the famous climb back up to Bellevue. Distances varied from 31 to 54.7 miles (50 to 88 km) with the possibility of recharging about midday. The shorter distances were of course reserved for the heavier vehicles.[10]

Out of this, a non-commercial Society for the Development of Electric Vehicles (SDVE) was created and following an agreement between the various manufacturers and the professional union of the electrical industries, a standard governing the batteries and their recharging was published. Charging was done at a voltage of 110 V, while lead-acid batteries had 64 elements and nickel-iron batteries had 120 elements. SDVE opened a garage and placed orders with various manufacturers for trucks and vans which it operated industrially on behalf of customers, including the Eastern Railway Company. SDVE was also responsible for organizing traction battery charging stations in the Paris region: by 1926, there were about 15. The company provided full equipment to individuals or garage owners wishing to install a public charging station, in return for the levy of a certain percentage on the current provided. The supply of the energy available from power stations during the off-peak hours for the charging of the accumulators enabled the producers to obtain a better output of the equipment installed. From 1927, it published a quarterly magazine, *The Electric Vehicle*, to promote the use of these vehicles.

Another company, the Société Lyonnaise pour Exploitation des Véhicules Electriques, SLEVE, founded in 1927, started with a garage of 36 units for service around Lyon. By 1929 a second garage was housing and recharging 66 vehicles. A decade later there were three garages in Lyon, one in Villebranche, and more than 100 trucks. By 1947, there were 411 vehicles, seven garages in Lyon, seven garages in Clermont-Ferrand, Montluçon, Roanne, Chambéry, Villefranche, Vienne, Grenoble, and a workshop in downtown Lyon. Since its foundation the SLEVE fleet had covered some 12.4 million miles (20 million kilometers).

Marc Vincent of SLEVE (Societé Lyonnaise pour Exploitation des Véhicules Electriques) developed its fleet from 36 to 411 commercial trucks in twenty years. Since its foundation, the SLEVE fleet had covered some 20 million kilometers (Collection J-N Raymond).

In 1926, the French family concern Fenwick unveiled a "truck with lifting platform"—the first pallet stacker. In its marketing, Fenwick said that the truck solved countless problems in the transport of materials and was suitable for loading heavy-goods vehicles, trains, and warehouse racking. Their worldwide success proved that they were absolutely right.

SOVEL

One company that emerged from this *dynamique* was to become a key player in French electric trucking, its success and lifespan on a par with Walker in America. It was born out of the ambition of École Centrale de Paris–trained

Louis Noyer, to revive the electric truck in France. With André Levy, who would become his close collaborator in the commercial branch, Noyer decided to start manufacturing accumulator trucks, believing that there was a possible market. Finance was provided by Maurice Schlumberger, and in April of 1925, the Industrial Electric Vehicle Company was established in Paris with a healthy capital of 600,000 francs, although it would be four years before they made a profit. In 1925 they changed their name to SOVEL (SOciété des Véhicules ÉLectriques).[11] A workshop was headed by Armand Jequier, with two Swiss, Messrs Noverray and Nussberger, in the design office. The first of many patents was obtained for a laterally attached battery case. During a very cold winter, two SOVEL chain-drive prototypes with a 3.5- and 5-ton payload were tested, one of them to transport coal to the Streichenberger house in Lyon, a city known for its unforgiving hills. The 3.5-tonner took part in the 1926 EV trials at Meudon, and the company received its first order for two trucks. It took further orders at the 1927 Lyon Fair where a pavilion was especially reserved for electric traction. A third truck was tested for the removal and transport of garbage in Villeurbanne. The local authorities were so impressed by how it could do the work of three horses that they put it into regular service: for the collection of garbage in the morning and for the transportation of materials in the afternoon. The average daily journey, including Sundays and holidays, was 25 miles (39.8 km), some days reaching 30 or 35 miles (50 or 62 km). To ensure the maintenance of the truck, the contract provided a reserve to stop the vehicle three half-days (afternoons) per month. Nineteen months later, the decision was made, given the results obtained and because of the work required, to use two 5-ton trucks to replace the 3.5-tonner. The Villeurbanne truck launched SOVEL, and 11 of the first trucks were delivered to the aforementioned SLEVE, of which the Schlumberger bank was a shareholder. These trucks were used for different services such as garbage disposal, coal and brewery deliveries, transport of benzol in tanks, and miscellaneous work. SOVEL began producing electric trucks for the Post, SNCF, Paris Airport, but also for private enterprises such as "Chocolat Poulain" at its factory in Blois, who required that there be no gas emanation that might alter the cocoa during its transportation between the station and the plant.[12]

Elsewhere, SOVEL provided the Paris Gas Company with ten electric trucks of five tons payload for coke deliveries in Paris. This agreement came after extensive testing with a 3.5 ton. In 1928, 27 trucks were produced. SOVEL quickly became the specialist in electric trucks for garbage collection. During meticulously controlled tests carried out in 1930 by the Paris Automobiles concern, a 5-ton SOVEL truck with a 4.2-ton (12 m^3) bucket and a SAFT battery worked without incident for 364 days, covering an average of 23 miles (37 km) per day. There was only one day off for setting a tilt device. In 1931, this resulted in an order for three trucks with a 5-ton chassis and a Ville de

Paris bucket of 4.2 tons (12 m³) capacity, then an additional six trucks in 1932. The same garage also operated three Vétra trucks.[13] Finally in 1936, a total of 31 SOVEL trucks were in use by the City of Paris. Finally, SOVEL made its first profits. The city of Asnières used ten frames of five tons and two of 3.5 tons. SOVEL installed a transformer substation, three switches and the necessary load tables for recharging its trucks. With the experience of Villeurbanne where the first truck, put into service in 1927, had done absolutely regular work for 365 days a year, by 1932, 16 French cities were equipped with SOVEL trucks for garbage collection, which had increased to 25 cities by 1935.

To the manufacture of electric chassis, SOVEL added sewage cleaning systems and tamping bins, patented in 1934, a formula that then replaced that of the old models known as Ville de Paris. A patent for a clamshell bucket was also filed in Belgium and the United States by Louis Noyer. The first 2.5 ton truck for the emptying of street catchers was sold to the city of Strasbourg in 1934. Chassis were also built for the maintenance of public lighting networks in Saint-Etienne and the city of Paris as well as the chassis for the sweeping and watering of public roads in Avignon. Subsequently, vehicles of 1 ton (1,000 kg) to 8 tons of payload would be built. In 1939, SOVEL manufactured some forty vehicles in the two Saint-Etienne workshops, by which time a total of 567 SOVELs were officially in circulation.

One of SLEVE's garages with a fleet of trucks made by SOVEL (SOciété des Véhicules ÉLectriques). These trucks were used for different services such as garbage disposal, coal deliveries, delivery of breweries, transport of benzol in tanks, garbage and miscellaneous work (Collection J-N Raymond).

1938: A fleet of SOVEL electric refuse trucks proudly lined up under the iconic Eiffel Tower in Paris (Collection J-N Raymond).

From 1926, the "National Fuels Rally" was regularly organized under the auspices of the Automobile Club de France to promote alternative fuels for energy independence. In 1933, during the seventh National Fuels Rally in Paris, four categories of vehicles were defined with, for each, a specific regulation: garbage trucks, buses, delivery vehicles and factory carts. Four SOVEL trucks participated in this rally: a 1929 Paris-based Société EC type lorry, a 1933 Bières DuMesnil EC type truck, a 1932 Paris dump truck and a 1933 wine tanker. At the end of the rally, a gathering of vehicles took place at the Place de la Concorde, Paris, headquarters of the Automobile Club. During the ninth National Fuels Rally of 1935, three SOVEL trucks were engaged in Paris along with a Vétra truck. At the same time, a competition was organized in Lyon on July 3 and 4. This competition was intended to highlight the possibilities of electric vehicles, especially their ability to climb steep slopes. The routes, from the garage of the SLEVE to the southeast Lyon suburb of Gerland, were laid out partly on flat ground, some sections in very narrow streets, and partly in very rough terrain. Out of Lyon's hills, two particularly challenging ones were selected: Choulans with a 6.7 percent average incline over 2,000 yards (1,800 meters) and unevenness of 130 yards (120 meters); and the rise of Dijon on the Croix-Rousse (8 percent grade on average over half a mile [800 meters] with a maximum of 18 percent).

The system of battery exchange for SOVEL trucks (Collection J-N Raymond).

SOVEL was not alone. The big truck manufacturer Berliet, also of Lyons, developed electric trucks such as the 8-ton *GTB*. From 1937, the SCCFE (Sociéte Central des Chemins de Fer et d'Entreprises), today's SNCF national railway company, made three types of electric trucks, 0.5-, 1- and 2-ton (500, 1000 and 2000 kg), at its Le Mans factory. As for batteries, in 1928, SAFT batteries were acquired by the Compagnie Générale d'Electricité (later to become Alcatel).

Across the border, in defeated Germany, after the end of the war, Bergmann of Berlin concentrated again on the production of power plant equipment and electrical goods until they were allowed to return to electric trucks. Several models appeared in 1928: the Bergmann BEL2500, Bergmann BEL4500, BELU and BEM. The 2-ton BEL2500, for example, was powered by a 6 kW motor, giving a speed of 10 mph (18 kph) and used for parcel delivery. It continued to use Akkumulatoren Fabrik AG's alkaline nickel-cadmium battery. From 1924, Hansa-Lloyd Werke AG began building "Electrolastwagen" e-trucks, based on Ipswich-based Belgian Paul Mossay's designs, and went on building them until the mid–1930s. One of these, Geestemünder Eiswerke of F. Busse & Co in Bremerhaven, was still being used in 1978, 54 years later.[14]

Between 1921 and 1922, the Deutsche Eleketromobil-u.Motoren-Werke AG at Wasseralfingen, Württemberg, produced their *Omnobil* electric truck, designed by Dornier aeronautical engineer Hans Keitel and using batteries from Fabrik AG Berlin.[15] By 1927, the German post office was using 1,632 electric vehicles, and in 1930 this had grown to 5,000 electric vehicles registered throughout Germany, including 1,500 for municipal services.

Joseph Vissarionovich Stalin came to power in the mid–1920s. Under Stalin's leadership, the Soviet Union transitioned from a market economy into a centrally planned economy which led to a period of rapid industrialization and collectivization. As part of this, trucks designed and built in the Union of Soviet Socialist Republics must be developed by the state, in particular the Central Scientific Research Automobile and Automotive Engines Institute (NAMI). From 1927, NAMI produced automobiles, trolleybuses and trucks, in particular for the Red Army. In 1929, due to a rapidly growing demand for automobiles and in cooperation with its trade partner, the Ford Motor Company, the Supreme Soviet of the National Economy established GAZ. In 1935, the first Soviet electric vehicle was built on the basis of the GAZ-A car. In the same period, a 2-ton electric garbage truck based on the ZIS-5 vehicle was created in the Laboratory of Electric Traction of the Moscow Power Engineering Institute (MEI) under the leadership of Professor V. Rezenford and engineer Yu. Galkin. Behind the cab, 40 accumulators with a total capacity of 168 A-h and a total mass of 1.4 tons (1400 kg) were placed in wooden boxes in the wooden platform. They powered the 13 kW electric motor located under the driver's cabin. In the outfitted condition, the electric vehicle LET, built in 1935, had a mass of about 4.2 tons (4200 kg). It could carry two containers with garbage weighing 1.8 tons (1800 kg). Top speed was 15 mph (24 kph) with a range of 25 miles (40 km). The ZIS-5 was built by the Spartak State Automobile Factory in Moscow.

Back in the USA

Considering the dwindling number of battery delivery vehicles in operation, in 1926 the Electric Truck Manufacturers Association was disbanded. Despite this, over one hundred light and power companies across the USA were using electric trucks. Some refused to accept defeat. One such was Charles Karl August Rudolph "Proteus" Steinmetz, a German-born American mathematician and electrical engineer and professor at Union College. A dwarf, hunchback, and an "outspoken Socialist," Steinmetz fostered the development of alternating current that made possible the expansion of the electric power industry in the United States, formulating mathematical theories for engineers. In 1915, he founded the Dey Electric Vehicle Syndicate (changed in 1916 to Dey Electric Corporation), in cooperation with Harry E. Dey, an electrical engineer from New York City. The smart design made use of one single electric motor, of which both the armature and the field (each connected to a driven wheel) could rotate so that a differential was not necessary. By 1917, the Steinmetz Electric Car Corporation's first vehicle went on sale but was considered too expensive. Then Steinmetz was sued by Patrick Hirsch, who claimed that he had helped fund the company but had not seen a cent for his efforts. In a full-page article in *The New York Times*, Steinmetz declared that it would dethrone the gasoline car and went about setting up the Steinmetz Electric Motor Car Company in 1920 to do just that. The first electrical Steinmetz truck hit the road in early 1922, climbing a steep hill in Brooklyn as a publicity stunt.[16]

At a meeting of automotive engineers, Steinmetz declared:

> I believe that the Electric will be the car of the future on account of its simplicity of operation and reliability. It is rare that it gets out of order. When it does so, it is an accident—not as with the gasoline car, an incident. The man of moderate means cannot afford a horse and buggy because of the attention required. He will be able to afford an Electric Vehicle to take him to business because it requires no attention—if equipped with an *Edison* battery. It often has to stand idle for several days and this is not good for a lead battery. I have tried to invent a lead battery that would not spoil but gave it up.

This quote was cited by Edison in an advertisement. In October, the company claimed to have developed a 5-passenger coupé. Steinmetz planned for the company to turn out 1,000 trucks and 300 cars annually, but that was cut short by his death in 1923. The company folded shortly after Steinmetz's death when a lawsuit from a shareholder revealed that the company had misrepresented the number of cars being produced. In March 1925, at the Annual Electric Truck Show held in the salesrooms of New York Edison, Steinmetz exhibited a truck with an improved appearance.

In 1925, Alfonso M. Leoni of Electromotive Devices Inc. of Philadelphia, formerly connected with the Steinmetz Electric Vehicle Company, innovated a gas-electric LEV, where the engine was part of the axle and all the bevel gears were eliminated, thereby insuring perfect balance, freedom from torsional twists and strains, with a resultant higher efficiency of power transmission.[17]

In 1922, George Bacon, Chief Engineer for the Detroit Electric Vehicle Company, designed a remarkable new milk delivery truck. It could be driven from four positions, front, rear, or either running board. But battery power was no match for winter weather, heavy loads (such as milk) or long days on the city streets. His employer balked at making a gasoline powered truck, so Bacon and other investors formed the Detroit Industrial Vehicle Company (D.I.V.CO.) to produce his invention using a LeRoi gasoline engine. After testing a prototype in 1924 and '25, Bacon and his investors were ready to go into business.

On September 28, 1929, the French journal *La Genie Civile, revue générale des industries françaises et étrangers*, published an article "History and Development of Electric Vehicles." According to them, there were currently 16,000 electric trucks in the USA used by Commonwealth Edison and New York Edison Company, who had 200 to 1,000 units in service for urban deliveries. The most important was American Railway Express Company, which replaced its 17,500 horses with 2,000 electric rather than gas trucks. (The article also commented on the 3,000 e-trucks in use in England across 60 municipalities, and 6,000 in Germany).

The best-documented fleet is Commonwealth Edison's exceptional fleet in Chicago which had acquired its first 5-tonner in 1902. With the retirement of the last of its horse-drawn wagons in March 1922, the evolution of the Commonwealth Edison service fleet reached its midpoint. In 1925, it had 350 to 375 Walker electric trucks in operation, whereas the total number of urban electric trucks in that city increased by 50 percent in two years. Over the remainder of the decade the company touted the benefits of electric trucks and expanded its stable of electric vehicles. It helped organize an "Electric Vehicle Course," twice-weekly lectures offered through the Automobile Continuation School of the Chicago Board of Education, intended for "drivers, mechanics, garage employees, battery-manufacturing employees and owners of cars." Then in 1933, Commonwealth Edison sold the Walker Vehicle Company to the manufacturing concern Yale & Towne. Thereafter, the utility bought no new electric trucks, and the number of electrics in the vehicle fleet began to shrink through attrition. In 1947, the last one was taken out of service, 48 years after the company had registered its first electric commercial vehicle.[18]

From 1930, UPS (United Parcel Service) used their first White electric delivery trucks for deliveries in Manhattan, NYC. Before long, their fleet had grown to several hundred.

During this time, Henry Ford of Detroit had been busy. In addition to his successful *TT* truck, Ford's new gasoline engine Model A (also colloquially called the A-Model Ford or the A) became the third huge success for the Ford Motor Company. First produced on October 20, 1927, but not sold until December 2, it replaced the venerable Model T, which had been produced for 18 years. Ford Model A production ended in March of 1932, after no fewer than 4,858,644 had been made in all body styles, including trucks. Its successor was the Model B, which featured an updated 4-cylinder engine, as well as the Model 18, which introduced Ford's new flathead (side valve) V8 engine. Like the Model TT, the Model AA was available exclusively as a chassis and cab offered in two lengths, with new power train and axle options for greater capacity. To stay ahead in what had become a hotly competitive business, Ford replaced the Model AA with the even more capable Model BB in 1933. Many were outfitted as mail and freight vehicles, ambulances and stake trucks. Two years later, Ford introduced the 1935 Model 50 pickup, powered exclusively by its famous Ford Flathead V8 engine.

By 1941, Ford had sold more than four million trucks. Changing over to war production resulted in the loss of consumer sales but a gain in experience building heavy-duty military truck chassis and four-wheel-drive personnel carriers. A year after consumer production resumed in 1947, Ford leveraged that knowledge to provide even more innovations for its customers, incorporated in their F-Series *Bonus Built* truck.

Walker Trucks made a brief foray into the field of gas-electrics in their early days but had much more success with their Model 500 Gas-Electric Dyna-Motive introduced in 1936. But in 1942, even this longstanding company had to close its factory doors for the last time. In October 1947, the Commonwealth Edison Company of Chicago, after more than 40 years of battery-recharging, also scrapped the last of its electric trucks. By 1950, the utility's transportation department owned and operated 824 vehicles, all of them gasoline-powered.

It would be the shortage of gasoline in countries occupied or blockaded by the armies of the Third Reich that would revive the electric truck.

FOUR

SOVELs to TAMAs

The Second World War led to the occupation of a large part of Europe by the Germans. France did not escape and was occupied as early as 1940. In order to feed the Eastern Front, the occupier put France under the yoke of rationing, making many products rare and several almost unavailable. Gasoline was available only to official users, such as the emergency services, bus companies and farmers. The priority users of fuel were always, of course, the armed forces. But the French were resourceful and recalled the days of the electric vehicle, 40 years before.

Whereas in 1939 there were fewer than 500 EVs in France, by 1944 this number would increase to 3,500. If the gasifier took the road uses, the electric was confined to urban uses. Many builders started up in this troubled period, but without reaching important series production. Even some gasoline car manufacturers tried to electrify their vehicles such as Laffly, Chenard & Walker, or Citroën with a *TUB* van, but all without much success. On the other hand, the established electric vehicle builders knew real success. Electric truck makers worked together closely—SOVEL with Chenard-Chausson, Fenwick with Citroën, Jourdain-Monneret with Delaunay-Belleville, and veteran campaigners Mildé-Kriéger with la Licorne.

During the summer of 1936, Pierre Boulanger, Chairman of the Citroën Car Company, received the results, photographs, statistics, sketches and comments on an extensive investigation of customer requirements that he had commissioned concerning what would make an efficient gasoline-engined truck. From this he laid down a specification which, characteristically, was both simple and demanding. In order to maximize available load space, the new van must position the driver as far forward as possible on the chassis. It must be equipped with a sliding side door and a low loading floor. So was born the Citroën *TUB* (Traction Utilitaire Basse or Traction Utilitaire type B). Production had only just gotten going when in 1940, the German army invaded and, in a few weeks, occupied almost half of the territory of

A wartime DC ammeter made by the French Compagnie des Compteurs. A fixed red needle indicated the discharge limit for the batteries (Collection J-N Raymond).

the metropolis, requisitioning on its way all vehicles that seemed useful, including the Citroën TUB. The few Citroën TUBs that managed to remain in the hands of their owners were quickly faced with rationing and fuel shortages. To overcome these disadvantages, Citroën had Fenwick, which had been supplying them with repair tools since 1932, retrofit the remaining TUBs in stock as electric trucks with their modified forklift truck motor and 1,190 lbs. (540 kg) of batteries. This reduced the payload of the TUB from 2200 lbs. (1,000 kg) for the gas version. Although the electric was originally planned to be marketed under the name of Fenwick Cittub, Citroën required Fenwick to change the name to Urbel (Urbain Electrique) just before the launch of marketing. The Urbel was equipped with large chests of drawers on each side, pierced with vents to cool the battery compartment and prevent the formation of flammable gases. Therefore, these doors replaced the TUB's sliding side door design while the spare wheel was moved to a new compartment located above the batteries. The Citroën grille was replaced by a sheet that sported the Fenwick logo. With a weight of about 1,825 kg, the Fenwick Urbel could reach a maximum speed of 30 mph (50 kph), but it was advisable not to exceed 15 mph (25 kph) empty so as not to unload the batteries unnecessarily. The Urbel was manufactured between 1941 and 1942, before production ceased due to the depletion of stocks of Citroën TUB parts. Many Parisian companies used the Fenwick Urbel. While postwar Citroën returned to gas-engined vehicles, Fenwick went on to become a major player in forklift truck manufacture and other material handling equipment.

In 1940, the SOVEL company equipped about 40 municipalities with waste collection vehicles; in 1941 the goal of 100 units was far exceeded. After the debacle of June 1940 and the shortage of gasoline it was causing, electric traction experienced considerable development and the best years so far in its history. Until the Liberation, this mode of propulsion rendered invaluable services to the national economy. In agglomerations, it was most common before the introduction of the gasifier, using town gas or acetylene. Lyon was not late in this field both for manufacturing and for the use of electric vehicles. SOVEL's prodigious output earned the city of Lyon, where it was located, the title of the capital of "the accumobile." In spite of the lack of raw materials, strictly limited by order of the German authorities, SOVEL's production would quickly reach figures higher than before war.

The powerful General Electricity Company (C.G.E.), founded by Pierre Azaria in 1899 and directed by Henry de Raemy, became interested in SOVEL and acquired half of the capital on September 30, 1940, sharing control of SOVEL with the Schlumbergerbank. C.G.E. then charged Jean Kauffmann, a 35-year-old polytechnician, to design a larger factory in the Lyon area. A subsidiary of the C.G.E., the C.G.E.E. (Compagnie Générale d'Entreprises Electriques) sold part of a large piece of land that it owned in Villeurbanne. The workshops were built in December 1940. The general management of SOVEL was entrusted to Kauffmann, while Armand Jequier was the technical director of the factories of Saint-Etienne and Villeurbanne, and founder Louis Noyer chaired the board of directors.

On January 30, 1941, the headquarters of SOVEL were transferred from Paris to the Villeurbanne factory. Artisanal production finally gave way to a more rational chain-line construction and a small industrial series. During the war years, SOVEL presented its models at the Lyon Fair in September 1941 and 1942. From 1941, SOVEL's total production increased from about 40

L'ELECTRIQUE SOVEL
VÉHICULE MODERNE - PRATIQUE - ÉCONOMIQUE
Pour tous transports de marchandises en ville

SOCIÉTÉ SOVEL — 1, RUE TAITBOUT — PARIS 9ᵉ
VÉHICULES ÉLECTRIQUES INDUSTRIELS

SOVEL's output was prodigious. From 1941, total production increased from about 40 trucks a year to 800. Of this total, 500 frames of 2.5 and 5 tons were manufactured at the Villeurbanne factory, which had to be enlarged in 1942 (Collection J-N Raymond).

trucks a year to 800. Of this total, 500 frames of 2.5 and 5 tons were manufactured at the factory Villeurbanne which had to be enlarged in 1942.[1]

Also in 1941, a third assembly site opened in Ivry-sur-Seine, near Paris, where the Compagnie des Lampes, belonging to the Compagnie Générale d'Electricité, made part of its factory available to meet the increase in demand.

The latter assembly site, headed by Fernand Dupuy, an engineer from Arts et Métiers, was more specifically responsible for assembling electric vehicles from mechanical elements supplied by renowned manufacturers of gas vehicles such as 200 Chausson pickup trucks with a payload of 600 to 700 kg, 400 Citroën (2.5 tonner), and 400 Latil (5 tonner) used for garbage collection and Chenard and Walker with a 1000 kg van.

SOVEL output was prodigious. A significant part of its business was also devoted to electric vehicle repairs. Their manufacturing programs were set by the Organization Committee for Electric Construction (COCELEC), itself affiliated as an "integrated industry" to the Organizing Committee of the Automobile (COA) headed by François Lehideux, nephew of Louis Renault. The occupiers were closely watching this organization, in order to force the constructors to work exclusively for the German war effort. But though these heavy and slow SOVELs with a small radius of action did not interest the Wehrmacht, other elements of the occupying forces beset the leaders of orders and requisitions, in vain. The issue of new motor vehicle purchase licenses gave rise to the collection of a fixed fee of 300 francs for the benefit of C.O.A. for the remuneration of its regional delegates and the amortization of the various costs entailed by the licensing formalities. The builders were responsible for collecting the corresponding sums and making the payment to the C.O.A. for the vehicles of their manufacture.

The copper and lead needed for batteries was also used for the manufacture of ammunition so it was necessary to recycle two used batteries to obtain a new battery. Users even had to return the heads of used spark plugs, these being required by the supplier in exchange for orders to the SOVEL factory. Also, to compensate for the lack of raw material, a decree of July 10, 1942, which was in fact an order by the GBK (the German organization managing industrial production in occupied territory), prohibited the manufacture of electric vehicles in France. The decree was applied on October 1, 1942, in the occupied zone and the prohibition would be extended to the free zone on January 1, 1943, thus leading to the closure of the plant at Saint-Etienne, where until 1942, 80 percent of electric trucks produced in France were manufactured. More than 1,000 battery-powered road electric vehicles left the SOVEL factory in three years, 800 of them in 1942 alone. Things were brought to a temporary halt on the night of December 31, 1943, with the destruction of the plant by Allied bombs.

Despite the sale of spare parts, turnover fell sharply as production stopped; only an order from the City of Paris for vehicles to make deliveries from the Halles de Paris was honored. To fulfill this order, SOVEL used all the 5-ton trucks built in Saint-Etienne and Villeurbanne. In the occupied zone, the maintenance and repair of SOVEL trucks circulating in the departments of Seine, Seine-et-Oise and Seine-et-Marne was provided by the Compagnie des Camions Electriques de Paris. In 1944, manufacturing difficulties were related to the delay of suppliers, the shortages of electricity and coal, and the transport crisis. During the four years of occupation, SOVEL declined all German orders and did not deliver any vehicles to the occupation authorities.

SOVEL was not alone in producing electric vehicles. Two veteran electric vehicle engineers, Charles Mildé, aged 90, and Louis Kriéger, aged 73 (see Chapter One), also pooled their resources to make an electric pickup truck, its electric motor driving the rear axle with electrical equipment and a battery pack mounted on the Unicorn chassis. The Mildé-Kriéger averaged 14 mph (22 kph) on the flat with a range of between 40 and 60 miles (70 and 100 km). Jean-Dominique Jacquemond electrified Renault ABF trucks by equipping them with trolley poles and electrical equipment placed at the front. Electric industrial truck builder Jourdain-Monneret in the rue Claude Decaen in Paris's 12th Aroudissement built a range of 3.5 hp *Autélec* delivery vans of 0.5 to 1.2 ton (500–1,200 kg). Hispano-Suiza, evacuated from Bois-Colombes to Tarbes in the Unoccupied Zone, made a type 351 electric tricycle truck with an 0.8 ton (800 kg) payload whose unique front wheel drive had a 13 ft. (3.90 m) turning circle, its batteries housed on either side of the car and mounted on a sliding trolley.

By the end of 1940, there were about 20 electric truck builders in Occupied France, including SOVEL, SCF, Labinal, Stella, Vetra, Laffly, De Dion Bouton, and Berliet. Post-war production would only resume between 1945 and 1947, when out of a total of 3,500 post-war electric road vehicles, some 1,600 were trucks of various descriptions.

It was similar for the islands of Great Britain. Gasoline shortages at an early stage of the war brought about a large increase in the number of electrically driven vans in door-to-door delivery; this particularly concerned dairy products (as is recounted in Chapter Five). But subsequent events, such as the Luftwaffe's bombing of cities and plants and the need to build up the number of RAF airplanes, brought such an increase to a standstill. During the first half of 1940 a number of exhibitions were held under the auspices of the Electric Vehicle Association at Manchester, Cardiff, Leeds, Glasgow and Birmingham, where a comprehensive range of electric vehicles was shown, including the electrically driven pedestrian pram. In a report in *The Electrician* on January 31, 1941, entitled "The Electric Vehicle—How the War Has Affected Manufacture," the writer states:

> The lack of new electric vehicles of all sorts is beginning to be felt and raises hopes that the outlook for 1941 for electric vehicles is brighter than the year just past. The difficulties of steel control as practised by the Ministry of Transport, the operation of the Purchasing and Acquisition Order both limit the substitution of electric vehicles for petrol cars and the restrictions now existing should be removed.

By 1943, as the result of problems with manufacturing materials, the Ministry of Supply Machine Tool Control (DIEE) suggested to the Electric Vehicle Association of Great Britain that a sub-committee should be formed to prepare a specification for a standard electric vehicle chassis with a one-ton payload capacity. BEVs (Battery Electric Vehicles) could only be supplied for essential use on the road or in works and in restricted numbers and all components had to be interchangeable. The 8 hp GEC motor specification was laid down, embodying British Standards Specification 173/1941 both with regard to rating and construction. By the end of the year, the first prototype of a national standard electric vehicle was completed and demonstrated to officials from the Ministry of War Transport and the Ministry of Supply. Application was made by the aging Sir Felix J.C. Pole, executive chairman of Associated Electrical Industries, to begin manufacture. Although 1,000 vehicles were proposed, the scheme was never fully realized due to the ongoing shortage of materials, particularly rubber, and also because of government restrictions on retail deliveries.

In 1943, as required by the British Ministry of Supply, the Electric Vehicle Association of Great Britain's 1-ton payload prototype standard electric vehicle was wheeled out. Although 1,000 vehicles were proposed, the scheme was never fully realized due to the ongoing shortage of materials, particularly rubber, and also government restrictions on retail deliveries (Wythall Transport museum).

In 1943 bus-manufacturer Crossley Motors Ltd. of Gorton, Manchester, had prepared a 12–15 cwt truck chassis. *Commercial Motor* commented:

> They had in course of construction when war started a vehicle of this type which, however, was, unfortunately, never put into production and still [*sic*] probably continue in this state until after our victory.[2]

May 26, 1944, was marked by Allied bombing of Lyon, France, causing many casualties in the neighborhoods of Guillotière and Vaise. Raffin, of the SLEVE concern, testing a new electric vehicle, was saved only by taking refuge in a basement of a building in Place Jean Macé. As the electric hearse of the Funeral Service could not cope anymore, SLEVE trucks were requisitioned for the transport of the bodies toward the cemeteries. SOVEL trucks were also used to transport the wrecks of seaplanes destroyed on the Grand Large Lake by American fighter planes on April 30, 1944, to the Lyon-Bron airfield. At the end of the war, SLEVE had a fleet of nearly 500 vehicles in seven garages, traveling 3,420,000 miles (5.5 million km) annually. Seven other garages were installed within a radius of 125 mi (200 km) around Lyon. But this prosperity would gradually decline in the next post-war period, the competition of gas trucks being suddenly felt. And the fight for liberation would cause the loss of three members of the workshop.

The total number of SOVEL electric vehicles in circulation (80 percent of the French electric fleet) had increased from 567 in 1939 to 700 in 1940. During this period, only a few trucks disappeared, casualties of war or through accidents, while all the others remained in service. One electric hearse was used in Roanne by the Resistance to smuggle machine guns inside a coffin. Only six trucks were considered looted by the occupation army. Paris was liberated during the fall of 1944, with General Von Choltitz signing his surrender on August 25. In his book *50 Years of the Automobile*, Jean-Albert Gregoire, inventor of the Tracta joint, recalled:

> Jacques Jourdain, president of the C.G.E, felt very lonely in the face of the serious problems that beset him. His director, his friend, the man in whom he had full confidence, Henry de Raemy, was stuck in Lyon for a month by the Allied advance in Normandy and the landing in Provence on August 15. By all the means of communication available, letters, telegraph, telephone, emissaries, Jordan sent desperate calls to his director:– Come home at all costs! I absolutely need you. Admittedly, he could have a car and enough fuel to reach Paris, but the country was in a dangerous mess. While fleeing, the Germans had requisitioned all the trucks and cars in running condition, sometimes executing the driver without *ausweis*. For their part, the Maquis occupied the ground as soon as it was released and also seized any vehicle in working order. In such an adventure, little chance of arriving in Paris and many chances to lose your life! J.K. did not lack ideas and persuaded Kauffman to loan him a SOVEL truck. "Come on, old man, you know that your machines have only sixty kilometers of autonomy! It's impossible." "Yes, sir, it is possible. Macon is fifty-one kilometers from Lyon. A wholesale grocer owns one of our trucks. He will be able to recharge the vehicle. You then reach Chalon-

1944: German soldiers stand beside a cleaner truck in Colmar, Occupied France. Sometimes these trucks were used by the Resistance Movement to smuggle arms and even Allied soldiers (Photograph Dalferth—Collection J-N Raymond).

sur-Saone after fifty-eight kilometers. There we have two customers. A wine merchant will take care of you. Macon and Chalon are warned. Kauffmann loaned de Raemy a 2.5 tonner, its bigger batteries giving it 70 km range. In addition, it has *ausweis* for all of France. And finally, a pass from the head of the Lyon resistance." Raemy hesitated. He knew the risks of adventure. The power outage on the road or a burst of machine gun from over-nervous fugitives. But he must answer the call of his president. The next day, at dawn, he climbed into the SOVEL with provisions for a week. Five days later, he arrived in Paris, his kidneys shattered by the hard suspension of the empty rolling truck—but quite proud of his feat. Though he was stopped several times on the road by Germans and

In 1950, rising up from the ashes of defeat, the Nippon Electric Automobile Company of Japan produced their Denka automobile and truck (Petersen Automotive Museum).

resistance fighters, they all waved on this strange vehicle that could not be of any use to them.[3]

Over in Germany, the postal services continued while the measures taken soon after the war caused the number of battery trucks to keep the Third Reich's transport and delivery infrastructure running to rise to 50,000 units.

In Mussolini's Italy, FIAT, which in the 1930s had built some electric refuse collectors for the municipal authorities in Milan, now converted their Fiat 621 gas truck, of which almost 50,000 units were made not only in Italy but also in Poland and the Soviet Union, to an electric version, the 621E. Former electric streetcar boss Adolfo Orsi of Modena bought the Maserati firm, more famous for its high-powered racing and sports cars, and built battery-electric trucks, the heaviest of which was a forward-control 1-tonner with truck, hearse or tank body, 6½ hp motor and single-plate clutch.

Following Japan's defeat and near destruction in 1945, Japan experienced a scarcity of gas, but there was plenty of electric power. Jiro Tanaka, aeronautical and automotive engineer, set up a branch of Tachikawa Airplane Company in a borrowed factory in nearby Tama, calling it the Tokyo Electric Car Company. Their mission was to build electric cars and trucks. Based on an Ohta Jidosha gas truck, the production model of the Tama EOT-47–2 electric truck, with 1,100 lb. (500 kg) load capacity and a top speed of 21 mph (34 kph), was launched in 1947 alongside a sedan auto. Both had a motor built by Hitachi replacing the engine under the hood with batteries by Genzo Shimadzu of the Yuasa Storage Battery Co. positioned under the cargo bed. In November 1949, the company name was changed to the Tama Electric Car Company. Alongside Tama, in 1950 the Nippon Electric Automobile Company produced their Denka automobile and truck.

However, in 1950 with the advent of the Korean conflict, the lead used in the batteries exploded in price, such that the batteries cost 400,000–500,000 yen. At the same time, with gasoline becoming freely available due to the U.S. forces in Japan, the era of the electric truck ended. Tokyo Electro Automobile in 1951 became part of Prince Motor that in turn became part of Nissan in 1966. Forty years later Nissan would return to the electric vehicle business with their Leaf and in 2014, their e-NV200 pickup.

FIVE

"Drinka Pinta Milka Day!"[1]

In August 1967, the UK Electric Vehicle Association put out a press release stating that Britain had more battery-electric vehicles on its roads than the rest of the world put together. All manufacturers of battery electric vehicles were, at one time, members of the Electric Vehicle Association of Great Britain, and they received returns from the manufacturers on a regular basis, so they were able to give accurate numbers of BERVs in use in the UK for a certain year. The EVA also had industrial truck manufacturers, battery manufacturers and component suppliers as members of the Association. Closer inspection disclosed that almost all of the battery driven vehicles licensed for UK road use were milk floats—30,000 of them.[2]

For a long time, doorstep milk delivery by electric trucks played an important part in daily life. Picture the scene, at 7:30 a.m., when usually a couple of foil-topped glass milk bottles, color-coded (gold for full cream, silver for half cream or red for ordinary), were at the front door, some having been pecked by the blue-tits. In his childhood, this author, with parental permission, would climb up onto the passenger seat of the open-door white and orange milk float and go for a ride with "Milkie." I remember the primitive control system, the quiet whirr of the engine and the bottles rattling in their crates. It was indelibly my first electric vehicle experience. This chapter pays tribute to the handful of manufacturers who supplied this way of life with milk floats in the British Isles and beyond.

For example, T.H. Lewis Ltd. of Watford had been building milk floats, milk carts and horse-drawn vehicles for London's Express Dairies Company since 1873. In the early 1930s Lewis switched over to electric. They designed two types, the first being a three-wheeled pedestrian-controlled vehicle with a 3.5 cwt payload, which had a fixed speed of three miles per hour (4.8 kph) on level ground. The battery drove a 0.75-horsepower (0.56 kW) motor that was connected to the rear axle by reduction gearing, and this configuration gave a range of around ten miles (16 km). They were one of the first companies to

The controls of an AER-4 milk float built in the 1950s by T.H. Lewis Ltd. of Watford for London's Express Dairies. As a child, the author had his first experience of driving a BEV when the milkman let him take the steering wheel (photograph de Astui).

provide storage for dry goods on their vehicles, and demonstrated a type AER 4-wheeled float with a grocery box behind the cab at the 1955 Dairy Show. Their exhibits at the 1958 Dairy Show included a standard 25 cwt milk float with a walk-through cab and a vertical steering wheel.

During this period, it became almost impossible to meet the demand for such vehicles. T.H. Lewis's Electruck ride-on vehicles, known as Rider Prams, formed a huge part of the Express Dairy fleet with more than 1,400 built over two decades. Perhaps surprisingly they were also supplied to other dairies, including the London Co-operative Society. In the mid–'50s T.H. Lewis simply could not keep up with the demand for the parent fleet. The production of 168 Rider Prams was, therefore, sub-contracted to Ross Auto & Engineering. Almost exact copies of the Lewis design, they carried a Helecs Vehicles Ltd. chassis plate and it is assumed that Ross had earlier acquired Hindle, Smart & Co. Ltd., which built battery electric vehicles badged as Helecs.

In 1933, A.C. Morrison of Leicester, England, whose family was running an electrical business, manufacturing stationary engines for generators, compressors and also for the film industry, had a discussion while playing a golf round at Leicester's Birstall links with Mr. Squires, a local baker who wanted a closed-door electric delivery truck with a good range. Morrison's firm designed and built their first prototype electric truck with an ENV axle within a month. Trials suggested that the vehicle needed a stronger chassis and a longer wheelbase to enable it to carry loads of 10 or 12 cwt (500 or 600 kg), and the baker took delivery of the first production vehicle later in the year. It was registered as JF 4231, and the company soon built up a large order book for such vehicles. Before long, these small vehicles were marketed as Terriers, and the company produced a larger model, called the Mastiff, with a 25 or 30 cwt. payload.[3]

Following the Armistice, in 1919 Electromobile Ltd. of Birmingham had taken over Edison Accumulators Ltd., continuing to supply their refuse truck with the name Electricar. They also supplied Liberty, the luxury department store on Great Marlborough Street in the West End of London, with six silent delivery trucks, which shared a garage with five gasoline trucks of the Albion and Dennis marques. During the 1920s, the cleansing departments of town councils across the UK continued to acquire Electricar's 30 cwt and 3½-ton low-loading trucks for refuse-collecting and road-gritting.[4]

In 1936, Lt.-Col. L. P. Winby of the Young Accumulator Company formed the business group Associated Electric Vehicle Manufacturers Ltd. (AEVM), of New Malden, Surrey, which held a large interest for the purposes of acquiring two electric vehicle manufacturers: Electricars of Birmingham and A.E. Morrison & Sons of Leicester, who made 70 percent of UK production of such vehicles; both were customers of Young's range of batteries: Renown, Super-Armoured and Exchange.

Following the formation of AEVM, A.E. Morrison worked closely with Electricars. The two companies rationed their products, with Morrison concentrating on vehicles with a payload of 40 cwt or less, and Electricars building heavier vehicles. By 1938 the city of Birmingham alone was using a fleet of 150 Electricars ranging from a 2½ ton to a 7-ton six-wheeler, including elevating platform, low-loading, tiering, crane and aircraft refueling types. The Bristol Co-operative Society was using 300 Morrison-Electricars up and down the hilly districts of both Sheffield and Bristol.

At the all-electric bakery garage of the Bristol Co-operative Society, the Morrison-Electricars were recharged using American-built Westinghouse units, supplied by Hants Electric Chassis Ltd., Bournemouth. The Westinghouse charging station, with its rheostats capable of charging up to 12 trucks at once, was also used for the Addlestone Cooperative Society's dairy delivery trucks.

As sales of Morrison-Electricars increased, the manufacture of stationary engines was phased out. Vehicles were exported to Australia, New Zealand and Finland, generally as a kit of parts, with bodywork and batteries being sourced locally, and a left-hand drive option was also available. In April 1939, Electricars received an order worth £15,000 from the USSR.

On the outbreak of war in 1939, Morrison-Electricars was competing alongside eight marques of BEV: Wingrove and Rogers Ltd. of Liverpool with nine models, four with elevating platforms; Erewash Electric Traction Co. Ltd. of Nottingham; Diamond Motors, Graiseley; Metrovick of Manchester; Midland; Wilson; Tilling-Stevens; and Murphy.

Despite the serious damage caused by the Nazi Luftwaffe bombers in most major British cities, milk deliveries continued, potholed roads permitting. When one milkman's float was destroyed by a firebomb, he appeared the following day transporting the milk in his private car.

In 1946, the Austin Motor Co. Ltd., well known for its Austin Seven automobiles, teamed up with Crompton Parkinson Ltd. and its associated companies—A.E. Morrison and Sons Ltd. and Electricars Ltd.

It was frequent to see customers shopping from a cooperative mobile butcher's shop, a Crompton Parkinson Morrison-Electricar. Four women are standing at the service hatch, and the butcher is inside the van, serving them. The side of the van has an open display. The body of the vehicle is in Co-operative Wholesale Society national red, with lettering in black, lined in silver and outlined in black.

Morrisons continued to make two of T.H Lewis's models, the Electruck Rider, which became the model E15, and a pedestrian-controlled vehicle, which became the model DPC3. A sizeable fleet of 127 Electrics was run by the Express Dairy Company Ltd. from its 37 branches in and around London. T.H. Lewis maintained them alongside 350 gas trucks (Austins, Bedfords and

Do you realise the full significance of the figures above? They mean that the great majority of the thousands of users of electric vehicles place the Morrison-Electricar above all others. They mean that its performance in service is such that these users give it their repeat orders again and again. And they mean that the accumulated experience of its makers excels that of all other electric vehicle makers put together. This experience continues to improve the Morrison-Electricar and perpetuates its superiority. It is the " electric " for all who realise that it is costly to gamble in transport. You can obtain it in 10 and 20 cwt. Utility Vans; 40 and 50 cwt. and 5-ton Flat Deck Vehicles and Refuse Collectors of 7 and 12 cubic yards capacity.

MORRISON-ELECTRICARS

BACKED BY A NATION-WIDE SERVICE

A. E. MORRISON & SONS LTD. *Sales Office :* Electra House, Victoria Embankment, London, W.C.2
In association with :   *'Phone : Temple Bar 5911 'Grams : Crompark, Estrand, London*

C R O M P T O N   P A R K I N S O N   L I M I T E D

213

Meanwhile in the English Midlands, Morrison-Electricars were equally prodigious as is shown by this advertisement. For example, the Bristol Co-operative Society was using 300 Morrison-Electricars up and down the hilly districts of that city (Wythall Transport museum).

With their men gone off to war, women continued delivering the milk in the Cots-wolds village of a besieged England (Wythall Transport Museum).

Fordsons) and afforded a 24-hour service. In addition, T.H. Lewis manufac-tured the Lewis pedestrian-controlled electric pram, many of which were operated by the Express Dairy concern. The maintenance workshops were in Claremont Road, northwest London, where the fleet was serviced every ten days. The Metropolitan-Vickers battery-charge timing relay was linked to the rheostat system imported from the Westinghouse Electric and Man-ufacturing Company of East Pittsburgh, Pennsylvania, which enabled 12 vehi-cles to be correctly charged simultaneously. Batteries used were Britannia, DP, Exide and Young. The fleet included machines made by GV, Lewis, Metro-vick and Morrison. The prams could carry up to 33¾ gallons of milk, equiv-alent to 6 cwt. The London Co-operative Society also had a large fleet of *Electruck Riders*, and continued to add to them with purchases of the E15. Birmingham Co-operative Society was locally very important in this field, also using Morrison-Electricar D1 battery-electric vehicles on laundry rounds, all their customers receiving a dividend on everything they bought from the co-op, to spend later. Seventy-two green and cream Electricar DV4 4-ton refuse vehicles were acquired by the City of Birmingham between 1938 and 1948, some in use until 1971. Their batteries were recharged with electricity generated from steam produced by burning the refuse they collected.

Between 1938 and 1941, more than 70 DV4 4-ton refuse trucks were purchased by the City of Birmingham Salvage Department. Most of them lasted until the late 1960s (Wythall Transport Museum).

There is a wartime picture of 24 Electricar 2-tonner pallet trucks lined up at Hall Green, Birmingham, for shipment to the USSR as part of Great Britain's gift aid for the Russian armaments industry. Each BEV has a woman proudly standing at the controls. During this period of hostilities, there was a serious shortage of manpower, and as well as working in the plants, women took on the duties of delivery drivers.

War was over in 1945, but with rationing still in force, the British Ministries of War, Transport and Supply displayed considerable interest in battery electric vehicles and in 1944 permission was given for the manufacture of a

The occasion was to celebrate the completion of a consignment of two-ton capacity electric trucks for the Russian armaments industry. The board wishes good luck and a speedy victory to our Russian comrades. George Smith, the last works superintendent at the site, kindly loaned his album of company photos to me for this book. His future wife Violet is on the front truck on the right as we look.

Top and bottom: In 1944, Brush of Loughborough shipped out this sizeable batch of industrial trucks to the U.S.S.R. Both women and men workers were photographed to publicize this event (Brush/Wythall Transport Museum).

Work underway on the final batch of Electricar refuse vehicles for Birmingham Corporation's salvage department in 1944. Sturdy seasoned oak and ash had been used for the timbers, but construction systems would soon change (Wythall Transport Museum).

few prototypes. Morrison rose to the challenge with chassis-less construction.

The 25-cwt D5 and 1-ton D4 trucks, combining chassis and body framework of the ACM, was constructed in chrome-molybdenum steel formed of three sections bolted together. Each truck carried on its roof a quick-release fitting to accommodate ladders.[5] One example of a satisfied client during the 1950s was Mills & Rockleys Ltd. of Coventry, one of the leading outdoor advertising contractors who had 30 Morrison-Electricars based in the following 18 depots: Bristol, Cambridge, Coventry, Derby, Doncaster, Gloucester, Hull, Ipswich, Leicester, Luton, Mansfield, Nottingham, Norwich, Oxford, Peterborough, Weston-super-Mare, Worcester and Yarmouth. Each depot foreman had to complete a course at the works of Crompton Parkinson Ltd. Service costs had been reduced by 5½ d per 16-sheet of advertisement. Morrison also supplied coal trucks to clients such as the Ipswich Co-op.[6]

For decades, the bodies of many trucks had been built of ash or of oak,

This tower truck on a Morrison-Electricar 50 cwt. chassis was purchased by the City of Coventry Gas Department in 1946. Such tower trucks became fairly commonplace in the 1950s (Wythall Transport Museum).

and later they were built from lightweight aircraft grade aluminum. On November 3, 1949, the first UK polyester resin technical forum was held by the Scott-Bader Company at their Wollaston Hall HQ in Northamptonshire. Here Dr. Irving E. Muskat, inventor/president of Marco Resins Inc., New Jersey, USA, gave a lecture to representatives of British industry on polyester resins. As the Marco process involved expensive vacuum molding, before long an easier, less expensive process of contact molding using glass chopped-strand matting impregnated with resin was adopted. The electric truck-building industry soon saw the power-weight advantages of glass-fiber.

For the 1960s Morrison developed the EH20 chassis with glass-fiber (Fiberglass is a trade name) roofs with raised channels, mainly to aid water flow during rainy periods, and also to strengthen the roof and avoid flexing. While they gave a pleasing appearance to the vehicle, the glass-fiber also improved their power-weight ratio and range. A fleet was supplied to the Port of London Authority to serve hot drinks and snacks to London dock workers. The body, of composite construction, had a fully fitted mobile canteen interior with cupboards and shelves for confectionary and other wrapped goods.

This Morrison-Electricar was converted into a canteen for dockers at the busy Port of London (author's collection).

In business terms, Austin had merged into the British Motor Corporation in 1952, which in turn merged with Leyland Motors in 1969, to become British Leyland. The electric vehicle business became Crompton Leyland Electricars Ltd.

In 1972, British Leyland sold their share of the business to Hawker Siddeley, better known for aircraft manufacture, and the company became Crompton Electricars Ltd. of Tredegar, Gwentwith. Its Thruline range came about when staff at one of their main distributors, Oxford Electrics Ltd. built a truck themselves and called it the Oxcart. They persuaded C.E. to build a number of them in Tredegar, but it was not a success and not many were made. Ten years later, with many Electricars being exported to India, Hawker Siddeley decided to sell the business, and it was bought by Mahindra & Mahindra Electric Vehicles, who were based in Atherstone, Warwickshire. This was effectively the end of Morrison-Electricar, although M & M subsequently adopted the Electricars name for the vehicles that they manufactured.

Where milk delivery was concerned, other companies also deserve mention. In 1931 Victor Electrics Ltd., a subsidiary of Outram's of Southport,

During the 1960s, Crompton-Leyland-Electricars Ltd. produced these smart garbage collectors (author's collection).

Merseyside, who had been in the bread delivery business for a decade, introduced a 27-cwt vehicle designed for the dairy industry. In the early 1920s, Outram's, a large bakery, had been running a fleet of steam trucks, Ford TT gas-trucks and horses and carts to deliver bakery products both nationwide and locally. They wanted to buy electric vehicles to replace some of the horses, but found that both home-produced and imported vehicles were considerably more expensive than they were prepared to pay. They were looking for something that was comparable in price to their Ford TT vans, and so formed Victor Electrics Ltd., appointing one of their directors, H.N. Outram, as its joint managing director. Their first electric van was completed in 1923, and they built several more to carry up to 800 loaf tins.

Their first vehicles had hoods, like conventional vans, which stored the batteries, but by 1935 all of their vehicles were forward control models, with the cab at the front. The chassis was constructed of wood, strengthened with some steel channel, and Ford components were used for the steering gear and rear axle, although the final gearing was modified to give a lower ratio. The motor was mounted in the center of the vehicle, and drove the rear axle through a propeller shaft and overhead worm drive. Power at 48 volts was provided by a 24-cell Kathanode unit rated at 143 Amp-hours, manufactured by the D.P. Battery Co. Ltd. at Lumford Mill, Bakewell. Control was through a four-stage series-parallel controller with starting resistances, and some electric braking was provided by using the resistances. The weight of the vehicle was around 17 cwt, with the battery weighing an additional 5 to 6 cwt. By 1929, Victor were making three models of bonneted van, all with similar basic dimensions, but differing in the length of the rear storage area. They were 5 feet 4 inches (1.63 m) wide, with a wheelbase of 10 feet (3 m). The Model A was designed for a 20-cwt payload and formed the basis for a number of vans supplied to the General Post Office in 1929. It came with a 3 hp (2.2 kW) motor running at 48 volts. The Model B had a larger 4.75 hp (3.54 kW) motor running at 40 volts, and was supplied with a 192 Amp-hour battery as standard, but extra batteries could be fitted at the rear of the vehicle, which carried 23 cwt. The Model C was the largest, with a 6 hp (4.5 kW) motor running at 80 volts. The batteries under the bonnet were supplemented by others which were mounted either under the driver's seat or at the rear. The payload was 30 cwt. In 1931, Viktor Electrics introduced a 27 cwt vehicle designed for the dairy industry with forward control and a walk-through cab without doors. The 40-cell, 168 Ah Kathanode battery, manufactured by DP, was located over the front axle, and supplied current to a Metro-Vick motor. The vehicle was designed to be driven while standing up, with the controls only enabled when the driver was standing on a spring-loaded floor button. The controls were also interlocked with the hand brake.

Midland Electric Vehicles Ltd. was established in 1935 and was based in

Leamington Spa, Warwickshire. They supplied chassis to both the Birmingham and Wolverhampton divisions of the Midland Counties Dairy in 1936, and the first production vehicle probably went to the Wolverhampton division, whose ride-on fleet of milk floats consisted almost entirely of Midland vehicles, apart from some bought elsewhere during the war years and some pram trucks. The chassis were supplied with a dashboard and glass for the windscreen, but the bodywork was built by the Wolverhampton body shop at Midland Counties Dairy, and their basic design remained unchanged until the demise of Midland Electric. The first design was a 10–15 cwt chassis, which was launched to the wider world in January 1937. It was designed by J. Parker Garner, who at the time was a well-known designer, having been involved in the manufacturing of vehicles for a number of years. Its chassis was made from channel section steel, with cross bracing and a dropped section at the front, in order to give a low floor height for the cab. The doorways were behind the front wheels, and were not fitted with doors, although doors were available as an option. The height from the roadway to the cab floor was just 10 inches (250 mm), and such a low height was desirable because of the number of times a driver would have to enter and leave the cab while delivering bread or milk. The batteries were mounted in trays on either side of the vehicle, which could be slid out on rollers for maintenance, or to exchange the battery if it was required to do more than one round in a day. The batteries fed a 60-volt motor, and a series-parallel controller gave three forward and reverse speeds. Transmission was by a layrub shaft to an overhead worm driven rear axle. The bodywork was designed so that any panel could be easily removed and replaced if it became damaged.[7] In 1939, the major milk producer in Birmingham, England, Midland Dairy, used more than 100 electric delivery trucks. Another Midland Electric innovation in 1940 was a tractor designed to haul a trailer, which could not only be used to tow a fighter airplane, but also to start its aero engine.[8]

In the mid–1930s, Diamond Motors Ltd. of Wolverhampton, who had previously made motorcycles, began producing battery-electric road vehicles (BERV). Having moved to new premises on Upper Villiers Street, Wolverhampton, in January 1937, Diamond Motors produced their first battery-electric road vehicle, under the Graiseley brand, a four-wheeled van with the cab in front of the front wheels, suitable for a payload of 8–10 cwt. The frame, which was made from 3.5-inch (89 mm) channel with tube and channel cross members, had a lower section for the cab floor, which was just 13 inches (330 mm) above the ground, to provide easy access for a roundsman. The vehicle was fitted with a 3.5 hp (2.6 kW) motor manufactured by the Electric Power Engineering Co. and powered by a 60-volt battery. Standard 162 Amp-hour batteries gave a top speed of 16 to 18 mph (26 to 29 kph) and a range of around 35 miles (56 km), but a larger range was available by fitting 216 Amp-hour batteries. A press statement announced that this was the first in a series of vehicles which would be produced by the company, and further details of other models would be announced soon afterwards.[9] These included a pedestrian-controlled model. They soon found that they could sell into other industries, and the vehicles were used in hospitals, factories and warehouses. The company went into liquidation in the early 1960s, although the Graiseley marque was used by two other companies until at least 1972.

From the mid–1930s, Tomlinson Electric Vehicles Ltd. manufactured milk floats and other battery electric road vehicles, which they also exported to the Benelux countries. They also built the bodywork for two streamlined vans supplied to the West Ham Electricity Department in 1934, on chassis manufactured by Partridge Wilson Engineering. They supplied another electric van to the East Ham Electricity Department the same year. In 1949 they were taken over by King's Motors of Oxford, keeping the Tomlinson name.[10]

Many of these milk floats used Exide Ironclad batteries developed by Montefiore Barak ("Monte") and a team at the Chloride Electrical Storage Co. at Clifton Junction, Manchester. Chloride, by far the dominant battery maker in the UK, had acquired other companies (Pritchett and Gold at Dagenham, DP Batteries at Bakewell, Tudor Batteries in Redditch, Lorival, who made rubber and plastic containers and separators in Cheshire, Alkaline and some emergency lighting and uninterruptible power supply makers). Chloride also had major plants in all the Imperial countries, some of them quite large.

Chloride did not have a monopoly. Britannia Batteries Ltd. in Redditch, Worcester, made both lead-acid and nickel-alkaline types. Fuller traction batteries produced by the Fuller Accumulator Co. (1925) Ltd. in Chadwell Heath, Romford, used an improved form of separation to withstand vibration through road shocks. After extensive research, Fuller adopted a triple-separation method. Positive and negative plates had between them glass wool, ebonite and treated wood in definite form and sequence acting as a cushion. Oldham and Son Ltd. of Denton, Manchester, used flat plates separated by Port Orford cedar and reinforced with vitreous felt giving exceptional resilience without an increase of internal resistance; the containers were ebonite. Finally, the Kathanode cell made by the DP Battery Company of Bakewell, Derbyshire, used spun-glass felt to protect the plates.

This was, after all, the era of streamlining in design. In 1938, the London and North Eastern Railway locomotive *Mallard*, with its streamlined body designed by Sir Nigel Gresley, set a world speed record for steam locomotives of 126 mph (203 km/h). Shown to the public in late 1930s, the Burney Streamliner automobile was the work of Sir C. Dennistoun Burney, an Englishman. The Comet DC-3 airliner was equally aerodynamic. The Art Deco style in fashion at the time "streamlined" both interior (toasters to flat irons) or exte-

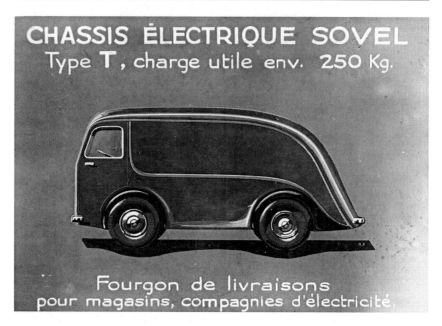

Top and bottom: During the late 1930s, both French and British electric truck manufacturers gave their latest models the fashionable aerodynamic look, even though
drag was irrelevant at their slow speeds. The SOVEL Type-T (top) remained on the
drawing board (Collection J-N Raymond), while the Electricar CY-2 Airline
remained a demonstrator (Transport Museum Wythall).

rior objects. It was quite natural for Metrovick, also builders of bomber airplanes, and Electricar to fall in with this styling approach with streamlined bodywork flowing right back from the cab front to the rear bumper, despite the fact that the 15 mph average speed of their vehicles did not exactly present any serious aerodynamic challenges.

Another company who took a streamlined approach to their e-trucks was Cleco Electric Industries of Leicester. Following the curvaceous Cleco Electric Eel industrial truck produced for the MoD for flameproof use inside ordnance depots and factories during the war, in 1948 Cleco produced the Bijou, its light-alloy body. Although of simple construction, it had attractive lines, the sweep of the cab paneling following the contours of the front wheels. The prototype, used on a baker's delivery round, covered 20 miles each day without any weaknesses in design, but the Bijou never went into production.[11]

In June 1938, "Electrics on the Farm" was one of the popular exhibits at the Royal Agricultural show in Cardiff, Wales. This all-electric farm included a poultry house and a milking shed. Electric trucks provided by Cleco, Metrovick, and Partridge, Wilson & Co. were garaged, maintained and charged on the farm and were engaged in transportation between the various farm buildings and for delivery duties to Cardiff retailers and Great Western Railway's railway station.

In 1940, Brush Traction, a manufacturer and maintainer of railway locomotives, based at Loughborough in Leicestershire, England, required some small battery-electric tractor units, but as none were commercially available, they asked AC Morrison of AE Morrison and Sons (later Morrison-Electricar) to produce a design for one. Morrison produced a three-wheeled design, which Brush then used to manufacture a number of units for internal use. Subsequently, they began selling them on the open market, and shipped a large order to Russia in 1941. They added battery electric road vehicles to their product list in 1945, buying the designs and manufacturing rights from Metropolitan Vickers or Metrovick, who made a range of "streamlined" models of 7–9 cwt (353.5/457.2 kg), and 15–20 cwt (762/1016 kg) load capacities.

Early Brush vehicles are almost indistinguishable from late Metrovicks. Three-wheeled vehicles were marketed as the Brush Pony, and they also produced four-wheeled vehicles. In 1948 they added a 2-ton chassis to their range, which could be supplied with a large van, standard van, flat truck or milk float body. The welded box-section chassis was fitted with semi-elliptic springs and a Lockhead hydraulic braking system. The 36-cell 290 Ah battery was mounted on both sides of the central spine. The electric motor was connected to a banjo-type rear axle by a Layrub propeller shaft. In common with other Brush vehicles, control was by a double-depression foot pedal, where the first depression gave two stages of control with the two halves of the battery connected in parallel, and the second depression gave a further two stages with the batteries in series. In early 1949, they reduced the prices of their electric vehicles by around 25 percent in an attempt to make them more competitive with petrol vehicles. One satisfied Brush client was the Dartry Laundry Company in Dublin, whose 2-tonner, registration ZH 2511, was used to move laundry in bulk to and from its branches. It also carried the large laundry baskets used by various institutions which would not fit easily into vans. A familiar sight in Dublin for nearly 34 years, the Brush was withdrawn in May of 1981.

Following his experiences of doorstep milk delivery in the South Downs area of Sussex, in 1947 Sidney Holes set up an electric vehicle company in Brighton, Sussex, to build both pedestrian-controlled three-wheeled e-trucks and ride-on models (BERV) which he called Manulectrics. They were fitted with a 1 hp (0.75 kW) motor and a 24-volt battery. The bodywork was fabricated from steel, and the vehicle could carry 24 milk crates, 16 in the body and 8 on the roof. Those in the body were mounted on runners, so that they could slide out to access the bottles. It had a range of ten miles (16 km). Manulectrics were used by both the Holes and Davidgor Dairies. Sidney Holes Electric Vehicles was bought by Stanley Engineering in the 1960s and sold to Crompton Electricars in 1972.[12]

A latecomer was Wales & Edwards, formerly a garage and salesroom for Morris and Wolseley cars, based in Shrewsbury. In 1951, Mervyn Morris designed and built an electric milk float for Roddington Dairy. A request from United Dairies saw the production of a three-wheeled chain driven vehicle, which was an immediate success. An order for 1,500 vehicles followed, and a new manufacturing base was set up in Harlescott, a suburb to the north of Shrewsbury. Larger models followed, although the three-wheeled design was retained for most of their subsequent output. Four-wheeled vehicles were introduced in 1966 for payloads which exceeded 1.5 tons, although they made 18 five-wheeled articulated milk floats from 1961, which could carry two tons. The company was acquired by Smith Electric Vehicles in 1989.

Harbilt electric vehicles were initially produced by the Harborough Construction Company Ltd., Market Harborough, near Leicester, which was formed in 1935 as a manufacturer of aircraft components by a Mr. Navarro. The business made products for the National Aircraft Company in Lancashire—the factory was known locally as The Aircraft—which moved into the former Hearth's Hosiery factory in Logan Street in 1935. During the Second World War they made engine mountings and gunner seats for Avro Lancaster bombers, fittings for parachutes sewn up at the nearby corset factory, known locally as The Factory, tail wheel forks for Hawker Siddeleys and bomb bays for Wellingtons. After the end of the Second World War, they diversified, and electric vehicles were the main part of their new product range. In 1945, the first prototype was designed by Tom Mather of Imperial College, London, and developed by Robert Matthews working with former torpedo engineer Bob Eastwood. The production model, launched in 1949, was the 4-foot (1.2 m) wide 551 pedestrian-controlled vehicle. For its charger they approached Partridge Wilson of Leicester, who was making their own range of Wilson battery vehicles.

In 1949, Harbilt of Markert Harborough, near Leicester, built this 4-foot wide 551 pedestrian-controlled vehicle. It became a bestseller. The Swiss bought some two thousand 551 chassis for hotel and postal use where gas vehicles were forbidden and where the lack of a differential gearing improved adhesion in snow and ice (Hakewill Collection).

One satisfied Wilson client was Johnston Mooney O'Brien of Dublin for bread deliveries from their bakeries at Ballsbridge and Jones's Road. Although they used gas trucks for long haul, the main business was done by a fleet of some 130 door to door delivery vehicles. The firm's first Wilson was so successful that a further 50 were bought up to 1954 when Partridge Wilson of Davenset Works, Leicester, ceased production after 20 years.

The Harbilt 551 was used at walking pace for the retail delivery of milk or bread. The British post office brought quite a few, boxed in for carrying parcels use, and local authorities bought them for street cleaning. The Swiss would buy some 2,000 551 chassis for hotel and postal use where gas vehicles were forbidden and where the lack of a differential gearing improved adhesion in snow and ice. Hundreds of 551s were built. The Harbilt 670 1-ton truck for light factory work was used in large numbers in the brick and tile industry. Its range at full speed was about 15 miles (25 km), and its speed was 31 mph (50 kph) in forward or reverse gear. A traction motor of 2 hp was used and driven from a locally produced Tungstone 12-cell battery, but other batteries were sourced to satisfy the customers' need.[13]

The other main plank of Harbilt's expansion was the ride-on milk float, with successive models from 735, 750, 760 to 850, 900, 924 and 936. In 1956 they built the 735, designed with 24 or 36 cell batteries that could travel 50 miles (80 km) and reach speeds of 22 mph (35 kph). This still tends to annoy morning commuters caught behind an empty float returning to its nest at the Kirby & West Dairy in Leicester. The 750 was a 72v wider body float, whereas the 760 was a 36v narrower body. Many old films feature these floats.

Constant development of ideas was a theme their salespeople stressed. Harbilt engineers would fall over backwards to create a prototype for a client to approve and order. The 551 mentioned above evolved with a seat and steering wheel added. The battery sat under the cushion. It had become a tow-tug for trailers. It then grew a hard-paneled shell to protect patients and, with a cab for the driver and a nurse, it was an ambulance for use on or off roads.

The company history is littered with prototype ideas that did not find a general market but were an engineering or design challenge. Their in-house design for a golf buggy looked like an invalid carriage so they bought Melux, a Polish design, and assembled and badged it as Harbilt. They then adapted it for a first aid ambulance for Caterpillar in Scotland.

In 1959 Harbilt was taken over by Crosby Valve and Engineering Co. Ltd., a U.S. operation with a European arm based in Wembley, north London, with a long history in contract milling work.

In 1974 Harbilt presented their HSV3 (Higher Speed Vehicle) commercial van, as designed by Bob Matthews, John Sanderson and the team at Market Harborough for delivery, hospital and factory use. Although heavier batteries meant its payload was reduced compared to the thousands of milk floats Harbilt were making, the HSV3 was extremely popular and helped Harbilt become the market leader. Also, assembled in Scotts Valley, California, 30 HSV3s were used by the United States Postal Service in Cupertino, California. The body was fiberglass, then unusual in the USA, linked onto chassis parts shipped out to await the construction team of four.

The Dairyliner range of eight milk floats was showcased at the Royal International Dairy Show held at Olympia in October 1970. At some point in the early 1970s, Harbilt and Morrison-Electricars reached an agreement for a product exchange and rationalization. All milk floats would be built by Morrisons at their Tredegar works, while Morrison and Manulectric trucks would be handed over to Harbilt. The electric vehicle facility was taken over

In 1973, Harbilt used fiberglass to build the bodywork of their HSV3 (Higher Speed Vehicle). Among the hundreds built, 30 HSV3s were used by the United States Postal Service in Cupertino, California (Bob Hakewill).

by a management buyout in 1975 and registered as Harbilt Electric Trucks. During this decade Harbilt trucks and milk floats would account for 80 percent of the 50,000 electric vehicles on the UK roads. In Ireland, there were more than 600 battery electric vehicles, nearly all milk floats and vans on the streets of Dublin, with smaller numbers in other cities and towns throughout the country.

For use off the roads where 100,000 electric vehicles were in use, Harbilt produced tugs, tractors, carriers and platform trucks, used at holiday resorts, exhibition centers, airports and elsewhere. Cranes and hydraulic platforms, special fitments for lifting and moving steel coil and plate were bolted onto a chassis but still serviced by the company engineers or their overseas agents. A subsidiary company Tri-Truk Ltd. marketed an electric refuse bin collection vehicle and another subsidiary, Powered Sports, marketed a range of golf caddie cars. Harbilt continued to make trucks for a variety of industries, until it was bought in 1987 for almost twice its share value by Fred W. Davies, a Canadian who wanted an MOD Licence for his Davies Magnet

Group Vehicles and York Trailers. Production moved to Corby, but the venture was short-lived, and it was sold again to M&M Electric Vehicles of Atherstone and was eventually liquidated in 1989.

Many housing estates were constructed during the decade or so after the end of the Second World War as part of the progressive, experimental establishment of the Welfare State in Britain. In the decade after 1945, 1.5 million homes had been completed. Prime Minister Clement Attlee's postwar Labour government built more than a million homes, 80 percent of which were council houses, largely to replace those destroyed by Hitler. To move around the building materials, electric trucks proved ideal. The 15-cwt Electrovan, developed in 1950 by Trojan Ltd. of Purley Way, Croydon, Surrey, became the workhorse for these building sites. Once built and occupied, the fleets of electric milk floats moved into the estates to deliver milk and bread to their doorsteps daily, followed by the council street orderlies under the control of the street sweeper.

Last but not least, another great name behind electric milk delivery trucks that was to outlive those mentioned so far was Smith Electric Vehicles Ltd. of Gateshead, founded by Berlin-born Horace William Heyman, who had trained as an electrical engineer in both Darmstadt and Birmingham. Following a spell as assistant chief electrical engineer for Morrison-Electricars, in 1940, Heyman moved to Metropolitan-Vickers, at Sheffield, where he worked on the development of industrial trucks and vehicles until the board abandoned the project. In 1944, the company sold its interest in electric vehicles to Brush and, because it was a subject that interested him, Heyman went to Loughborough too. However, it was a move that did not entirely please him and before the year was out, he had heard of Northern Coachbuilders' battery-vehicle project and won himself an appointment which offered the scope he needed. He assumed charge of the new enterprise and began to build vehicles to his own design in a couple of ex–Army Nissen huts on the Team Valley estate at Gateshead. He had one secretary and fewer than a dozen men. Mr. Heyman found himself designer, sales manager, engineer and accountant. Determined to build a good vehicle in quantities sufficient to maintain a competitive price, he succeeded in winning a 208-truck order from Thomas & Evans, the Corona fruit drink manufacturers in South Wales. This was followed by other big orders from the Co-operative Wholesale Society. Soon his small factory, named after his directors Douglas Smith and his son, was turning out 300 vehicles a year. In 1949, electric vehicle and bus production were separated, with buses continuing to carry the Northern Coachbuilders marque, and all NCB electric vehicles being manufactured by Smith Electric Vehicles, still in Gateshead. The Smith Electric Vehicles business in the 1950s and '60s focused on the milk float. In the mid–1960s, Smith launched the Smith Cabac, the first float to have a rear entry cab so the milkman could exit the vehicle on either side. Smith produced four versions of the Cabac: the 65, 75, Jubilee 77 and 85.

In the 1960s, Smith Electric Vehicle Company of Gateshead became synonymous with the image of the milk float. This 1966 example was used by the West Midlands Co-operative Society. Unusually, the fleet included a large number of the 2-ton S95 model. Smith also launched their Cabac, the first float to have a rear entry cab so the milkman could exit the vehicle on either side. Smith produced four versions of the Cabac; the 65, 75, Jubilee 77 and 85 (Transport Museum Wythall).

Smith took its first steps into North America in 1962 when the Smith family signed a partnership with Boyertown Auto Body Works and the Exide Division of Electric Storage Battery of Philadelphia, Pennsylvania, in order to produce a state-of-the-art electric-powered route delivery truck called the Battronic. At that time there were more than 14,000 Smith Electrics in service across the United Kingdom and Western Europe. The Boyertown-Smith connection had been made in the late 1950s, when the British firm's managing director was in the United States exploring a partnership with William and James Conway, the owners of "Mister Softee," whose mobile ice cream trucks were built by Boyertown. Smith eventually secured the United Kingdom rights to the Mister Softee brand from the Conways and started producing Mister Softee electric ice cream floats in 1959, in partnership with a J. Lyons & Co. subsidiary named Glacier Foods Ltd.

For the Battronic, Exide's parent company would produce the batteries,

During the 1960s, Smith Electric Vehicles Ltd. linked up with Boyertown Auto Body Works and the Exide Division of the Electric Storage Battery of Philadelphia, Pennsylvania, in order to produce a state-of-the-art electric-powered route delivery truck called the Battronic (Boyertown Museum of Historic Vehicles).

Smith the electric delivery vehicles, and Boyertown its high-strength, light-weight multi-alloy body. Early Battronics had a top speed of 25 mph (40 kph) and could carry a 2,500-pound (1,100 kg) payload up to 62 miles (100 km) on a single charge. The Potomac Edison Company of Hagerstown, Maryland, took delivery of the first production Battronic in March 1964. Smith withdrew from the partnership in 1966. Battronic worked with General Electric from 1973 to 1983 to produce 175 utility vans for use in the utility industry and to demonstrate the capabilities of battery-powered vehicles.

The ultimate fate of Smith is told in a later chapter of this history.

Phoenix

In 1975, 94 percent of milk was put into glass bottles delivered from door-to-door. By 2012, door-to-door milk delivery had dropped to 4 percent. The inevitable decline had set in with the introduction of home refrigerators in the 1950s, along with the 1990s deregulation of the milk industry. Supermarkets started to sell cheap milk in plastic containers, and in 2014, it was announced that the British concern Dairy Crest's last glass milk bottle plant was to close, no doubt starting a wave of nostalgia for a lost way of life. Some dairies in the UK, including Dairy Crest, had to modernize and replaced their electric milk floats with gasoline or diesel fuel-powered vehicles to speed up deliveries and thus increase profit.

At the time of writing, despite ongoing slumps in sales of cows' milk, as people switch to nut, rice and soy options, the market for glass bottles of milk appears to be holding steady, and even slightly increasing. After Theresa May, the British prime minister, announced plans to scrap all avoidable plastic waste by 2042, milkmen are reporting an increase in interest for the traditional "pinta." Dairy UK, which represents the milk industry, has stated doorstep deliveries of glass bottles are now around one million per day. Just two years ago the figure was estimated to be nearer 800,000. Mark Woodman, 56, who runs Woodman's Dairy in Rumney, Cardiff, has recently spent thousands refurbishing his old milk float to meet the new demand, which he puts down to recent pledges to tackle plastic waste by the government and industry.

Patrick Müller has been investing a further £20 million in the UK and Ireland division of Milk&More business, headquartered in Chicago, revamping IT, upgrading machinery and—most visibly—rolling out a new fleet of more than 200 electric floats to replace many of the older diesel vehicles used on longer rural rounds. In May 2018, Milk&More further expanded its UK EV fleet with 200 new StreetScooter electric vans. These are already in use by Germany's Deutsche Post, which operates 5,500 of those on its own. The StreetScooter has a 1-ton (1,000 kg) payload and a 9-yard (8 m) cube box, enabling Milk&More to carry 860 pints of milk at a time. The new floats have zero emissions and a range of up to 75 miles (120 km).

Patrick Müller, CEO of Milk&More, explains:

> Our customers are at the heart of every decision we make and that includes our investment in the *StreetScooter* milk floats. As a business, we are committed to making this great British tradition relevant to 21st century consumers and therefore the delivery vehicles we use must also meet those needs. We are already seeing the results of this strategy with a significant increase of 40,000 new online customers since January 2018, 90% of whom are ordering milk in our iconic one-pint glass bottles. We deliver 100 million of these glass bottles every year, and each is reused on average 25 times.[14]

Also in the tradition of the electric milkfloat delivery truck, in 2012 a start-up calling itself Picnic bv. was formed by a team of IT specialists, led by Joris Beckers, Frederik Nieuwenhuys, Bas Verheijen and Michiel Muller in Amsfoot, the Netherlands. Backed by these four investors, it planned to come up with a new business that would be able to gain a position dominated by giant companies in the grocery market. The idea was simple. Clients ordered their dairy products and groceries using an online app only, which would then be delivered for free within a one-hour timeslot of their choice, using an electric truck with a 110 km range called the E-Worker, built by the French company Goupil. Starting off with 150 customers in Amersfoot, by 2016 Picnic was serving over 30,000 households in several cities in the middle of the Netherlands. In March 2017, having received €100 million in funding, Picnic announced an aggressive expansion in the years ahead, including five new warehouses, 70 distribution hubs, and the procurement of a staggering 2,000 electric delivery vehicles. In 2018, Picnic entered the German market, selecting Kaars, Neuss, Meerbusch and Oberkassel (part of Düsseldorf's district four) with further expansion, starting in North Rhine–Westphalia which has a population of about 18 million people. Picnic is also expanding its delivery service in the Netherlands, to Noord Brabant, starting with Breda and Tilburg. Up to 185,000 families will be able to use the grocery delivery service. There is no reason why Picnic should not eventually serve the 28 countries in the European Union.

SIX

The OPEC Effect

Post-war, tens of thousands of electric industrial trucks were still being produced in various versions for use in factories and warehouses. Some names lived on. Baker, for example, was still in business after 50 years, manufacturer of the Hy-Lift truck with special tilt-type platform, 24 of which were supplied in 1947 to the Hammermill Paper Company in Erie, Pennsylvania. With an annual production of well over 100,000,000 lbs. of paper, a new warehouse was built around the trucks and tractor-trailers with a substantial saving in handling time and cost. In 1951, industrial trucks in the USA comprised 44,000 units (of which 70 percent were forklift trucks) excluding the 21,000 "driver walk" trucks. In 1954, Baker Industrial Trucks merged with the Otis Elevator Company and continued as the material-handling division. Over in Hamburg, Germany, STILL launched their EK 2000 electric trolley, marking the entry of STILL into the industrial trucks business. In England, Ransomes, Sims & Jefferies of Ipswich, known for their pre-war Orwell urban utility electric trucks, continued in business. Lansing Bagnall of Basingstoke, Hampshire, run by Emmanuel Kaye and John R Sharp, joined the electric forklift truck business. Beginning in 1954, now in the reign of Her Majesty Queen Elizabeth II, the Royal Mail's PEDT (Pedestrian Electric Delivery Truck), a Bradshaw Carryall, went into service.

During World War II, with gas rationing, Merle Williams of Long Beach, California, had built a small electric vehicle for his wife to drive to the market. As others saw his creation as a solution to their short distance transportation needs too, he received requests to build additional vehicles which he called Marketeers. Moving his Nordco Company to Redlands, California, before long Williams had enlarged his range to include two-wheeled electric bicycles, invalid vehicles, an industrial tote truck called the Model 311 and a utility truck called the Model 211.

In the 1950s, the U.S. Post Office Department began motorizing city delivery routes. In 1959, tests began with 13 electric Westcoaster Mailsters in

139

Miami and Houston, and in 1961 they ordered 300 electric Mailsters from Highway Products Company for use in Florida. Highway Products, Inc., of Kent, Ohio, was formed by Joseph Thomas "Joe" Myers in 1960 to manufacture truck bodies for specialty markets such as mobile post offices. Often known as "mail scooters," Mailsters worked best in areas with warm climates and flat terrain. By 1961, more than 8,400 Mailsters were being used to deliver mail and more were on order. The Post Office Department was also increasing their studies on electric vehicles, and four-wheeled vehicles were put into experimental use in 1962. The Department stated there were benefits of the electric Mailsters, including, "the absence of a conventional engine permits redesign of vehicles to incorporate excellent driver visibility and operational accessibility." In 1963 the design was improved so that e-Mailsters increased their top speeds to 25 mph (40 kph). But these BEVs had a high cost of operation, twice that of a gasoline vehicle, which went against the idea of the Mailster. The electrical components could malfunction, sometimes catching fire. Most problematic, though, was that the vehicles were so slow that they could not safely travel on main roads, which they often needed to do to travel to the delivery route and back to the sorting office. Although most e-Mailsters were still in service as of December 1964, they accounted for only about 2 percent of the Mailster fleet (298 of 13,754 vehicles), mostly gas vehicles manufactured by Westcoaster. They did not accelerate as well as the gas-powered models and could travel only about half as fast, at about 16 rather than 35 mph (35 to 50 kph). The Department began phasing out Mailsters altogether in 1967, and by the early 1970s they had largely been replaced by gasoline-engined Jeeps.[1]

In immediate postwar France, the long-awaited fuels such as gasoline and diesel did not flow as fast as users wanted and propulsion by electricity still knew good times. Until the end of the 1940s, the Villeurbanne factory managed to maintain a production rhythm that was essentially the same as during the occupation. On June 30, 1947, the SOVEL Company still held the first place in France in its sector with 3,250 vehicles in circulation. To maintain this position, it was present with large stands both at the Spring Fair in Lyon which took place in 1946 and at the Salon de l'Auto. The year 1947 was marked by a strike and the relocation of the workshops. Competition became more intense with gasoline trucks. The year was in deficit due to continuing difficulties in the supply of non-ferrous metals and continual delays with subcontractors. Production was slightly lower than the previous year: 256 chassis were produced, 75 percent of which had 2.5 tons of payload. Half of the vehicles produced were for the private sector, the other half for the administrations. In 1948, SOVEL recorded an order for "special equipment" for the SNCF. That year, with a drop of 10 percent in production, 235 vehicles were manufactured, 75 percent of which were 3-ton and 11 percent 6-ton dumpsters. The share for the private sector represented 35 percent, for the administration 50 percent, and 15 percent of the production was intended for spare parts. In 1949, the city of Paris organized the first contest for the hermetic collection of household garbage. The production rate was ten electric vehicles per month, or only 47 percent of the 1948 production. However, less subcontracting was used and 95 percent of the trucks were bodied by SOVEL against 54 percent in 1948. The 3-ton chassis represented 60 percent, but those of large tonnage were increasing. The production share for the private sector was less than 10 percent. The material produced was more varied and lower in output. Then demand declined with the reappearance of fossil energy sources in sufficient quantity. By 1950, the private clientele had disappeared almost completely. SOVEL, which had to adapt, not without difficulty, ironically became dependent on the suppliers of gas-engined chassis. In 1951, a survey showed that 10 to 25 percent of SOVEL trucks were no longer in service with customers.

A SOVEL truck at Paris's Orly Airport, its bodywork by Laforge (Collection J-N Raymond).

In 1952, Compagnie Générale d'Electricité owned a large majority of SOVEL. The latter had built 80 percent of electric road vehicles circulating in France at the time when a decline in this technology was confirmed, stabilizing at about 20 pieces per year in the 1960s. Three quarters of the turnover was then composed of equipment intended for local authorities and mounted on gas-engined chassis. From 1964, business was bad. The main shareholder had to hand over the business in 1969 to SEMAT, which in 1974 handed over the construction of electric vehicles to a group made up of, among others, Renault Saviem, EDF and CEM. Finally, SOVEL closed its plant in 1977. It was the end of an era which had begun half a century before.[2]

In the USSR, in 1948, electric vehicles with a payload capacity of 0.5 ton (NAMI-750) and 1.5 ton (NAMI-751) were developed by AS Reznikov at NAMI. Four prototypes were used to transport mail around Moscow, then ten more, manufactured by the Lviv Bus Plant, were operated from 1952 to 1958 for mail cargo around Leningrad. In the design of these vehicles, many non-standard solutions were applied: for example, a frame in the form of a spatial truss, a carcass of a body made of aluminum profiles. For the loading and unloading of the mail, there were two side elevation hatchways on the right side (in the open position they moved under the roof) and an additional tailgate for the NAMI-751. The drive was by hub motors and iron-nickel batteries were used. The engine power for the NAMI-750 was 2 × 2.85 kW and 2 × 4 kW for the NAMI-751.

In 1957, under the presidency of Nikita Khrushchev, NAMI developed new models of electric vehicles of the same carrying capacity. In the same period, the first Soviet electric bus was built on the basis of the SVARZ trolleybus with a capacity of 70–80 people. The reason was the need to equip the Exhibition of Economic Achievements with new transport in return for the old not meeting the spirit of such a representative institution. However, in the following years electric vehicles once again failed to compete with trucks using the internal combustion engine. During this time NAMI helped the People's Republic of China to start its own automotive industry.

Following the discovery of rich deposits of lead ores in Southern Bulgaria in the mid–1960s, this communist state got the role of supplier of forklift trucks and batteries to the USSR and other Eastern Bloc countries. In 1950, the automobile repair factory "Vasil Kolarov" was founded for the refurbishment of Soviet, Czech and East German cars. It was initially planned that about 500 cars would pass through the halls, but later plans expanded and 3,500 units were processed. In 1952 the first Bulgarian platform electric truck was produced, followed in 1957 by the first 150 electric low-forklift trucks, which were exported to Russia and Czechoslovakia. In 1964 the first joint-venture companies for sales of industrial trucks with the trademark of Balkan car were established. The following year it was decided to change the activity of the company to forklift production, in parallel with the repair of cars. The first forklift model BV 2733 was presented to the public. For the next 40 years diesel dominated, then in 2010 electric platform model ET2 with loading capacity of two tons was presented at the Plovdiv Technical Fair.

Under Leonid Brezhnev's presidency, in 1968 researchers at the Karl

Marx Polytechnic Institute with Yerevan Motor Works in Armenia initiated work on the sedan type Electromobile called YERPL-1 with a carrying capacity of 800 kg, speed of 75 kph and range of 60 km. Also, they unveiled UAZ-451-M1 AC-drive e-truck delivery vans by Moscow trade centers.

Back in the USA, smog had become so thick in the Los Angeles basin that local politicians were talking about banning the internal combustion engine. In response, all of the "Big Four" Detroit automakers started working on electric-vehicle technology. In 1967 Ford developed a molten-sodium battery that was so unconventional it broke a research logjam.

Then a political event occurred which brought electric vehicles—with trucks—back onto center stage, albeit temporarily. The oil crisis began in October 1973 when, led by Sheikh Yamani, Saudi Arabia's oil minister, the members of the Organization of Petroleum Exporting Countries (OPEC) proclaimed an oil embargo. The embargo was targeted at nations perceived as supporting Israel during the Yom Kippur War. The initial nations targeted were Canada, Japan, the Netherlands, the United Kingdom and the United States. The crisis skyrocketed gasoline prices and also sparked interest in alternatives to fueled vehicles. The quest for better fuel economy, lower fuel bills and so-called energy independence brought diesel and ethanol, and alternative powertrains, such as hybrid and electric vehicles. The 1973 oil embargo triggered a mad rush of electric-vehicle research.

On the same scale as the British milk float manufacturing boom, the U.S. Postal Service was seriously determined to change their huge fleet over to electric propulsion. In 1973, Frank M. Sommerkamp III, the dynamic Senior Assistant Postmaster General in Research and Technology who was leading this initiative, enthused that tests of a number of BEVs "could result within several years in our replacing conventional mail delivery trucks [with electric vehicles] at the rate of 5,000 per year."[3] Among those vehicles, Battronic worked with General Electric from 1973 to 1983 to produce 175

During the 1970s, Frank M. Sommerkamp III, the dynamic Senior Assistant Postmaster General in Research and Technology, led an initiative to change the U.S. Postal Service's huge fleet over to electric propulsion (U.S. Postal Service).

utility vans. West Coast Machinery, founded by S.S. Moore, had been manufacturing electric tilt dozers, power control units and rough terrain fork
trucks since 1946, with one of the first golf carts in the United States in 1950.
In 1973 West Coast Machinery, now part of Otis Elevator Co., manufactured
a limited number of electric delivery trucks for the USPS trials around Santa
Ana, California. In 1974, Electromotion, Inc., of Lowell, Massachusetts, produced a number of BEVs built with Saab parts which could carry about 660
lbs. (300 kg) of payload. The American plant of the British manufacturer
Harbilt in Scotts Valley, California, contributed 30 of their HSV3s. From 1977,
Sebring-Vanguard Inc. of Sebring, Florida, was producing the electric Citi-
Van, a variant of their CitiCar, modifying it and renaming it the Comuta-
Van. In 1981, 231 Comuta-Vans were delivered to post offices in south Florida,
but motor failures and a dispute with the company over warranty terms
grounded the fleet less than a year later. The vehicles were left parked during
a legal dispute with the company over contract terms, and the remaining
vehicles ordered were never delivered. Jet Industries of Austin, Texas, provided ten of their Ford Escort–based Electricar trucks, their 16 96-volt GC
batteries linked to a Prestolite MTC-4001 motor with PMC MOSFET controller.
Airplane manufacturer Grumman converted a GM Chevrolet S-10 Blazer to
a Long Life Vehicle (LLV) they called the Kurbwatt, using 14 golf cart batteries
replacing a 2.5L I-4 TBI Iron Duke motor to achieve a reported 40-mile-per-
charge range; a small fleet went into service in Evansville, Indiana, and were
also trialed by Canada Post. Nearly all of these vehicles used lead-acid batteries.

In the fall of 1972, M. Stanley Whittingham, an English-born chemist
working with a team at the Exxon Research & Engineering Company,
announced that they had come up with a new battery, and patents were filed
within a year. Within a couple of years, the parent company Exxon Enterprises
wheeled out a 3W 45Ah prototype lithium cell, and linking it to a diesel
engine, started work on hybrid vehicles. When solid-state physicist Professor
John Goodenough became head of inorganic chemistry at Oxford University in 1976, his research group included assistant Dr. Phil Wiseman, Dr.
Koichi Mizushima and Dr. Phil Jones. They set themselves to the task of looking at the potential of rechargeable batteries which began by simply "kicking
around ideas on a blackboard." "We looked at it in a different way using
lithium cobalt oxide at the positive terminal and pulling the lithium out;
this produced a huge cell voltage, twice that of the Exxon battery," Dr. Wiseman explained. It was this spare voltage that allowed alternatives at the other
terminal where Exxon had been forced to use lithium metal which was
fraught with problems. Instead, lithium-ion material could compose both
electrodes. The group's research was published in the *Materials Research Bulletin* in 1980. In 1977, Whittingham teamed up with Goodenough to publish

a book called *Solid State Chemistry of Energy Conversion and Storage.*[4]

In 1976, Congress had made a large appropriation for electric vehicle research, but as soon as oil prices fell in the 1980s, companies and governments shut down all those battery-research projects they had started in the 1970s. Exxon closed Whittingham's shop, appointing him director of their chemical engineering division, responsible for technology, for synthetic fuels in those days, chemical plants, and refineries. When Exxon stopped their R&D, the U.S. government largely got out of clean-energy research as well.

Another person looking at the potential of the lithium battery was Canadian geophysicist Geoffrey Ballard, with a mission to replaced the gas-engined automobile. Ralph Schwartz of Arizona convinced Ballard that they should try to come up with a way of recharging. They formed American Energizer and

In the 1970s, British-born chemist M. Stanley Whittingham (left) and a team at Exxon Research & Engineering Company, then American-born solid-state physicist John B. Goodenough (right) and a team at Inorganic Chemistry Faculty at Oxford University, did the groundwork that led to today's universal lithium-ion battery. This photograph of the two pioneers was taken in July 2018 (courtesy Whittingham).

recruited Keith Prater at the University of Texas chemistry department. Working in a trailer, Ballard and Schwartz built a simple battery and Prater brought a sample of the lithium dithionite, and when they were placed together and charged, a weak current was produced. After further development the system was able to be recharged about a dozen times. With the technology looking like it could be made into a commercial enterprise, Ballard purchased an abandoned motel in Arizona for $2,000 and set about turning it into a lab. After obtaining some private bridge financing, they won a contract for a non-rechargeable lithium battery with a shelf life of ten years for the fire detector company, Firenetics. After about a year the battery was ready and production was going to be started in Hong Kong, when, to Ultra's surprise, Firenetics filed for bankruptcy after a long lawsuit with General Electric. The rechargeable version never matured and Ballard began to look elsewhere for a clean source of energy.[5]

Fuel Cells

During this same period, another energy source was seen as a solution: the fuel cell.

In the early 1950s, an English engineer, Professor Thomas Bacon of Cambridge University was making considerable progress developing the first practical hydrogen-oxygen fuel cell to present large-scale demonstrations. One of the first of these demonstrations consisted of a 1959 Allis-Chalmers farm tractor powered by a stack of 1,008 cells. With 15,000 watts of power, the tractor generated enough power to pull a weight of about 3,000 pounds (1,360 kg). Allis-Chalmers maintained a research program for some years, building a fuel cell-powered golf cart, submersible, and a forklift truck. Interestingly the U.S. Air Force also participated in this program.[6]

In 1966, 24-year-old Jürgen Garche, studying electrochemistry with Kurt Schwabe at Dresden University of Technology (TU Dresden), worked on an industrial 3 kW hydrazine-air fuel cell forklift truck developed by BAE Berlin and TU Dresden. The main challenge was developing the hydrazine anode with a relatively low activity.

The same year another prototype fuel cell vehicle was developed in Detroit, Michigan. General Motors decided to expand on the experience of their battery-powered converted Corvair auto, the Electrovair, and install a cryogenic hydrogen fuel cell system in a GMC Handivan: the Electrovan. The rather sizable van had continuous and peak outputs of 32 kW and 160 kW respectively. But GM soon discovered that a leak with the electrolyte used caused "brilliant fireworks," and that it weighed 550 lbs. (250 kg) and needed to be housed in a larger vehicle. There was also an incident of an exploding hydrogen tank, which injured no one but sent pieces flying a quarter of a mile, which was of great concern. Extra safety precautions needed to be taken.

The Electrovan project was led by Dr. Craig Marks who headed up most of General Motors' advanced engineering projects. In 1957, Marks had received the Society of Automotive Engineers (SAE) Horning Memorial Award for his research on engine combustion noise. He worked in the 1960s to develop advanced-performance alternative power plants, including that of the fuel-cell-powered Electrovan. Marks, along with a staff of 250, modified the van for over two years before attaining a drivable vehicle. In NASA's Gemini spacecraft, fuel cells had powered onboard systems, producing drinkable water as a by-product. The Electrovan used a fuel cell produced by Union Carbide, which was fueled by both super-cooled liquid hydrogen and liquid oxygen. Today's fuel cells use less pure oxygen than is native in the outside air. The Electrovan had one large tank for the liquid hydrogen, one for the liquid oxygen and a third for the electrolyte, potassium hydroxide. It contained 550 feet (168 m) of piping throughout the rear of the vehicle, turning this six-seat van into a two-seater with barely enough room for two passengers. Both the liquid oxygen and the liquid hydrogen were kept at subzero temperatures, and the potassium hydroxide once again produced "brilliant fireworks" when it leaked. Given the highly flammable nature of both liquid hydrogen and liquid oxygen, this must have been anything but reassuring, and accidents did, occasionally, happen during the Electrovan's development.[7]

The Union Carbide 5 kw fuel cell (rated at 1,000 hours of use) was able to propel the Electrovan for top speeds of 63–70 mph (100–113 kph). It also had a respectable range of 120 miles (200 km). Because of safety concerns, this prototype was only used on company property, where it had several mishaps along the way. GM's team showed it off to journalists in October 1966 but did not allow them to drive it, as it was perceived to be far too complex (and potentially dangerous) to leave in untrained hands. The project was scrapped largely because it was cost-prohibitive. The platinum used in the fuel cell was enough to "buy a whole fleet of vans" and there was absolutely no supporting hydrogen infrastructure in place at that time. However, in some quarters, it was seen as the most advanced electric vehicle yet built.

This period also saw the creation of the small electric aircraft tug. In 1945, Wilt Paulson founded Willamette Aircraft and Engine Company in Beaverton, Oregon, to repurpose military aircraft for crop dusting and other civilian uses. Moving his company in 1948 to Warrenton, Oregon, to be closer to family, his business quickly morphed into the electric vehicle company now known as LEKTRO. Under Paulson's creative genius, LEKTRO developed products for the logging, farming, golf, theme park, and aviation industries. Some of these inventions were the first of their kind, including the first portable wind machines for logging slash burns and the first battery-powered vehicle to feed mink. In 1967, Paulson's friend, Si King, owned an MRO called Flightcraft at Portland PDX International Airport. Si and Wilt noted that tow bars often caused damage to the nose gear of planes and were overall problematic. Si wondered if the nose gear could be lifted with a scoop to cradle the gear, eliminating the tow bar. From this idea, Wilt produced a small electric aircraft tug by turning around the mink feeder chassis and attaching a hydraulic scoop and winch and tow bar-less towing was born. He called it the Airporter, and some 5,000 were built in airports in 93 countries across the globe. As a testament to their quality of construction and reliability, their second tug ever manufactured is still in operation (the first unit was recently taken out of service so it could be displayed in LEKTRO's Warrenton museum).[8]

In 1973, Elton Cairns joined General Motors Research Labs as assistant head of the Electrochemistry Department responsible for R&D on fuel cells, high temperature cells including LiAl/FeS2. He was responsible for the development of a Zn/NiOOH (zinc–nickel oxide system, also known as the nickel–iron battery or Edison cell) battery for electric Chevettes and electric Chevy LUV Trucks. (LUV is an acronym for light utility vehicle.) The Electrovan and the Chevy LUV truck EVs had been prepared for market entry, but when the oil embargo ended and gasoline prices and availability improved, the electric truck risked taking back stage again. The field tests were successful, but the EV project was discontinued when the price of oil dropped in the late 1970s.

In 1978, the U.S. Congress passed the Electric and Hybrid Vehicle Act and the government shared the cost of electric vehicle programs, funding their development to the tune of $30 million in 1979 and $41 million in 1980, enabling the construction of 575 electric cars and trucks. Jet Industries of Austin, Texas, with a workforce of 25, planned to build 600 electrics, all Dodge trucks and vans. AM General built nearly 350 delivery trucks for the U.S. Postal Service. American Telephone and Telegraph Company (AT&T) began to use 20 trucks as part of its 40-vehicle fleet for telephone installation and repair service in and around Culver City, California.[9] Working with the University of Alabama, UPS road-tested an electric delivery truck in 1980. General Motors announced that its breakthrough in a new zinc-nickel-oxide battery would enable it to begin producing electric cars by 1985. But soon after, GM executives stated that their battery would need further improvement before electric cars could compete with high-mileage, conventionally powered gas or diesel trucks.

The USA was not the only country attempting to free itself from OPEC dependency. Around the same time as General Motors was experimenting, Volkswagen in the Federal Republic of Germany was developing a number of powertrains for its popular Type 2 light commercial vehicle. The VW T2b Elektro Transporter aroused great media attention to the potential of cleaner transport. Its lead-acid batteries weighing 850 kg were housed in a voluminous compartment under the loading floor between front and rear axles. Power came from a 17 kW/23 bhp continuous output electric motor, with a peak output of 33 kW. Range was around 50 mi (80 km) with a top speed of 46 mph (74 kph). A single-speed drive transmission put the batteries' power down to the wheels, with regenerative braking. In 1972, an initial "10 to 20 vehicles" were built. Stadtwerke energy supplier was the first client. From 1974, VW decided to increase manufacture and about 150 vehicles were created for use in urban areas. VW also developed prototype hybrid-electric microbus taxi and gas turbine T2 variants. The German press was skeptical, not least considering the cost of acquiring the electric vehicle, amounting to around DM 60,000 compared to DM 15,000 to DM 17,000 for a conventional T2. At about the same time, it was reported that the U.S. space agency NASA was testing batteries with longer life nickel-zinc alloys and the possibility of longer driving distances.

In 1972, Daimler-Benz designed an e-truck to transport passengers and equipment to and from the Munich Olympic Games. The LE 306 and 307 were equipped with a quick-change battery system: through a flap fitted on the side between the axles, the set of 12-volt Varta lead-acid batteries, mounted beneath the cargo area, could be pulled out on one side in no time at all, while on the other side a new set of batteries was being inserted. The van, which was from the Hanomag-Henschel range, could handle a payload of exactly one ton with a maximum GVW of 3.5 to 3.9 tons and a battery weight of 860 kg. Depending on the style of driving, one battery charge

In 1972, Daimler-Benz designed an e-truck to transport passengers and equipment to and from the Munich Olympic Games. The LE 306 and 307 were equipped with a quick-change battery system used through a flap fitted on the side between the axles for the set of 12-volt Varta lead-acid batteries (author's collection).

enabled a radius of operation of about 30 miles (50 km). The electric motor developed 35 to 56 kilowatts; top speed was 50 mph (80 kph), climbing ability was 13 percent. The electronic controls were from Kiepe.

At the same time, BMW used the same battery swap system with a Bosch-engined converted 1602 sports sedan used at the Munich Olympic Games to outpace long-distance runners. All in all, 59 Daimler-Benz LE 306 and LE 307 units were manufactured. Trials were carried out by both Stadtwerke Aachen AG (STAWAG), which supplied energy to the city, and RWE, which was the regional energy supplier in Dortmund, North Rhine–Westphalia. The German postal service used 22 vehicles of this type in a practical test in Bonn in 1983. The results, however, were rather sobering: the energy costs were almost twice as high as the cost of comparable diesel vehicles.

In 1971, Linde presented its first electric forklift truck at the Hanover Fair. Six years later, they purchased the Baker forklift business, so continuing the Baker heritage. In 1984 Fenwick, still a French family business, was acquired by Linde, establishing Fenwick-Linde S.A.R.L.

Across the border in the French Republic, in 1970, Electricité de France (EDF) launched its research program for electric vehicles, with a budget of 4.7 million francs in collaboration with major car manufacturers. Between 1972 and 1975 EDF tested a hundred light vehicles as well as some buses. These included the electrification of 80 Renault R4s and five Renault R5s making it possible to achieve the first fleet on an industrial scale. Two types of batteries shared the market: lead-acid and nickel-cadmium. SAFT and CNRS (National Center for Scientific Research) also tested many new and more exotic electrochemical couples: nickel-iron, nickel-zinc and even lithium-iron-sulphide. In 1975, French Prime Minister Jacques Chirac decided to set up the Interministerial Electric Vehicle Group. Three years later, the French created a European Association of Road Electric Vehicles (AVERE) in Brussels. This was to become a center for information, exchanges and expertise. Its mission is to promote the acquisition and use of electric and hybrid vehicles, in particular by stimulating and accompanying the deployment of electric mobility to local authorities and businesses.

In 1986, Citroen's C15, equipped with SAFT NiCd batteries, was trialed in the towns of La Rochelle and Brussels. The commercial version was launched in 1990 at the Paris Motor Show. With its 0.35-ton (350 kg) payload and 62+ mi (100 km) range, the C15 continued to sell until the end of the century. Another experiment took place in the town of Châtellerault, center-west France, where with the leadership of its mayor Edith Cresson, a dozen medium-sized Renault Master trucks were tested in urban conditions. With their range of 50 mi (80 km) using lead batteries to 75 mi (120 km) with nickel-cadmium, by 1991 these Masters had traveled a total of 155,343 miles

(250,000 km), the most active having reached about 6,214 miles (10,000 km) per year. At the same time, Renault's traditional competitor, PSA Group, had installed 43 kW motors with ABB batteries in their Peugeot J5, FIAT Ducato, and Citroën C15 and C25 service trucks and were offering them to corporate or community fleets.[10]

The world was becoming concerned about global warming and pollution. Following the Earth Summit at Rio in 1992, the United Nations Framework Convention on Climate Change entered into force on March 21, 1994. Then the Kyoto Protocol of 1997 came into force in 2005. If the transport world was to meet the new requirements and go electric, then a battery couple with high enough energy density would have to be commercialized.

In 1993 the French Ministry of the Environment issued a call for tenders and called on local authorities to set an example. The goal was to create the beginning of a vehicle market by promoting acceptance by users and by preparing the physical and organizational infrastructure. Through these experiments, cities could identify interested populations and have vehicles tested by volunteers.

In addition, they could also determine the required parking spaces and charging stations. Twenty-two French cities became "pilot sites" for the introduction of electric vehicles, including la Rochelle, Bordeaux, Tours, Saint-Quentin-en-Yvelines, Strasbourg, Sophia-Antipolis, Besancon, Nancy, Toulouse, Douai, Lyon, Nanterre, Grenoble, Avignon, Montbéliard, and Rouen. Four hundred thirty charging points were installed by EDF in these 22 cities.

In 1992, a former schoolteacher, Achille Salvan, and his wife Caterina, set up a plant to build innovative service trucks in the ruins of Villa Mistrello in Padua, 40km far from Venice, northeast of Italy. By 2000, their company Alkè was producing an electric version; the AT 100e, and four years later, the 635 kg, 8 kW ATX 320E series was soon selling worldwide. In the 1970s Soviet Union, many organizations conducted experiments in the field of electric vehicles. The focus was on batteries and control systems, which contributed to a more economical energy expenditure. A fairly wide range of organizations joined the experiments. Among them were the Research Institute of Road Transport (JARI), the All-Union Scientific Research Institute of Electromechanics (VNIIEM), the All-Union Scientific Research Institute of Electric (VNIIETO), as well as automobile plants VAZ, ErAZ, RAF and UAZ. Road tests of the batch of electric vehicles NIIAT-A.925.01 with a DC power system were held in 1975 in Podolsk. A year before, five U-131 electric vehicles based on the UAZ-451 DM entered experimental operation at Avtokombinat No. 34 in Moscow. These machines were the result of joint efforts of the Research Institute of Glavmosavtotrans and VNIIEM Minelectrotechprom. They worked on alternating current with asynchronous motors.

In the UK

One of the problems that the UK electric vehicle industry has had to face is that of the "milk float image" (see Chapter Five). To many people the electric vehicle had become associated with the milk float as a 15 mph (25 kph) mobile traffic jam. One way of surmounting this prejudice would be to develop an electric-powered vehicle that could try to compete with the internal combustion-engined variety on performance, range, and economy, as well as providing acceptable ergonomic standards for the driver. Hence the current breed of electric vehicles built around conventional chassis or panel vans.

During the 1960s there were major advances in semi-conductor technology which opened the way for the efficient and infinitely variable control of electric motors; this was coupled with modest advances in the energy density of lead-acid batteries which made higher performance drive systems a more realistic possibility. Pioneering research work undertaken by Lucas Industries in the UK on electronic controllers for Direct Current (DC) motors led to the creation by Lucas of a dedicated Electric Vehicle (EV) project team with the aim of developing fully integrated drive systems for "traffic compatible" EVs, meaning with competitive speed and acceleration in city and urban driving conditions.

During the 1960s, Vauxhall-Bedford became the only division of General Motors outside of the U.S. to experiment in any meaningful way with electric vehicles. This was not a wholly Vauxhall project and was done in a joint development with the Lucas EV group and their then competitor Chloride. The first fruit of these joint projects was a conversion of an 18 cwt (914 kg) Bedford CA petrol engine truck to electric power in 1968. The biggest problem with this prototype was the sheer weight of all the batteries under the raised rear cargo floor which meant there was virtually no capability to carry any sort of load without overloading the suspension, unless the truck was going to deliver polystyrene blocks. Vauxhall uprated the suspension several times but the project was eventually dropped. Only one prototype was built; its fate is unknown but it was more than likely just scrapped.[11]

In September 1969, the Bedford CA had been replaced by the much sturdier CF van range, and with the Middle East oil crisis in 1973, once again in conjunction with Lucas EV Group and Chloride, development work commenced on converting 20 Bedford CF Vans to electric power on similar lines to the CA project. By this time the battery development had improved the output in relation to size and Lucas had developed a higher output electric motor as well as improved control technology. These vehicles were trialed from 1974 onwards by a select group of fleet operators who were chosen specifically because their work suited a light payload, short-haul, stop/start vehicle such as the Electric CF. Vauxhall liaised closely with Lucas EV Team and the vehicle operators as to the suitability and performance of the vans in service. While the trial was relatively successful, the one other barrier to series production was cost—the price of an Electric CF would be double that of a comparable diesel CF at the time and its payload would be smaller, and therefore it would take a mountain of years for the electric version to counter the initial outlay of the diesel versus the reduced running costs of the electric version. Despite this, trials with selected fleet operators continued for the rest of the 1970s.

Neither Vauxhall nor Lucas Chloride gave up on the electric van project and prototype building and testing continued throughout the rest of the 1970s, as is shown by the spy photographs taken in 1977 showing a heavily modified CF in Lucas livery undergoing tests at Millbrook proving ground. Lucas EV Systems Ltd. obviously felt confident enough to issue a book in 1978 detailing the projects they were working on.[12]

In 1981 Lucas, with its competitor, Chloride Group, established a joint venture company, Lucas Chloride EV Systems (LCEVS), to pool their systems technologies and resources and create a unified British EV programme. Given the limitations of the technology of the time (lead-acid batteries were still the only viable power source), Lucas and Chloride realized that electric cars were not a viable proposition, but research showed that around 50 percent of medium vans (1 ton/1,000 kg payload) rarely covered more than 50 miles (80 km) per day—a range which existing technology could satisfy. At the same time the two companies did not want to get involved with vehicle design and production and so in order to minimize investment in tooling, they needed to persuade vehicle manufacturers to fit their drive systems to existing petrol and diesel models with as few modifications as possible. The design brief thus became to produce a fully integrated drive system that could be fitted to a production van on a production line alongside conventional petrol and diesel models, giving the van a top speed of 50 mph (80 kph) and a range of at least 50 miles (80 km). This design specification required a 30 kWh battery pack, hung underneath the chassis, which weighed around one ton (1,000 kg). But, by fitting the heavy-duty suspension components from a long wheelbase model to a short wheelbase chassis, a 1-ton payload was maintained. Detailed research into 1-ton van usage in the UK highlighted a wide range of target applications, such as postal delivery, maintenance (e.g., Electricity Board jointing vans), newspaper delivery, and short-range people carriers. LCEVS embarked on a major strategic offensive, negotiating supply contracts with any vehicle manufacturers, although Bedford, which had played a pioneering role with the CF and been involved in the project almost from the start, was the only volume manufacturer still interested in a production EV van. Vauxhall-Bedford was also working hand in hand with Lucas Chloride's

EV Group to campaign for government support both for R&D and vehicle subsidies, persuading fleet managers to participate in market testing, and establishing a nationwide service capability for battery maintenance and drive system support. The latter involved recruiting a team of home-based service engineers with national coverage. The marketing proposition was more complex. The production cost of the vehicle would be greater than that of a conventional vehicle due to the lack of economies of scale. The cost of "fuel" (electricity) would be much less than petrol or diesel fuel (typically 2p per mile at the time), but the battery had a finite life and would be costly to replace. The LCEVS strategy was to offset the higher initial cost with a government subsidy and to lease the battery so that the combined battery lease and electricity cost more or less equated to the cost of petrol/diesel fuel over the life of the vehicle to the first owner.

In November 1980, working to Lucas and Bedford's specifications, Wilsdon & Co. Ltd. coachbuilders of Solihull were made responsible for the preparation of 100 Bedford CF electric vans as part of the Lucas/Bedford electric vehicle program with the vehicles being offered for sale from 1982 onwards. The work involved completion of vehicles from van shells supplied by Bedford, and the installation of the Lucas drive system components. Many of the vehicles assembled in Wilsdon's workshops were placed in commercial service with select fleet operators both in the UK and overseas. On January 7, 1984, Bedford announced the CF 1-ton electric van had gone into full-scale production at the Luton van plant. Using the same production line as the normal CF variants, 175 panel vans were scheduled for the end of May. Although this initial run would consist entirely of panel vans, Bedford was looking at introducing chassis-cab and chassis cowl variants. The provisional performance figures claimed for the CF included an urban range of 50 to 60 miles (80 to 100 km), a top speed of 50 mph (80 kph) and a 0 to 30 mph (0 to 50 kph) time of 11 seconds.

Thus, the CF joined the Renault R4 in France in launching the electric truck in Europe into serious production. The new van was part of a £70 million investment in the Luton facility and was claimed to be the first phase of what Bedford's General Manager, Mr. J.T. Battenberg III, described as "the biggest facility and product development programme in Bedford's history." It was also the culmination of nearly 15 years of joint development with Lucas, by now renamed Lucas Chloride EV Systems. The new CF Electric Van featured the latest electric drive technology, coupled with the highly developed practicality of the Bedford CF panel van.[13]

The other factor that had made the series production of the electric CF possible was that the UK Government's Department for Trade & Industry had agreed to provide financial support to both Bedford and Lucas Chloride EV Systems for R&D and sales subsidies and other financial support starting

In November 1980, working to Lucas & Bedford's specifications, Wilsdon & Co. Ltd. coachbuilders of Solihull were made responsible for the preparation of 100 Bedford CF electric trucks as part of the Lucas/Bedford electric vehicle program. The line-up shows the CF's range of applications (author's collection).

in 1982 for an initial five-year period. In November 1984, Bedford announced that more than 300 electric CF vans had already been built at its Luton plant and further models were being evaluated in Europe, Australia and the U.S. The UK Post Office was already running 40 electric CF vans as part of their own electric van test program. In 1985, Lucas Chloride also provided electrical propulsion equipment to Sherpa for their conversion of a small batch of Freight Rovers, classified as K2–250 Electric.

Other companies had also been busy. In 1981, following the satisfactory performance in service and the favorable operator reaction to a demonstration program involving 71 electric vans and buses, known as Dodge Silent Karriers, Dodge (Chrysler Europe) went ahead with its 50-Series, based on the 6.6 ton (6,600 kg) gasoline-engined Dodge 566, later known as the Renault 50 Series. The 50 kW EDC motor was mid-chasis mounted, and being of frameless construction the 50-series was 198 lbs. (90 kg) lighter and 40 percent cheaper than the Silent Karrier. The battery pack incorporated 80 cells of the lead-acid type from Chloride with a total weight of two tons. Body-building companies converted many into various wheelbase configurations from tipper trucks to buses. Many were built as "chassis cabs" to have box bodies fitted; these were widely used by utility companies in the UK. This Dodge had the distinction of being the first high-performance electric lorry to be manufactured on a normal automotive production line. The original Walk Thru had a range of about 35 miles (56 km), which compares with the 45 to 55 miles (72 to 88 km) on one charge being achieved by the 50 Series. On the braking side, the conventional vacuum-assisted system from the standard Dodge chassis was retained in contrast to the Clayton Dewandre full power system used previously. Dodge claimed that the slight increase in electrical power needed had a negligible effect on range, and balanced against this there was a significant saving in initial cost.

Then came the joint effort of Leyland Vehicles providing a G-series Bathgate-built chassis into which Wales & Edwards of Shrewsbury installed an electric drive. The Terrier TR738 filled the gap in Leyland's light vehicle range for a model to meet the recent changes to heavy goods vehicle driving license requirements. An inquiry had come from a large milk float operator as to whether a larger electric vehicle was possible than that on the market at the time and whether such a vehicle would be traffic-compatible. That inquiry led Leyland to initiate a study into electric power for the 3,500/7,500 ton (3,556 to 7,620 kg) goods sector. Whereas most manufacturers settled for one power system (usually from Chloride), the 7.5-ton Terrier TR738 was offered with the choice of drivelines based on Oldham or Chloride batteries. The original prototype was built around a cassette of batteries as Leyland did not want to have the batteries distributed all around the chassis. This left little room for the motor in the conventional mid-wheelbase position, a problem which Leyland solved by turning the motor over and mounting it behind the rear axle and driving it forward. The range was 50 miles (80 km) and it had a top speed of 40 mph (65 kph). As a change from Electricity Boards, the first electric Terrier went into service in February 1983 with the surveyor's department of the West Midlands County Council. Fitted with a Linktip tipping body, it was used for sign erection and litter collection. The West Midlands Terrier was one of three to be built as part of a Department of Industry–sponsored program, with the other two scheduled for Southern Electricity and North Western Electricity. Because of the lack of a conventional internal combustion engine, an auxiliary power pack was required on the Terrier to provide the braking effort. An air compressor was driven by the motor as was the power-steering pump via pulleys and a toothed belt.[14]

The Bedford saga continued. In October 1985, following the success of a single evaluation vehicle, Bedford Commercial Vehicles received an order to supply a further 35 electric CF vans to the United States for extended operational trials. The purchase of the vans was coordinated by the U.S. Electric Vehicle Development Corporation, which represents public utilities. The

EVDC chose the electric CF, branded GM Griffon in the U.S., following independent tests carried out with four other manufacturers of electric vehicles from Chrysler, Ford, AMC and Toyota. Phase two of the EVDC program was carried out jointly with the Electric Power Research Institute, General Motors, Vauxhall Motors Ltd. and Lucas Chloride EV Systems. It was to assess the suitability of the Griffon van for fleet operations in America and establish a system for servicing it in North America and Canada. The project would also identify potential electric van customers and develop marketing strategies to attract them. The first six electric vans would go to the Detroit Edison power company.

In May of 1986, Bedford reaffirmed its commitment to the electric panel van market with the news that in October 1986 it would start regular on-line production of electric CF2 vans, with a production rate of up to 500 a year, at the Luton van plant. Over 300 1-ton payload CF2 electric vans, produced in two batches, had already been sold, with the last of them built at the end of 1985. Questions were raised at the time as to whether or not Bedford would be able to sell 500 electric CF e-vans a year, although Bedford's electric vehicle manager Ken Malis claimed at the time that more than half of 1987's production was already covered by firm orders from electricity boards across the UK. Although the level of government subsidy given to electric vehicle manufacturers fell by 60 percent from the original figure of £4,200 per vehicle, Malia claimed that the CF2 would keep its original April 1984 launch price of £10,280 including battery pack and charger. Other UK manufacturers adopted a "wait and see" low profile in the electric vehicle market. Bedford, on the other hand, decided to launch a series of nine one-day electric vehicle roadshows in conjunction with the East Midlands Electricity Board and Lucas Chloride Electric Vehicle Systems. They were held at Bedford dealers in the East Midlands for the whole of June. Interest in the CF2 electric van continued to increase outside the UK, despite its relatively low overall sales in Britain. More than 30 GM Griffons were being evaluated in the United States with the development trials being coordinated by the American Electric Vehicle Development Corporation. They had reached the second stage of a four-part trial involving fleet users in the U.S., which could have ultimately led to production of a GM electric van being set up in America. More than 70 operators in Denmark, Sweden, West Germany, Japan and China were assessing the CF2 Electric at the time. Two vehicles were ordered by the Mitsubishi Corporation with one to be used by Kyushu Electric, while another two were shipped to the major Japanese utility company Chuubu Denryoku. Bedford claimed in June 1986 that it would begin development trials with a CF2 Electric fitted with sodium-sulphur batteries in early 1987 that could triple its 50-mile (80 km) range currently provided by a 1-ton lead-acid battery pack. Production of the sodium-sulphur battery-powered CF could even start before 1990. Compared with the standard lead-acid battery pack in the CF2 Electric, the sodium-sulphur battery pack would give better flexibility in payload and range owing to the varying number of cells that could be used.

Then came the bombshell on July 26, 1986. Bedford announced that it was to discontinue the electric CF2 just two months after announcing plans to produce up to 500 vehicles a year at its Luton plant from mid–October. The electric model had fallen under the axe in a rationalization program to try and curb losses of up to £1.5 m per week sustained over the past two years by Bedford in the UK. Bedford said it would continue to provide backup for the 300 electric vehicles already in service with operators. The decision came as Chloride Silent Power was on the point of fitting a sodium-sulphur pack in place of lead-acid batteries which would have extended the range for the CF2 to 100 miles (161 km) with a payload of about one ton (1,000 kg). But for Bedford worse was to come, and by 1990 the name had disappeared forever.[15]

Meanwhile in the USA, in 1989, Ford Motor Co., having progressed further with battery propulsion technology than either General Motors Corp. or Chrysler Corp., unveiled a battery-powered Aerostar mini-van, the ETX-11, at the Ninth Annual International Electric Vehicle Symposium in Toronto. General Electric and the U.S. Department of Energy were Ford's partners in the seven-year, $20 million venture. The ETX-11, a riskier program than previous efforts but with a potentially bigger payoff, incorporated an advanced sodium-sulfur battery built by Powerplex Technologies Inc., a subsidiary of Magna International Inc., Toronto. Ford had reduced its size, weight and cost, while increasing reliability. Though the electric Aerostar's gross weight was about the same as the gasoline version, about 5,000 lbs. (2,268 kg), its payload was only about half that of the gasoline version. The rest of the payload was taken up by the battery, which weighed about 1,270 lb. (576 kg). Recharge time was approximately eight hours.

The Energy Policy Act of 1992 directed federal agencies to add alternative-fuel vehicles to their fleets in increasing numbers beginning in 1996. In the early 1990s, the Postal Service continued to experiment with a number of electric vehicles, primarily in California where state law mandated the production of zero-emission vehicles.

In 1992, Ford of Detroit began to develop a small delivery truck fitted with lead-acid batteries and a 56 kW motor. With a state-of-the-art ABB sodium-sulfur battery pioneered by Wilfried Fischer in Heidelberg, Germany, the Ecostar was tested with encouraging results. Over 100 Ecostars were produced and trialed in fleet tests between 1992 and 1996 with over 1,000,000 miles (1,609,344 km) driven. The Ecostar averaged 94 miles (151 km) on a full charge, and demonstrated 155 miles (249 km) range in one test. The trials ran for 30 months. The Postal Service leased six Ecostars from the Ford Motor

Company, in cooperation with the Los Angeles area utility company Southern California Edison, for use at Huntington Beach, California. These were the first electric vehicles used by the Postal Service with a driving range that was extended through the use of regenerative braking. But throughout the trials there were problems with the system and the sulfur in the battery was flammable, a serious safety risk. ABB introduced a new version of the battery, but was unwilling to guarantee performance beyond one year. On several occasions the battery burst into flames during recharging. For this and several other reasons, Ford lost interest in the sodium-sulfur battery and turned to fuel cell concepts instead.[16]

Since their unsuccessful venture to develop a rechargeable lithium-ion battery, Dr. Geoffrey Ballard, Professor Keith Prater, and Paul Howard had been developing the fuel cell. Feeling the technology was ready for commercial use, in 1989 Ballard raised $4 million in public money from the British Columbia government to build a fuel cell powered bus, introducing it at Science World in 1993.[17] He took the bus to energy fairs around the world. In late 1997, Ford announced a partnership with Daimler-Benz and Ballard Power Systems to introduce car-ready fuel cells and their experiments with the sodium-sulfur batteries ended. Although the Ecostars performed well, concerns raised by Ford of catastrophic battery failure ended their evaluation as delivery vehicles. The development of the Ecostar led to other companies experimenting with similar vehicles, including Citroën in France with its Berlingo électrique, which was almost identical in looks, performance and range, but used 162 V SAFT NiCd batteries for power to a 28 kW Leroy Somer motor. In September 1996 Pascal Duclos, an electrical engineer previously with Schneider Electric, and Thierry Zerbato, specialist in self-propelled aerial work platforms, based in Bourran, started to develop their first short-range electric truck prototype, naming it Goupil, the French slang word for fox or for something small. The Goupil V2 was launched in 1999, while the G3 was homologated for on-road use six years later. More than one thousand units would be sold, with the option of a lithium-ion battery introduced with their G5 in 2015.

At the same time General Motors had produced the S10 Chevrolet EV pickup for a speed of 73 mph (118 kph) and a top range of 90 miles (144 km). It had a three-phase AC motor with 15 kW continuous and 50 kW peak power, and there were lead-acid and nickel–metal hydride battery options. The 1997 Chevrolet S-10 EV used a lead acid battery pack. Manufactured by Delco Electronics, the 1,400 lb. (635 kg) pack consisted of 27 batteries, with one being designated as an "auxiliary" cell. These reportedly offered 16.2 kilowatt-hours for propulsion. In 1998, an Ovonic nickel–metal hydride (NiMH) battery pack was also available; these batteries were lighter at 1,043 lb. (473 kg) and had a combined 29 kilowatt-hours of storage for a longer range.[18] NiMH also had longer life but cost more than the lead-acid option. The battery pack was located between the frame rails, beneath the pickup bed. On all battery types, a passive battery monitoring and management system was used; this meant that excess energy was wasted from cells with a higher charge, while the remainder of the cells reached the same state of charge. It was introduced in 1997, updated in 1998, and then discontinued. The USPS soon began testing six S-10s in Harbor City, California, and Merrifield, Virginia. In 1997, two more were put in service at Westminster, California. In March 1999, another two were delivered to Westminster; these were transferred to Harbor City in September 1999. The vehicles were taken out of service by the end of 2000 at the request of General Motors, which had cancelled its electric vehicle program.

Unlike General Motors' EV1, of the 492 S-10s assembled, about 60 were sold to fleet customers rather than just leased through restrictive programs, mostly due to the prior Department of Transportation crashworthiness evaluations done on stock S-10 pickups. As a result, unlike the fleet of EV1s that was repossessed and destroyed in 2002, a few electric S-10s can still be found in use today.

The Solectria CitiVan used a GM chassis, with a body by the Union City Body Company and electric propulsion by the Solectria Corporation of Wilmington, Massachusetts. In June 1998, the USPS began testing two 2-ton Solectria CitiVans owned by the New York Power Authority for deliveries and pickups in Manhattan. In 2001, USPS purchased 20 CitiVans for use in Manhattan. In 2004, eight CitiVans were put in service in the Bronx, and in 2005, two were placed in service in Queens. Approximately 400 vehicles were converted. The North Jersey District Water Supply Commission procured a 1996 Solectria Force that is still in service today. The original 13 12-volt lead–acid gel cell batteries lasted until April 2011, when they were replaced after nearly 10,000 miles (16,000 km).

In 1999, Daimler-Chrysler launched its EPIC (Electric Powered Interurban Commuter), based on the Dodge Caravan/Plymouth Voyager. Its SAFT nickel-metal hydride batteries gave the vehicle a 90–100 mile (145–160 km) range between charges, a marked improvement over lead-acids. While the standard Level II off-board charger (208/240 volt, 60 amps) recharged the vehicle in four to five hours, the EPIC could also utilize a new Level III (440 volt, 3-phase, 60 kW) charger which shortened the recharge time to a mere 30 minutes. In September 1999, twelve EPICs were added to the delivery fleet of the Harbor City, California, post office. A $60,000 grant from the Department of Energy helped offset the added cost of leasing the vehicles. Together with five electric LLVs, these EPICs comprised the Harbor City post office's entire delivery fleet for a short time, making it the first post office to have an all-electric fleet since the Cupertino post office in the 1970s. Although they performed well and were well liked by letter carriers, the EPICs were returned to Daimler-Chrysler in 2001 at the end of their three-year lease at the request of the company.

At the same period, Mercedes-Benz had developed hybrid-electric prototypes of their diesel trucks under the name of Mercedes-Benz T2, then changed to the Vario and the Atego as a result of a new face. The diesel engine of the Vario814D Hybrid had an output of 100 kW (136 hp); that of the Atego1217 Hybrid, 125 kW (180 hp). The diesel engines were assisted by electric motors with outputs of 55 kW (75 hp) and 60 kW (82 hp), respectively. Depending on requirements, the maintenance-free lead-gel batteries of the vehicles were charged either by the vehicle's diesel engine or with electricity by means of an onboard charger. They existed in a multitude of different versions and chassis, from the simple van to the dump truck to specialized models such as the armored truck. The breakthrough was not achieved, however, owing to excessive restrictions in relation to weight, range, and cost.

But as all electric vehicle designers and manufacturers during the 1980s and 1990s realized, neither the lead-acid nor the promising nickel-cadmium nor the sodium-sulfur battery options had yet shown energy densities high enough to compete with OPEC gasoline on which the world was still dependent. The solution, waiting for commercialization, was lithium-ion.

SEVEN

The Lithium-Ion Advantage

The past two decades have seen the development and series production on three continents of trucks with electric and hybrid-electric drives.

In 1993, funded by the Northeast Alternative Vehicle Consortium, the Grumman Corporation of Bethpage, Long Island, a leading manufacturer of military hardware and a nuclear-bomb factory, teamed up with the Long Island Lighting Company (LILCO) to install a hybrid compressed natural gas/lead-acid electric batteries system in an aluminum-bodied Route-Mate delivery van. Six vehicles were to be converted at the Allied Assembly plant in Sturgis, Michigan, and LILCO would put four of them into its 2,900 strong fleet. In 1994, Electricar Inc. teamed up with the Itochu Corporation, one of the world's largest trading companies, to target Tokyo's market for light delivery trucks. The first scheduled were the Grumman Long Life delivery truck as used by the U.S. Postal Service and the retrofitted Chevrolet S-10 pickups, 200 of which had been converted from gasoline by Electricar, headquartered in Santa Rosa with production facilities in Los Angeles, Redlands, Hawaii and Florida. Unfortunately, this period coincided with the end of the Cold War, reduced defense spending and a wave of mergers, including Northrop's acquisition of Grumman. The hybrid van project was wound down.

The Los Angeles Department of Water and Power, in cooperation with Southern California Edison and other utilities, issued requests to auto manufacturers to provide proposals for plans to manufacture, market, distribute and finance up to 10,000 electric vehicles in Southern California by 1995.

But as Thomas Edison had understood back in the 1900s, if the battery was right, everything would fall into place for all forms of electric transport, including trucks. Although the nickel-cadmium battery and its sister the nickel-metal-hydride had been more promising than the lead-acid, the grail discovery came in the increased development and commercialization of the lithium-ion (li-ion)battery.

In 1985 Akiro Yoshino of the Asahi Kasei Corporation in Japan created the commercial prototype lithium-ion battery. Two years later, Sony of Japan entered an agreement with Eveready USA to develop mass-market rechargeable lithium batteries. Many alternative cathode and anode chemistries have been discovered since those first commercial li-ion batteries hit the market in 1991. The original Cobalt Oxide cathode's vulnerability to overheating, producing oxygen, and possibly catching on fire led to the 2006 "era of flaming laptops." Meanwhile, other cathode types such as Lithium Manganese Oxide (LMO) and Lithium Iron Phosphate (LFP) were developed, offering greater resistance to overheating but having less energy density (measured in kilowatt-hours per kilogram, or kWh/kg). These types have become the principal players in the electric vehicle field.

Development continued. By the late 1990s, Japanese companies, in particular Sony, had made great strides in the commercialization of lithium rechargeable batteries. In 1997, Tsuyonobu Hatazawa, R & D Manager at the Sony Corporation, Kanagawa, invented the polymer-gel-electrolyte and lithium-ion polymer battery.[1] In 1997, Nissan Motors produced its Altra, an electric car, equipped with a neodymium magnet 62 kW electric motor and utilizing lithium-ion batteries manufactured by Sony. The following year, Ji Joon Kong in South Korea founded Kokam to manufacture polymer processing equipment, including polyester film and polarized film manufacturing systems, and breathable (porous) film casting systems. In the late '90s, Kokam expanded its business to designing and manufacturing li-ion secondary batteries and succeeded in developing the world's first commercial products. The same year, tests were carried out in France of vehicles equipped with li-ion batteries where an encouraging range of 124 miles (200 km) was observed by such authorities as the Inter-Ministerial Committee for Clean Vehicles.

Founded by Winston Chung, Shenzen Battery Ltd. based in Shenzhen, Guangdong Province, China, had produced its first batch of white Thunder Sky lithium ion batteries in August 1998. Thunder Sky (based in Hong Kong) built lithium-ion batteries used in trucks.

In late 2005, Mitsubishi Fuso Truck and Bus Corporation of Japan presented their Fuso Canter Eco Hybrid, commercially. It combined a compact clean-burning diesel engine, an electric motor/generator, and advanced li-ion batteries in a drivetrain that utilized a high-efficiency automated transmission. The result was a medium-duty truck that achieved up to 30 percent better fuel economy in delivery applications and also produced significantly less emissions than its standard diesel-only model. DHL Japan has been using the Canter Eco Hybrid truck for collection and delivery of small and medium-sized packages in Ohta-ku, a ward of Tokyo, since July 20, 2006.[2]

Two thousand six also saw the creation of a joint venture between SAFT and Johnson Controls Inc. to develop, produce and sell advanced-technology batteries for hybrid electric vehicles (HEVs) and electric vehicles (EVs). Two years later, Johnson Controls–SAFT opened the world's first production facility for lithium-ion hybrid vehicle batteries in Nersac, France.

Another pioneer of li-ion trucks was Power Vehicle Innovation (PVI) of Gretz-Armainvilliers. In the early 1990s, PVI had become the first to build electric and dual-mode garbage trucks called the Puncher. In 2005, PVI chose to invest in the development of complete solutions to equip industrial vehicles (buses and trucks) with all-electric power transmission, coupled with li-ion batteries. Under the Gépébus brand, they produced Oréos 22 and Oréos 55E, used for example by the RATP on a tourist bus line in Paris, the Montmartrobus. More than half of the French electric buses in circulation in 2003 were distributed by PVI. In 2007, PVI began to work with Renault to develop a li-ion truck for transportation of goods in urban areas. The result was the Maxity, a light commercial vehicle with a cab-over-engine, launched in 2011 after trials with a 2-ton (2,000 kg) payload prototype around Paris with drinks distributor Tafanel. Renault Trucks stated that between 10 and 30 pre-series Maxity Electric vehicles would be put on the road with pilot customers in France in 2010, and the vehicle was scheduled to be on the market by 2011. In 2013 Renault Trucks delivered a 4.5 ton (4,500 kg), 47 kW Maxity Electric equipped with a mini waste collection to Provence Benne Environment (PBE), also Nicollin for operation in Lyon. Almost as if they had taken on the mantle of the legendary SOVEL of Lyon (see Chapter Four), in the 2010s, PVI focused on 100 percent electric and developed a new generation of electric vehicles, including new models of electric buses (some being equipped with the Watt System), the first truck to collect electricity, the latest-generation CLESS (Centre Lyonnais d'Enseignement par la Simulation en Santé) garbage dumper (BOM) with a 26-ton (26,000 kg) Postes et Telecommunications 100 percent electric waste, and the 16-ton. Renault Midlum, in partnership with Renault Trucks for the Carrefour Group 6. In 2012, PVI opened a subsidiary in Shandong Province, China. The Chinese market, the world's largest automotive market, is a strategic issue for the internationalization of PVI's electrical solutions.[3]

In 2004, FedEx became the first global company to invest in hybrid-electric commercial trucks; six years later, they introduced the first all-electric Navistar Modec trucks to be used in the U.S. parcel delivery business for the Los Angeles area, ordering ten more for London and five more for Paris. As it had done at the beginning of the 20th century, now in 2012, La Poste (France's Post Office), launched its program of deployment of electric vehicles for postmen for the collection and distribution of mail and small goods. Postmen and women were equipped with electric four-wheelers, two-wheelers and electric carts. Within three years, the La Poste fleet had grown to 25,000 yellow electric vehicles, including 5,000 Renault Kangoo ZE and 18,000 electric-assisted bicycles produced by the manufacturers Arcade and Cycleurope. Each day, the world's first significant fleet of electric vehicles traveled around Earth five times. To further develop electric mobility, La Poste is also testing a Renault Maxity Electric 4.5 tons (4,500 kg) hydrogen truck and Renault Kangoo ZE equipped with a fuel cell developed by Symbio FCell. With autonomy extended to 124 miles (200 km), the prototype was tested for a year in the Dole region. Similar developments had been going on elsewhere in the European Union.

The decision of global logistics company DHL, the biggest buyer in the world of trucks, to design and build its own range of electric trucks is a game changer. Having received negative responses from a whole series of truck manufacturers to design and build electric trucks for them, they decided to do it themselves. In 2011, a team led by Professor Günther Schuh at the RWTH Aachen University in Germany produced the electric StreetScooter and began manufacture. Following extensive trials, Deutsche Post DHL purchased the concern and a fleet of 50 30 kW StreetScooters were put into service. The StreetScooter firm has gone on to develop fully electric pickups, vans, bikes, and trikes, which it also sells to third parties. An estimated 5,000 e-vehicles have driven 8.5 million miles (13.7 million km) so far. The plan is to have 35,000 of them on the road by 2023.

Between 1988 and 1995, Daimler-Benz had been manufacturing the MB 100 truck, equipped with a front engine and front-wheel drive. In 1994, the Stuttgart firm converted an MB 100 to fuel cell propulsion, calling it the NE-CAR 1 (New Electric Car), following it in 1997 with a NE-BUS. However, the electric version only had room for the driver and front passenger in the otherwise spacious truck. The 0.8-ton (800 kg) fuel cell filled the entire cargo area. However, the electric motor provided impressive performance: its 41 hp accelerated the vehicle to up to 56 mph (90 kph). One charge was enough for approximately 62 mi (100 km). The next stage for the Mercedes-Benz team was the Vito E-CELL with an operating range of around 80 miles (130 km) with a payload of around 1,984 lbs. (900 kg). The vehicle's top speed was limited to 50 mph (80 kph) to maximize the operating range of the batteries. The electric motor, a permanent synchronous unit, developed a continuous output of 60 kW and a peak output of 70 kW. Maximum torque was 280 N·m. Power was transferred to the front wheels via a single speed transmission. The li-ion battery in the Vito E-CELL could be loaded from 0 to 100 percent in about 6 hours. The usable capacity of 32 kWh proved sufficient to cover journeys of up to 60 mi (100 km) on a daily basis. Regenerative braking served as a plus for the high-frequency stopping for deliveries. The industrial truck also benefited from this fuel cell technology as evidenced by the Linde E20 and E50 forklift trucks.

The series-manufactured Mercedes-Benz Atego Hybrid was premiered in November 2007 during the opening event of the "Shaping Future Transportation" initiative in Stuttgart. It used the Eaton developed Parallel Electric system, with the Fuller Automated Manual replaced by the Daimler G45 automated transmission. Five examples of 7.5 (7,500 kg) and 12 tons (12,000 kg) GVW were trialed with the Deutsche Post DHL. The following year Mercedes-Benz presented a concept study of the Econic NGT Hybrid, which combines natural gas propulsion and hybrid propulsion at the IAA Commercial Vehicles Show in Hanover.

During this time, Smith Electric Vehicles Ltd. had not been idle. Acquired by the Tanfield Group in northeast England in 2004, R&D was now evaluating new transmission systems and batteries. A proof of concept vehicle called the Faraday was launched in October 2005, with a top speed of 50 mph (80 kph), a range of up to 60 miles (100 km) in urban operations and payload capabilities of up to two tons (2,000 kg). Built on Smith's own all-steel chassis, the Faraday had a Gross Vehicle Weight (GVW) in excess of five tons (5,000 kg). Early adopters such as TNT N.V. and Sainsbury's wanted an electric vehicle that better matched UK driving license restrictions. In the UK, anyone with a valid license can drive a light commercial vehicle up to 3.5 tons (3,500 kg) GVW.

Based on this feedback from the Faraday, Smith launched the *Newton* 7.5 ton (7,500 kg) truck in 2006, which housed the electric drive line technology in an established truck chassis from Aviain in the Czech Republic. The Newton came in three GVW configurations: 7,500 pounds (3,400 kg), 10,000 pounds (4,500 kg) and 12,000 pounds (5,443 kg). Each is available in short, medium or long wheelbase. The truck was launched with a 120 kilowatt electric induction motor from Enova Systems, driven by li-ion iron-phosphate batteries supplied by Valence Technology of Austin, Texas. In 2012, Smith re-released the Newton with new driveline and battery systems that were developed in-house. Smith offered the battery pack in either 80 kWh or 120 kWh configurations.

Leading express and mail operator TNT N.V. took the first Newton, for assessment in its London fleet. Also, in April, TNT N.V. ordered a fleet of 50 Smith Newton trucks, following its successful trial of the first Smith Newton. A few months later, in February 2007, Prime Minister Tony Blair officially opened the new Smith Electric Vehicles production facility in Washington, Tyne & Wear. "This will be a company that will really make its presence felt not just in the North East but actually throughout the world," Blair told *Ver tiKal.net* in February 2007. In April the same year, Smith Electric Vehicles unveiled the Smith Edison. Based on the Ford Transit, this was the first electric light commercial vehicle to have a GVW of less than 3.5 tons (3,500 kg)— meeting the "everyman" driving license requirement of UK fleet operators. First movers to deploy the Edison included the retailer Sainsbury's and utility company Scottish & Southern Energy. In December, the company also showcased its Newton truck in North America and announced ambitious plans to establish a U.S. production facility.

Recognizing the company's key role in this emerging sector, Smith was one of several electric commercial vehicle companies invited to the Department for Transport (DfT) in London, for discussions on how the UK government could help stimulate the market for commercial electric vehicles. This led to the announcement of the Low Carbon Vehicle Procurement Programme, in the government's Energy White Paper of May 2007.

By now, well-managed li-ion batteries were available for other transport systems. In 2007, Torqeedo of Starnberg, Germany, were building up their range of electric outboard engines with an integrated li-ion battery pack. The same year, pioneers in the USA, France, Germany and Slovenia built and flew their first electric prototypes using li-ion batteries. The same year, Zero Motorcycles of Santa Cruz, California, were pioneering the safe use of li-ion batteries in their two-wheelers.

The year 2008 began brightly, with Smith appointing its first full-service distributor, Electric Vehicles Ireland, and in April, Smith and Ford of Europe announced an "official collaboration" on the future development of commercial electric vehicles, starting with the Smith Ampere, a pure electric version of the Ford Transit Connect and built in America. The Ampere took the long-wheelbase Transit Connect and replaced the internal combustion engine with a 50-kilowatt electric motor and a bank of lithium-ion iron-phosphate batteries developed specifically for the vehicle. The batteries were covered by a five-year/1000-cycle warranty. Smith claimed the Ampere was good for 100 miles (161 km) per charge, could reach 70 mph (113 kph) and could carry close to 1,800 pounds (816 kg) of cargo. Smith was set to roll out the larger Faraday II, based on Ford's mighty F-650 medium-duty truck. The Ampere and Faraday II would join Smith's Ford-based Newton in the American market. Smith already had a small facility in Fresno, California, but in December, the company announced that it would open a much larger U.S. factory in 2010 with a production capacity of 10,000 vehicles per year.

However, by the end of June 2008, the world recession had started to bite. Smith's parent company, Tanfield, reported the cancellation and postponement of customer orders. In November, Smith Electric was shortlisted for the DfT's Low Carbon Vehicle Procurement Programme, a subsidy scheme that offered select public sector bodies the opportunity to buy electric and low carbon vans for the same price as the equivalent diesel vehicle. The economic downturn interrupted the company's fast growth; electric vehicle sales for 2008 were relatively flat at £25.1 million (2007: £26.1 million), reflecting a positive start to the year followed by a difficult second half. Tanfield cited a combination of supply chain constraints and fleet operators reducing spending in line with their own decline in sales, plus the lack of available credit for those who did want to purchase. Furthermore, the recession set back the company's plans to open a production facility in the USA.

In January 2009, following some market research, Bryan L. Hansel co-founded Smith U.S. Corp in Kansas City, Missouri, purchasing SEV Group Limited from Tanfield Group two years later for $15 million. In the United States, Frito-Lay was one of the main customers, with 176 Newton delivery trucks in operation by January 2011, representing about 1 percent of Frito-Lay's total fleet. Other American customers included Coca-Cola, AT&T, Pacific Gas and Electric Company (PG&E), Staples and the U.S. Marine Corps.

The Newton was named Green Commercial of the Year in the electric vehicle section of *Fleet Transport* magazine's Irish Truck of the Year Awards 2010, sponsored by Castrol. As of October 2012, the Newton was sold worldwide and available with three different payload capacities from 6,100 to 16,200 pounds (2,800 to 7,300 kg). The li-ion battery pack was available in varying sizes that delivered a range from 40 to 100 mi (60 to 160 km) and a top speed of 50 mph (80 kph). CEO Hansel built a second factory in New York City and planned to have as many as 20 around the country. But by Spring 2014 Smith Electric had stopped production, having sold only 800 Newtons in total.

Then in 2015, Smith Electric linked up with FDG Electric Vehicles Inc. in China. The chassis would be produced in China and shipped to the U.S. as semi-knocked down kits. Smith would then assemble and install the drivetrain. The battery would be produced by Sinopoly, part of FDG, a Hong Kong–based battery company with plants in China. By this time, Bryan Hansel was head of Chanje, a company based in California that had produced the V8070 all-electric van. The latter has a 100 mi (160 km) range with 7.5-ton (7,500 kg) gross vehicle weight (GVW) and can handle a 2.8-ton (2,800 kg) payload. It features a 10.4-inch (26.4 cm), Android-based touchscreen display with LTE connectivity to control most of the van's features. It runs dual liquid-cooled synchronous permanent magnet motors with battery capacity of 70 kW. In 2017 Ryder System Inc. placed an initial order for 125 vans ready to charge and service them in California, New York and Illinois, increasing this to an order for 500 in June 2018. Ryder is also acquiring a number of electric step vans from Ohio-based Workhorse Group and has ordered 2,500 of Workhorse's W-15 electric pickup trucks.

Sadly, in February 2017, back in the English county of Tyne and Wear, Smith Electric Vehicles (Europe) Ltd. was shut down. It was the end of a 70-year-old saga.[4]

Li-ion had been proven the way to go. In 2011 Liotech, a joint venture between Russian state-owned firm Nanotechnologies (RUSNANO) and Chinese holding company Thunder Sky Limited, opened the world's largest lithium-ion battery factory. The sprawling 40,000-square-meter plant near Novosibirsk was built in nine months. Electric transport equipped with lithium-ion batteries of the Liotech Company was exhibited at the "Transport of Russia" Exhibition in Sokolniki, including a truck for community services.

Solar energy has begun to provide assistance. From January 2014, the Coop in Zurich Switzerland developed E-Force One, a li-ion 18-ton t e-truck with 18 square meters of photovoltaic elements on the truck roof. Based on an Iveco Stralis chassis, together with regenerative braking, the solar panels provide 23 percent of the total energy of the vehicle. The battery can be replaced within ten minutes. The range of the truck is 149 mi (240 km) per day. In 2014, the Coop solar-truck was awarded both the Euro Solar European Solar Prize in the transport and mobility category and the German Federal Ecodesign Award. Two E-Force One trucks went into service at the Lidl store and with Feldschlösschen Beverages Ltd. followed by one with the company Pistor and others with Meyer logistics as a refrigerated truck.

There have also been developments in the Netherlands. In 2012, a Dutch company, Emoss Mobile based in Oosterhout, made a 100 percent e-truck with a 93–124 mi (150–200 km) range, payload-customized units which went into service with DeRooy, Deudekom, Heineken, Mondial Movers, Sligro and TopMovers for use in Switzerland, Austria and Lichtenstein. The following year, Emoss provided the German discount company TEDi with a 12-tonner whose opportunity-charging system increased range to 186–249 miles (300–400 km). Emoss has converted MAN and DAF trucks for work in Amsterdam and Tampere (Finland), their li-ion batteries rechargeable in only 3.5 hours.

The family firm of Terberg, based in Benschop, have developed their 138 kW Siemens-engined YT202-EV, a 40-ton yard tractor designed for moving trailers in distribution centers, transport depots, container terminals. The result of a partnership between BMW and service provider Scherm, the truck has a range of 62 miles (100 km) on a full battery and can be fully charged in three to four hours.

EIGHT

In Recent Months—
2016 to Present

In 1943, when Stanley M. Hills published the seminal "Battery-Electric Vehicles" in war-torn London, he was presenting the state-of-the-art technology of his time.[1] While Chapter One of this book chronicles some 70 years, Chapter Two 30 years, as this history has progressed, more and more successful applications of e-trucks are taking place. It therefore seems only right that the past four highly productive years should be given a chapter of their own.

In the same way that the OPEC crisis acted as a catalyst for electric vehicles, the United Nations Climate Change Conference, COP21, held in Paris in December 2015, should have proved a tipping point for electric vehicles. One hundred ninety-five nations signed the historic Paris Agreement on Climate Change with the objective of keeping temperature rise well below two degrees Celsius. At the High Level Transport Day on December 3, Segolene Royal, the French Minister of Ecology, announced the Paris Declaration on Electro-mobility and Climate Change and Call to Action.[2] It called for at least 20 percent of all ground transportation to be electrified by 2030. Twenty-four companies and organizations from around the world signed on to support the commitment. The COP 21 Agreement went into force on November 4, 2016, right before COP22 that took place in Marrakech where it was announced that the number of electric cars on the roads around the world had risen to two million.

In July 2017, the UK government followed France in announcing it would ban the sale of diesel vehicles by 2040, while the mayors of Paris, Madrid, Mexico City and Athens plan to banish fossil fuel trucks from their city centers by 2025. This of course includes gasoline-engined delivery trucks.

In my history of electric motorcycles,[3] I chronicle how legendary brand names such as Harley-Davidson, Curtiss, Ducati, Saroléa, and Royal Enfield have converted to electric propulsion. The same trend is being followed by truck brands. We resume the history of Daimler-Benz.

In 2017, Daimler's plant for manufacturing the Fuso eCanter went into operation, with the delivery of the first batch of e-trucks to UPS. The German automaker claimed that this was the first all-electric urban truck with a range of 62 miles (100 km) in "series production" and that they were planning to deliver about 500 more over the next two years before starting volume production.[4] Fusos were soon in service in New York City and Japan, with big companies such as 7-Eleven and UPS already signing up to try EVs in their fleet on both sides of the Atlantic. The Mitsubishi Fuso Truck and Bus division of Daimler then announced its plans for the E-Fuso Vision One, an electric heavy-duty truck, whose 300 kWh of batteries would make it capable of up to 217 miles (349 km) on a charge after hauling 11 tons. By March 2018, Fuso Trucks of America was trialing its medium range e-truck using about ten organizations—including the City of New York and the University of California, Irvine—to obtain data on how they are used, how drivers like them and what recharging habits develop. The same month the municipality of Houten, Netherlands, put 12 Fuso eCanters into municipal service. In July, John Deere Electronic Solutions (JDES) surprised the industry by becoming supplier of the PD400 inverter for Fuso eCanters produced by Daimler's sub-

Production of Daimler's Fuso eCanter is seriously underway, with plans to deliver 500 units worldwide during the next two years (Daimler-Benz).

sidiary. By July 2018, the Fuso eCanter was in use in six major cities around the world: Tokyo, New York, Berlin, London, and Amsterdam, as well as Lisbon.[5]

Daimler also unveiled two versions of its e-Actro truck, an 18-tonner and a 26-tonner, aimed at the European market. These were the fourth version of the Daimler range. Electric versions of the Mercedes-Benz Metris and Sprinter vans arrived on Europe's roads later that year, filling both the light-duty and medium-duty needs of small van and panel van customers.

In June 2018, Daimler unveiled its Freightliner eCascadia semi-truck at its North American headquarters in Portland, Oregon. This was part of its new unit called the E-Mobility Group to consolidate its electric truck efforts. The Freightliner eCascadia was based on the Cascadia, the most successful heavy-duty long-distance truck (Class 8) in the North American market. An impressive 730 hp was almost silently generated under the characteristically long, U.S.–style hood. At 550 kWh, its batteries provided enough energy for a range of up to 250 miles (400 km), and could be recharged to around 80 percent within 90 minutes to cover a further 200 miles (320 km).

This program was originally led by a 43-year-old French engineer, Jérôme Guillen. Guillen was born in 1973 in Avignon, southern France. Having earned a BSc. in mechanical engineering at the National Advanced School of Advanced Techniques (ENSTA) in Paris, the 20-year-old graduate attended a year of training in nuclear engineering at the Polytechnic University of Madrid in Spain. He then went on to earn his Ph.D. at the University of Michigan. After starting his professional career at McKinsey & Co., a New York–based management consulting firm, Guillen moved to Freightliner where he led an innovation group.[6]

To the eCascadia, Daimler has recently added the Freightliner eM2, a medium duty, all-electric semi. Its battery produces 480 horsepower via a 325-kilowatt hour battery and can run up to 230 miles (370 km) once it is fully charged. The battery can recharge up to 80 percent in one hour.

In late June 2018, Daimler announced that it would present a lineup of electric trucks by 2021 and that by the end of the year, it was planning to deliver a 20-strong fleet of eCascadias and eM2s to Penske Truck Leasing and NFI who had agreed to partner in operating the "Freightliner Electric Innovation Fleet," part of the development seeking feedback for the kind of applications the trucks can be used for. Penske began by taking delivery of ten eCascadias and ten eM2s for use in California and the Pacific Northwest, while ten eCascadias were delivered to NFI for drayage activities from the ports of Los Angeles and Long Beach to warehouses in California's Inland Empire. The two ports' joint Clean Air Action Plan envisions a majority of the 17,000 trucks operating at the facilities running on zero-emission powertrains by 2036.[7]

In 2012 MAN (Maschinenfabrik Augsburg-Nürnberg), established in 1758 and now part of the Volkswagen Group, laid the foundations for their eTruck, with the research and development for a MAN Metropolis hybrid vehicle. In September 2016, MAN presented the new eTruck, a TGS semi-trailer tractor with electric drive. Two years later it showcased its CitE all-electric concept truck, designed for last-mile delivery tasks in city centers; its design incorporated low entry, with a display of safety features and cameras for the surrounding environment. In December 2018, MAN Truck & Bus presented a 15-ton CitE delivery truck and the 3.5t eTGE electric van—both for inner city delivery of cooled groceries and parcels but also for garbage collection. Nine of these were already on trial, to prepare for serial production.

To help e-truck development, the German Ministry of Transport announced funding for firms purchasing trucks and semitrailer tractors at least 7.5 tons gross weight (7,500 kg) with natural gas drive (CNG), liquid drive (LNG) or certain electric drives (pure battery electric vehicles and fuel cell vehicles) intended for freight traffic.[8]

Meanwhile in France, Citroën (established in 1919) has introduced a new Berlingo Electric L2 550 LX van, which joins the existing L1 635 LX, bringing an extra 0.87 foot (250 mm) more load length, 6.7 feet compared to 5.9 feet (2,050 mm to 1,800 mm) while also extending the load volume to 130.7 cubic feet in comparison to 116.5 cubic feet (3.7 m^3 to 3.3 m^3).

Renault Trucks (established in 1957) is now selling "a range" of electric trucks following many years of testing based on the Maxity. Manufacture is at its Blainville-sur-Orne plant in Normandy, France. By October 2017, Renault's factory at Maubeuge in the Nord department in northern France had produced some 30,000 Kangoo ZE vans. A new model, equipped with a 33 kWh battery (against the 22 kWh for the 2011 model) offered an autonomy of between 93 and 124 miles (150–200 km) in real conditions. In June 2018, Renault SA announced that, during the next four years, it would invest more than one million euros ($1.18 million) to boost production of electric vehicles in France. It would equip four French sites with new electric car production capacity to increase output and update its models, including increasing the range of the Maubeuge-built Kangoo ZE to 168 mi (270 km). For the Festive Season (2018/2019) the London luxury store Fortnum and Mason integrated two Kangoo ZEs into its fleet.

For 2019, Renault Trucks unveiled the D.Z.E. and D Wide Z.E. with payloads of 16 and 26 tons (16,000 and 26,000 kg) respectively, so completing the electric UV line-up starting with the Master Z.E. at 3.5 tons (3,500 kg). The Master Z.E. comes in six variants and is designed for urban environments with an operating range of up to 75 miles (120 km). The 16-ton D.Z.E. is powered by a 185 kW electric motor (130 kW continuous output) and Renault Trucks specified a range between 124 and 186 miles (200 and 300 km) for the

Renault Trucks' wrap-around cab design (Renault Trucks press portal).

medium-duty EV that can also be used for temperature-controlled deliveries, e.g., groceries. They have two wheelbases available, 14.4 feet and 17.4 feet (4,400 mm and 5,300 mm). The Renault Trucks D.Z.E. and D Wide Z.E. will be produced at the Renault Trucks plant in Blainville-sur-Orne, Normandy, France in the second half of 2019.

The Toyota Motor Corporation (established in 1933) is running an FCHV (Fuel Cell Hybrid Vehicle) program named Project Portal to test at ports in Southern California. In April 2017, the company installed two fuel cell units (114 kW each) as used in their Mirai fuel cell automobile in a converted 18-wheeler Kenworth T680 electric Class 8 semi-trailer heavy truck for trials around in the Port of Los Angeles. The Alpha truck has two motors for a combined 500 kW (670 hp) and 1,325 lb·ft (1,795 N·m) of torque, a 200 kW 12 kWh battery, and a fixed gear ratio of 15.5:1. It has a range of 200 mi (320 km) determined by the size of the hydrogen tanks. It accelerates (empty) from 0 to 60 mph (0–97 kph) in seven seconds. In August 2018, Toyota unveiled the Beta, a second prototype semi-tractor that will use passenger-car fuel cell technology to haul freight in Southern California. The truck is lighter than its predecessor and can travel 50 percent farther—300 miles (480 km)—before it needs to be refueled. The project is part of a $41 million grant preliminarily awarded by the California Air Resources Board.[9]

The Truck & Bus division of Volkswagen (established in 1937) is working with Toyota's utility subsidiary Hino Motors to produce trucks through the former's subsidiaries MAN, Scania, Volkswagen Caminhões e Ônibus and Rio, taking account of Hino's presence in Asia and the Japanese market.[10] VW is spending 34 billion euros on electro mobility by 2022. In August 2018, the company received an advance order for 1,600 of its VW eCrafter truck from Ambev, an important Brazilian brewery. Although production of the e-Delivery was scheduled for 2020, VW had delivered its first vehicles to Ambev for trials by the end of 2018. In January 2019, Volkswagen went into partnership with U.S. rival Ford to focus on developing electric and autonomous vehicles. The two carmakers would work together on commercial vans and medium-sized pickups for the global market as early as 2022, in order to tap into a rapidly growing electric vehicle market.

Hyundai Motor Co. is working with Swiss H2 Mobility Switzerland Association, a consortium of private companies, to build 1,000 XCient commercial fuel cell trucks for operation in Switzerland beginning in 2019. Among the consortium is Coop Cooperative, which operates the largest gas station chain in Switzerland. The XCient is equipped with up to eight hydrogen storage tanks providing energy to two parallel fuel cell stacks on board. The Swiss order will be completed by 2023.[11]

In the post–World War II U.S. road building boom, the N Series manufactured by Cummins gasoline engines of Columbus, Indiana (established in 1919), became the industry leader, with more than half the heavy duty truck market from 1952 to 1959. Cummins sells in approximately 190 countries and territories through a network of more than 600 company-owned and independent distributors and approximately 6,000 dealers. Cummins has now produced the Aeos, an electric-powered semi-truck tractor unit named after Aeos, the flying horse of Greek mythology, one of four that pulled the chariot of the god Helios across the sky. It is the first fully electric heavy-duty truck revealed to the public, and the first electric model from Cummins. The aerodynamic semi-truck body was designed by Cummins partner Roush Industries, while Cummins focused on the battery and driveline systems. The Aeos is an 18,000-pound (8,200 kg) short-haul day-cab two-axle Class 7 tractor unit (prime-mover). It is to have a 140 kWh battery pack that will allow a range of 100 miles (160 km) when hauling the maximum load of 44,000 pounds (20,000 kg). The li-ion battery is to have a one-hour recharge time. Additional battery packs could extend the range to 300 miles (480 km). It is equipped with regenerative braking and low rolling resistance tires to maximize the range. An option for a range extender engine (the Cummins B4.5 or B6.7 motors) could be added for additional range. The big rig truck would have a gross vehicle weight rating of 75,000 pounds (34,000 kg). Solar panels can be equipped onto the trailer to increase range. Production will begin in 2019, with OEM production partners.

Peterbilt Motors Company of Denton, Texas (established in 1939), is working on an all-electric Class 8 truck, teaming up with Meritor and Trans-Power who will supply the all-electric drivetrain systems for 12 Peterbilt all-electric Class 8 Model 579 day cab tractors and three Model 520 refuse trucks. The program is being funded by the California Air Resources Board and a consortium of California's regional air quality districts, including the South Coast Air Quality Management District, Bay Area Air Quality Management District and San Diego Air Pollution Control District.

In 2014, Walmart showcased its Advanced Vehicle Experience tractor-trailer, with an advanced Peterbilt turbine-powered range extending series hybrid powertrain. By placing an aerodynamic convex cab over the engine, with the driver in the center, the AVE's wheelbase was greatly shortened, resulting in reduced weight and better maneuverability. There was a one-piece, fiberglass-reinforced floor panel with a 16,000-pound forklift rating. For use in urban areas, the truck would run on electric power alone until the battery state of charge hit 50 percent, when the turbine would automatically kick in.[12]

DAF (established in 1932 and producing gas trucks since 1993) of Eindhoven in the Netherlands has teamed up with VDL E-Power Technology to produce the 210 kW CF Electric, a 4 × 2 tractor unit developed for up to 40-ton distribution applications within urban areas in which single or double-axle semi-trailers are standard. With a 170 kWh li-ion battery pack, the CF Electric has a range of approximately 62 miles (100 km). Quick charging of the batteries can be executed in 30 minutes or a complete full charge can be accomplished in as little as one and a half hours. In December 2018, DAF delivered a CF Electric to Dutch supermarket chain Jumbo as part of their test program.

For 2019, using experience gained from their successful electric bus, VDL Translift designed and built three production electric garbage collecting vehicles, going into operation later that year in cooperation with three Dutch public waste collectors. In addition to the VDL vehicles, the Dutch research institute TNO was also part of this living lab project, using the knowledge and experience gained from this pilot to draw up a plan outlining how the sector can scale up the electrical waste collection and make it fully sustainable.

Volvo Trucks of Gothenburg, Sweden (established in 1928), produces and sells more than 190,000 gasoline-engined units annually. In 2017, Volvo announced its intention of working with battery manufacturer Samsung SDI of South Korea for an electric truck design it was preparing. This would include a safety system with a wireless camera attached to the front grille of the truck. The image it is recording is sent to a four-panel video wall on the rear of the truck. Drivers behind the truck are then given a clear view of the road and traffic conditions in front of the truck. This image will let drivers make better decisions about passing the truck safely.

In April 2018, Volvo introduced its first all-electric truck for pickup and delivery, refuse and recycling and other applications in Europe starting in 2019. The Volvo FL, which offers up to a 186-mile (300 km) range through a 185 kW motor, can be charged in one to two hours with a DC fast charger or in ten hours with AC charging via the main grid (22 kW). Volvo Group also controls the Renault and Mack truck brands, among others. Just weeks after their first model was announced, Volvo announced a second model, the ten-meter Volvo FE Electric, to take on more heavy-duty urban loads such as rubbish collection. The battery electric truck has a 125-mile (200 km) range. In late 2018, Swedish retailer Coop began to use the Volvo *FE* for temperature-sensitive food transportation to 13 stores in the city of Gothenburg. In the fall of 2018, Volvo began to trial eight "multi-configuration" Class 8 trucks as demonstrators, as well as 15 "commercial and pre-commercial" models in California's South Coast Air Basin. The California Air Resources Board awarded $44.8 million to the project. The ultimate plan is to sell Volvo FL and FE trucks in North America by 2020.

Another brand name is Leyland Motors of England (established in 1907), now owned by the Hinduja Group headquartered in Chennai, India. Founded in 1948, Ashok Leyland is the second largest commercial vehicle manufacturer in India and 12th largest manufacturer of trucks globally. In January 2018, Ashok Leyland signed a letter of intent with Phinergy of Israel to use the latter's hybrid lithium-ion and aluminum-air/zinc-air battery systems in a new line of electric trucks.

In 2019, Mahindra & Mahindra (M&M), India's second largest commercial vehicle maker, launched the Furio range of five intermediate trucks, designed by Italian design house Pininfarina (an M&M owned company). These trucks will play in the 9–14 ton segment.

Opel (established in 1929), once known for its Blitz gasoline trucks, now owned by PSA, was also looking into electric power for its Vivaro, available as a purely battery-electric variant from 2020.

In 2011, Kenworth Truck Company (established in 1912), a division of PACCAR, introduced its T270 Class 6 and T370 Class 7 hybrid-electric Medium trucks. Power is from a PACCAR 6.7-liter PX-6 engine and features a parallel hybrid system developed with Eaton Corporation, a frame-mounted 340-volt battery pack, and a dedicated power management system.

The mining industry has some of the biggest and toughest vehicles in the world and they are going all electric. Liebherr was established in 1949. The 600 ton (600,000 kg) Liebherr T284 with its 363 ton (363,000 kg) payload requires so much power that the cheapest way to run it as well as the most efficient and effective way is to use its Litronic electric drive. The electricity is generated using a huge diesel generator—3 MW in size—which is enough to power 200 homes. It can still travel at up to 40 mph (64 kph). Atlas Copco (established in 1873), world-leading manufacturer of underground mining equipment, headquartered in Örebro, Sweden, is building its Green Line zero-emission and battery-driven load haul loaders Scooptram EST1030 and EST14, drill rigs and EMT35 and EMT50 mine trucks. Epiroc AB, also of Orebro, Sweden, has also begun to electrify all its machines for underground use starting with an 18-ton loader and medium-sized drill rigs with battery options. The manufacturer launched a new range, including the largest battery-powered vehicle for mining below the Earth's surface: a 42 ton-capacity truck that can haul blasted rock through narrow tunnels. This is part of the company's latest series of mobile excavators, including drill rigs and loaders, designed to cut emissions and lower energy costs for miners.

In March 2018, Artisan Vehicles, based in California and Kirkland Lake, Ontario, unveiled the yellow Z40, a battery-electric 40 ton underground haul truck. The Z40 is equipped with four electric motors and it comes with a battery swap system to effortlessly change the battery pack and extend the operation time of the vehicle and make it comparable to a diesel truck. With its all-electric powertrain, Artisan Vehicles claims that the Z40 has almost twice the peak horsepower of a comparable diesel machine and it generates only one-eighth the heat of its diesel equivalent. The vehicle will be used at the Kirkland Lake gold mine. The electrification effort in the mining industry is especially interesting since the advent of electric vehicles requires larger mining efforts for minerals like nickel, cobalt, lithium, and others. The Z40 ushers in a new era in underground hard rock mining. In January 2019, Sandvik Mining and Rock Technology's load and haul division acquired Artisan Vehicle Systems.

In December 2018, the push for electrified mining got a further boost last month from an industry lobby, the International Council on Mining and Metals, which plans to minimize the impact of underground diesel exhaust by 2025.

Isuzu Commercial Trucks (established in Japan in 1934) of America showed a battery-electric N-Series cabover at the Work Truck Show to allow the manufacturer to gauge interest from fleets who would use the truck for certain applications. The truck was modified by Nordresa, developer and manufacturer of electrified powertrains for commercial vehicles based in Laval, Québec, Canada.

Spartan Motors is using e-chassis supplied by Motiv Power Systems to convert Ford E-450 trucks to electric drive. Motiv, led by Jim Castelaz, a manufacturer of all-electric powertrain control systems for commercial vehicles, based in Foster City, California, has redesigned its offering to work in delivery vans. For example, electronic controller boxes previously placed outside the frame rail were repositioned on the inside. This allows for the chassis to be used in a wider variety of vehicle configurations. The vehicles will be configured with two sodium-nickel battery pack choices. The larger 106-kWh battery offers a range of up to 90 miles (145 km). He said the cost of the battery is rapidly declining. A lithium-ion battery pack version of the chassis is planned for the future. In 2019, BMW began to supply their i3 battery packs to Motiv Power Systems, who will integrate them into their Electric Powered Intelligent Chassis (EPIC) for commercial vehicles. The contract involves the latest BMW i3 batteries, which now have a total capacity of 42.2 kWh following an upgrade with 120 Ah cells from Samsung. In February 2019, Motiv began delivering seven Ford E-450–based all-electric step vans to the United States Postal Service (USPS) for deployment in California's Central Valley.

The City of London is electrifying its vehicles. Electra, a 26-ton (26,000 kg) refuse truck, capable of a ten-hour shift, has been in service in the capital and also trialed in two other cities. City Corporation refuse vehicles collect over 1,500 tons of household waste and more than 850 tons of recycling a year. The City is also running a cargo bike scheme with zero-emission delivery operator Zedify, which has gone into service in both the Smithfield and Farringdon areas. Couriers are using electric cargo pedelecs and trikes with load capacities of 220 lb. and 550 lb. (100 and 250 kg) respectively to make deliveries to and from a hub located at West Smithfield. The cargo bikes can drop the goods off anywhere within the Congestion Charge zone. The aim is to fill a gap diesel vans may leave as running one through the city center is becoming increasingly costly.

In May 2018, Sadiq Khan, Lord Mayor of London, launched a new Electric Vehicle Infrastructure Taskforce, bringing together industry, businesses and the public sector to work together to deliver electric vehicle charging infrastructure in the capital. Khan explained,

> London's filthy air is a public health crisis, and encouraging more Londoners to switch from diesel to electric vehicles is critical in tackling it. We've already made some great progress with the rollout of electric buses, electric taxis and rapid charging points, alongside launching the Toxicity Charge (T-Charge) for the oldest polluting vehicles in central London and bringing forward the introduction of the world's first Ultra-Low Emission Zone. We are installing rapid charging points across London, only licensing zero emission capable taxis and by 2020 all single decker buses will be zero emission. However, we recognise more can be done and we are working hard with boroughs and the private sector to ensure London has the infrastructure needed to become an electric city.[13]

In September 2018, despite the ongoing Brexit crisis, at a Zero Emission Summit in Birmingham, UK, Prime Minister Theresa May announced a £106 million funding boost for the research and development of zero-emission vehicles to help meet a target for UK roads to be free of petrol and diesel vehicles by 2050. Included in this was £2 million in new funding to support the uptake of electric bikes for last-mile delivery in towns and cities and the Faraday Battery Challenge, a £246 million investment program to support the development of new battery technologies. The "Birmingham deceleration" was signed by Italy, France, Denmark, the UAE, Portugal, Belarus and Indonesia and the UK.

IKEA, the renowned Swedish home furnishing giant, has teamed up with Gayam Motor Works in Hyderabad to provide blue and yellow electric three-wheeler cargo bikes to a customer who opts for a home delivery of his or her purchased products. The electric three-wheelers support a battery swapping mechanism and the swapping of batteries takes just one minute, which will prove beneficial for the drivers.

Since the late 1990s, Thomas Grübel of Munich had been developing an electric scooter with one of the first interchangeable lithium-ion battery management systems for scooters. He founded Govecs GmhH in Munich, Germany, firstly to make electric scooters. He then teamed up with the Danish energy supply company Trefor to produce the Tripl urban cargo trike, which was presented at the Post Office Expo in Paris in 2015. The battery packs are Samsung SDI lithium-ion developing 5.5, 6.7, or 8 kWh. In August 2018, Govecs signed a letter of intent with a UK company regarding the delivery of 6,000 e-scooters for the London shared-vehicles market. The letter of intent included the potential order of 3,000 e-scooters (Schwalbe) in 2019 and a further 3,000 in 2020. All the e-scooters are to be used in a shared-vehicles system in London.[14]

In Shenzen China, the BYD (Build Your Dreams) start-up was founded by Wang Chuangfu (Chinese: 王传福, described as a "Chinese Edison"). Coming from a family of poor farmers, after high school Wang attended the Central South University of Technology, obtaining a bachelor's degree in metallurgical physical chemistry in 1987, progressing to a master's degree in metallurgical chemistry from the Beijing Non-Ferrous Research Institute. In 1993, his institute set up a company in rising Shenzhen, where he took on new responsibilities as deputy director, then as general manager in Shenzhen Bi Ge Battery Co. Limited. He then decided to create his own company. A cousin from his hometown in Anhui Province, Lu Xiangyang, had also headed south, looking to do well in investments and trade. Wang, believing that Japanese battery suppliers were leaving the market, got Lu to lend him 2.5 million yuan (then about $350,000) to set up their own maker of rechargeable batteries. They founded BYD Company Ltd. in 1995 with 20 employees, which rapidly became the world's biggest li-ion cell phone batteries manufacturer, making Wang one of the richest men in China. In 2003, Wang took what appeared to be a U-turn when he bought Tsinchuan Automobile, a failing Chinese state-owned auto manufacturer. But that purchase gave Wang a shortcut into an industry he hoped to transform: battery and hybrid automobiles, buses, forklifts, rechargeable batteries and trucks sold under the BYD brand.

BYD took the first fully plug-in electric vehicle to the Detroit Auto Show in 2008. Soon after, billionaire Warren Buffett's Berkshire Hathaway invested $230 million into buying a 10 percent stake in BYD Auto. By 2010, *Businessweek* ranked it as the eighth most innovative company in the world. The Chinese company opened its Los Angeles headquarters in 2011 with just ten BYD employees. The team then established a manufacturing foothold in the Americas with the procurement of the Lancaster, California, BYD Bus and Coach Factory. BYD brings its battery cells into California, and then they are assembled into battery modules in the adjacent battery module assembly plant. In November 2017, Loblaw, the largest Canadian food retailer, trialed the BYD Class 8 truck to deliver groceries from their Vancouver Distribution Center to a local store in West End, Vancouver. By 2018, BYD was able to open its first assembly plant in Ontario, Canada, in anticipation of the surge in demand for electric trucks from municipalities and businesses.

BYD's T7 is over 20 ft. (6 m) long and has a GVWR of 10.5 tons (10,500 kg). It features a 175 kWh battery capacity and has an estimated range of 124 miles (200 km) with minimal battery degradation. To their range they added the T9 and T10ZE (both Class 8 electric trucks). In 2018, BYD delivered a fleet of T7 all-electric Class 6 trucks to San Francisco Goodwill at the annual Advanced Clean Transportation (ACT) Expo in Long Beach, California. Seeing the surge in demand for battery vehicles, BYD began construction of the world's largest battery factory in the western province of Qinghai. With an annual capacity of 24 GWh, this new battery factory should enable them to significantly increase production with a total battery production capacity of 60 GWh. The entire process consists of nearly 100 robots, intelligent logistics system, and improved information management system. Meanwhile, in July 2017, BYD won the largest pure electric truck order in Latin America—200 vehicles to be delivered to Brazil's Corpus Saneamento e Obras Ltda (Corpus). The first 20 trucks were delivered at the end of May 2018, while the remaining 180 will gradually arrive by 2023. (The history of BYD's building of hundreds of thousands of buses will be chronicled in a subsequent book.) Other companies in China are manufacturing electric trucks. In 2017, the number of electric light-duty commercial vehicles—both all-electric and plug-in hybrids—sold in China was roughly 200,000, a mere 6 percent of the market for trucks under six tons. Beijing banned heavier trucks from entering the city center between 6 a.m. and 11 p.m. The Dongfeng Motor Corporation in Wuhan, Hubei, central China, is traditionally one of the "Big Three" Chinese automakers. At the 2010 Beijing Auto Show, Dongfeng displayed an electric vehicle concept car, a physical representation of its vow to bring an electric car to market by 2015. In November 2017, a grand ceremony was held to mark the delivery of 600 units of Dongfeng electric logistic vehicles to their customer, Ronghe Rental, to put into service across the People's Republic. Chongqing Ruichi Automobile Industry Co, Liangjiang New District, Chongqing, southwest China, has a product range of 103 electric vehicles including a cargo van, box van truck and postal van. Guohong Automobile Co. Ltd., located in Tianjin City, northern China, has a 76-strong product range with the Hongfengtai brand, including an electric cargo van, electric stake truck, electric postal van, electric self-loading garbage truck, electric garbage truck, caravan trailer, electric crew cab cargo van, electric crew cab stake truck, electric crew cab postal van, refrigerated trailer, electric sprinkler truck, box van truck, electric hooklift hoist garbage truck, oil tank trailer, and sprinkler machine (water tank truck).

In November 2018, with work underway on a new factory in the southern Chinese province of Hunan, the automobile start-up Singulato Motors announced its plans to build up to 50,000 electric trucks per year and ride the crest of a wave for e-truck demand in China. Singulato envisioned two main models that would appeal to e-commerce and logistics firms: a small intra-city delivery van the size of the Ford Transit or the Toyota HiAce, and a delivery truck under two tons. Foton, part of Beijing-based BAIC Group and China's biggest maker of light-duty trucks under six tons, was also looking at expanding further into mini delivery e-trucks and electric delivery vans, working with a highly regarded engineer, now retired from a Japanese automaker. Nissan Motor Co., one of the first global automakers in China to develop an e-truck lineup through its venture with Dongfeng Motor Co. Ltd. Group, believed that demand for light-duty e-trucks would quadruple in four to five years. Dongfeng aimed to lift its electric commercial vehicle sales six times to 90,000 by 2022.[15]

In November of 2018, FedEx ordered 1,000 Chinese-built Chanje V8100 electric delivery vans for use in California. The company owns 100 of them and leased the other 900 to Ryder Systems. The V8100 has a range of 150 miles and a maximum capacity of three tons (6,000 pounds).

Nearly two dozen cities including Beijing, Shanghai and Guangzhou have put in place restrictions on fossil-fueled trucks entering city centers.

Earlier in this history, the Walker Company of Chicago made the Walker Balanced Wheel and became one of the most successful electric truck companies in the first half of the 20th century. A century later, the Workhorse Group and commercial vehicle supplier Dana Inc. have unveiled a Class 5

Medium Truck powered by the e-Drive eS9000r, a jointly built 400-volt electric axle, adaptable for Class 4, 5 and 6 vans, trucks and buses. The fully electric vehicle is a combination of the chassis and battery pack from a Workhorse E-Gen van, the body of a Morgan Olson UPS delivery truck and the new Dana axle. The truck has a gross axle rating of six tons and a gross vehicle weight rating of 8.7 tons. It can travel up to 67 mph (108 kph) on the highway. The concept vehicle was not slated for production. However, interest from potential customers might bring it to market. Workhorse and Dana developed the axle in tandem, through the supplier's Spicer Electrified brand. From spring 2018, Dana's E-Axle has entered production as a joint venture with Dongfeng Motor in Xiangyang, China, its first application on a medium duty Dongfeng commercial vehicle. The eS5700r, designed for Class 3 vehicles, is rated at 174 hp (130 kW) and weighs 673 lbs. (305 kg).

eS9000r electric axle (photo Workhorse)

Top: **Close-up photograph of the Walker Balanced Wheel (Berliet Foundation).** *Bottom:* **Like the revolutionary impact the Walker Balanced Wheel had on electric trucks from 1918, this integrated axle, developed by Dana Inc., the eS9000r, increases the efficiency of Workhorse Group's Class 5 electric vans by 14 percent (Dana Inc pp).**

The Triumph of the Electric Postal Vans

The U.S. Postal Service, continuing its century-old quest to electrify its delivery trucks, is currently looking to replace the old Grumman Long Life Vehicle trucks, which have been serving as the standard delivery truck since 1987. Of the 215,000 in operation, 140,000 are at least two decades old. Nearly 100 truck engine fires in fiscal year 2017 alone have underscored the need to replace the aging fleet. The changeover, which may be incremental replacing 12,000 trucks at a time, could take place over the course of seven years. In March 2018, Ford Motor Company (established in 1903) announced that it is working with the Oshkosh Corporation on an electric version of its Transit cargo van. Other proposals are from Karsan Otomotive, a Turkish truck maker, which is working with Morgan Olson, a Sturgis, Michigan, manufacturer of walk-in vans that has a longstanding relationship with USPS. The pair submitted a plug-in hybrid van that was spotted alongside the Oshkosh vehicle. VT Hackney/Workhorse Group is also participating as a duo to offer up an electric mail truck. The Hackney prototype shares many components with the Workhorse W-15 electric pickup truck. Two bidders were overseas companies. Both would assemble the vehicles in the U.S., but it was hard to see how the Trump administration's "America First" outlook would allow this important government contract to be captured by businesses such as India-based Mahindra or the Turkish-owned Karsan.

For postal deliveries in other countries, BEVs are still the most desired. China Post is using a fleet of 64 provided by Naveco. Canada Post's fleet are made by Navistar Inc., an American manufacturer of medium and heavy trucks. The eStar, a Class 2c-3 light electric truck and the first in its category, has a range of 100 miles (160 km) per charge and can be fully recharged within six to eight hours. Canada Post has the largest delivery fleet in Canada—more than 7,300 vehicles traveling more than 49 million miles (79 million km) a year. Posten Norge has introduced more than 900 electric vehicles and trailers into its mail distribution operations. Over the course of one year, almost 300 new electric cars were introduced into the mail distribution fleet throughout the entire country as part of Norway Post's extensive program to reduce its CO2 emissions. This includes a truck made by the Chinese car manufacturer SAIC. After the test in Norway, the electric car will be tested in Stockholm, where it will be used by Bring to deliver goods for Ikea. Since 2017, le Poste Italiene have been using 70 Nissan e-NV200s trucks for deliveries in different national urban areas, representing the most important fleet of zero emission commercial vehicles in Italy to date. DHL and GLS are also using the Nissan. With a new li-ion battery of 40 Kwh, the range of this van will be extended for long-distance deliveries. Voltia, based in Bratislava, created a 580 kg payload version of the Nissan e-NV200.

In 2017 Royal Mail, an important postal service and courier company in the UK, unveiled a new electric truck made by Arrival. The company started a trial with three versions of the vehicle to transport packages between its mail and distribution centers around London. Arrival, formerly known as Charge Auto, built the trucks at their new 110,000 sq. ft. factory in Banbury. Royal Mail is beginning trials in London of nine fully electric vans with ranges of up to 100 miles (161 km). The vehicles, which come in various sizes, are distributing mail from the central London depot. Another batch of 100 electric vans for Royal Mail was also ordered from Peugeot and was put into service at 18 depots in Belfast, Edinburgh, Essex, and Kent. Other areas would get the vans later. Having already been trialed by Royal Mail, these will enter service in December. Arrival says the nine vehicles it has supplied come in sizes of 3.5, 6 and 7.5 tons.

Postal fleets in other countries are going from strength to strength. In Germany DHL, with plans to ramp up production of StreetScooters to 10,000 a year, built a second factory in 2018, allowing it to sell more vehicles to third parties. Officials hope eventually to replace Deutsche Post's remaining 30,000-unit fleet of internal combustion vans with electric vehicles. The long-term goal is to have the complete fleet of 70,000 delivery vehicles electric.

Alongside this, DPDHL and ZF, one of the world's largest automotive technology suppliers, have been working together to deploy a test fleet of autonomous delivery trucks. The first prototype delivery vehicle was shown this week at the GPU Technology Conference (GTC) in Munich. The "last mile" of courier delivery to the final destination is the costliest part of the delivery equation and DPDHL is keen to automate the process as much as possible by upgrading its fleet of up to 3,400 StreetScooter vehicles with autonomous last-mile capabilities to permanently reduce delivery costs. And by applying artificial intelligence to the equation, the aim is to continue the optimization process. The autonomous StreetScooter prototypes are equipped with ZF's ProAI self-driving system, which is based on Nvidia's DRIVE PX technology and jointly developed by both companies.

In December 2018, UZE Mobility ordered 500 StreetScooter Work and Work L trucks for use in a car-sharing scheme, enabling private citizens to use the StreetScooters to move larger items around town. In a curious twist, the new network aimed to make the trucks available to customers at no cost, though initially there was a fee as UZE Mobility ramped up its operations. Ultimately, the company planned to generate revenue through advertising and data-gathering from customers, which would enable customers to use the vehicles without having to pay.

Ever innovative, the StreetScooter team, led by Achim Kampker and a team at the RWTH University (Rheinisch-Westfälische Technische Hochschule), has developed their primotype for a modular electric delivery van with a 7.5-ton capacity. Designated the LiVe 1, it is based on a conventional Isuzu truck chassis with a *modular* electric drivetrain, where a battery pack can be as little as 20 kWh and up to a maximum of 200 kWh. The individual cells in each battery pack can be replaced as needed instead of discarding an entire pack. The LiVe 1 uses an electric drive axle provided by BPW. It offers customers the opportunity to specify precisely what attributes they need for their vehicles.

UPS has several ongoing electrification efforts to convert its massive fleet of delivery vehicles and they have announced a new step in their partnership with Workhorse to build 50 all-electric 100-mile range (160 km) delivery trucks and another for 1,000 electric vans. Workhorse is a Loveland, Ohio–based truck maker that has been developing several different electric powertrains and electric vehicle programs. The company is working on its upcoming plug-in electric W-15 pickup truck and it recently unveiled an electric van geared toward delivery with a drone for the last mile. Trialing in Atlanta, Dallas, and Los Angeles, the new vehicles will join UPS's pre-existing fleet of more than 300 electric vehicles deployed in Europe and the U.S., and nearly 700 hybrid electric vehicles. According to Ananth Srinivasan, a mobility expert with research consultancy Frost & Sullivan, "Postal business in the UK, Germany, France, Italy and Spain have the potential to convert significant chunks of their fleets to electric vehicles in the coming years."

According to a recent report from America's Commercial Transportation Research Co., LLC (ACT), based in Columbus, Illinois, there are more than 20 manufacturers offering more than 50 electric models of Class 4–8 commercial trucks in the U.S. alone. Regional air-quality regulations are a principal reason for the scope and variety. While a number of these are long-established firms, there are also newcomers, a number of them outside America. With so many well-established and startup electric truck building companies heading onto the highways and auto routes, an industry alliance wants to establish a global charging standard. The alliance, called CharIN, wants to extend the fast charging standard to the higher power heavy- and medium-duty vehicles of today. The group was launched in 2015 to promote the Combined Charging System, or CCS, for electric vehicles. CCS is an AC and DC electric vehicle charging standard that was widely adopted in Europe, the United States, Australia and parts of South America. The idea of the standard was to make charging an electric vehicle as seamless around the world as using a mobile phone as it bounces between cell towers. That goal faces skepticism from trade groups such as the American Trucking Association and the North American Council for Freight Efficiency, or NACFE. Both worried that with electric trucks barely in their infancy, there is not enough data to point the way to the most effective charging system. Tying truck charging to a system developed for passenger vehicles also might turn out to be the wrong approach. Time will tell.

Alongside the traditional truck brand names converting to electric, hybrid-electric and fuel cell systems, there are a number of dynamic companies that have only "started up" during the past decade.

In 2007, the newly established American Electric Vehicle Company took an Italian design for a light electric vehicle and built it in Michigan as the Kurrent. When the AEVC closed down, several of the team, led by Ray Leduc, founded a new company in Milford, Michigan, which they called GGT Electric, the name coming from GreenGo Tek. GGT began to produce a new line of four-door electric pickup trucks, electric passenger vans, and flatbed electric trucks with tilt and dump capability called the E-Dyne and the Scout. Based on their reliability, GGT Electric's vehicles became part of fleets operated by such organizations as the U.S. Bureau of Land Management (BLM), the U.S. Veterans Administration, the Federal Aviation Administration (FAA), Grand Canyon National Park, the University of Memphis, the U.S. Forestry Service, and the state of South Carolina.

Backed by Hollywood *Terminator* star and former governor of California Arnold Schwarzenegger, the Austrian firm Kreisel Electric of Rainbach im Mühlkreis (started up in 2014) has developed the first fully functional fire truck with an electric motor, in conjunction with Rosenbauer and Linz AG. The initiative began two years before under the orders of the firefighting supplier Linz AG. The basis for the electric fire truck, named KLF-L, was a Mercedes Sprinter. This is not the first time Kreisel Electric used the transport vehicle as a basis for the electrification of utility vehicles for transport and bus companies. Within two months the vehicle was rebuilt at the Kreisel factory in Rainbach. A 120 kW electric motor was installed to provide the necessary power. A modular construction mode made space for four Kreisel batteries, with a total capacity of 86 kWh. The weight was set to be around 620 kg by the manufacturer. The batteries can be charged via a type 2 or CCS charger. DC fast charging enables a 90 percent charge to be made with a 50 kW charge in about one hour and 20 minutes.

John R. Bautista III, who previously specialized in electric race cars and then in electric motorcycles at Zero Motorcycles, has moved into the low-speed electric vehicle (LSV) market. He launched Tropos Motors, based in the Silicon Valley suburb of Morgan Hill, California. Tropos has produced the ABLE line of electric compact utility vehicles, assembled in California and New Jersey, from components shipped from China, where they are built for New Jersey–based Cenntro Automotive Corporation. With a payload capacity of 2,000 pounds (900 kg) and a towing capacity of 3,000 pounds (1,361 kg), among the line are a fire response vehicle and an emergency medical services vehicle. In August 2018, Tropos Motors introduced a new version of its ABLE

XR, with a 26 kWh pack that increases the range four times to 160 miles (257 km) at speeds of 25 mph (40 km/h).

Tod Hynes and XL Hybrid Electric Drive Systems of Boston, Massachusetts, started up in 2009, have produced a gas-electric version of the Ford F-250 pickup truck after talking to 50 potential customers and garnering hundreds of pre-orders.

In 2012, Asher Bennett, a former Deputy Commander of a diesel-electric submarine in the Israeli Navy, started Tevva Motors Ltd. in Chelmsford, England (Teva in Hebrew means "Nature"). His plan was to build an e-truck in the 7.4 ton to 14 ton range (7,400 to 14,000 kg), with range extenders based on technology used in submarines: an on-board generator with sophisticated patented software to ensure minimum emissions in low emission zones and city centers. The motor is powered by a li-ion battery pack that charges from mains electricity in approximately three hours to give a 100-mile (160 km) range. In 2017, Tevva raised $13.5 million (£10 million) from India's Bharat Forge Limited (BFL), an auto ancillary maker. Tevva Motors received its first orders for range-extending the trucks of delivery giants UPS, DHL and Switzerland's Kuehne+Nagel.

Denis Sverdlov, the founder of Kinetik, served as the Deputy Minister for Communications and Mass Media for the Russian Federation for 18 months. In 2006, as co-owner of the St. Petersburg–based company Korus, Sverdlov and Bulgarian businessman Sergey Adonev established the first provider of WiMAX, a new data transfer technology. In 2006, WiMAX was used in China, India, Indonesia, Taiwan and the United States. He then founded Yota and invented the YotaPhone, a Russian smartphone. Moving to London, the billionaire venture capitalist co-founded the autonomous electric car racing series, "Roborace." With this experience, Sverdlov next set about adapting his technologies to the electric truck and founded Charge Automotive in Yarnton, Oxfordshire. The lightweight prototype claimed an all-electric range of 150 miles (240 km), with the option to utilize a "dual mode" that can be used to recharge the truck's batteries, thus allowing for a range of up to 500 miles (805 km). Changing his company name to Arrival, in 2016 Sverdlov partnered with UPS to develop a fleet of 35 modular electric delivery vehicles for trial in London and Paris. UPS expected to deploy the first vehicles before the end of 2018. The Arrival has an advanced vehicle display, and features Advanced Driver Assistance Systems (ADAS) that aids driver safety and helps lower fatigue. Sverdlov also set up a deal with the Royal Mail to trial nine Arrivals in the ranges of 3.5, 6 and 7 tons (3,500, 6,000 and 7,000 kg) GVW.

In 2010, Michael Simon, who had run ISE, a leading electric and hybrid vehicle technology company for 15 years, started up TransPower in Escondido, California, to adapt ElecTruck battery-electric technologies to large vehicles.

As developed by James Burns and Paul Scott at TransPower, the Maximum Power Transfer Solution (MPTS) device is based on patented dynamic impedance matching and synchronous processing through solid state electronic switching, dynamic, accurate and precise correction using patented multitasking algorithm controls to optimize each phase to attain maximum efficiency. When connected to electrical AC inductive and other balanced or unbalanced phase loads, the MPTS device dynamically matches the source and load impedances resulting in reduced total power consumption and significant improvement and electrical efficiency. From 2013, the ElecTruck system accumulated over 80,000 miles (128,748 km) of Class 8 heavy duty use in a variety of commercial applications: on-road trucks, yard tractors, port cargo handling vehicles, and school buses. In 2015, working with IKEA, Trans-Power developed the Kalmar electric yard tractor at the IKEA Distribution Center in Tejon, California. Peterbilt also used ElecTruck in their Model 520 refuse truck. In 2018, Meritor Inc. of Troy, Michigan, makers of drivetrain and brake components, teamed up with TransPower.

Elon R. Musk, a South African–born Canadian-American business magnate, investor, and engineer, is best known for the Tesla electric automobile. In 1995, Musk dropped out of his studies in applied physics and material sciences at Stanford University to launch Zip2, an online city guide providing content for the new websites of both *The New York Times* and the *Chicago Tribune*. In 1999, a division of Compaq Computer Corporation bought Zip2 for $307 million in cash and $34 million in stock options. Musk then founded X.com, an online payment company. It merged with Confinity in 2000 and became PayPal, which was bought by eBay for $1.5 billion in October 2002. In May 2002, Musk founded SpaceX, an aerospace manufacturer and space transport services company, of which he is CEO and lead designer.

He then invested millions in Tesla Motors, a tiny electric automobile company, begun by two other Silicon Valley engineers, Martin Eberhard and Marc Tarpenning. The company, named after the electrical engineer and physicist Nikola Tesla, was started up after GM recalled and destroyed its *EV1* electric cars in 2003. Following the global financial crisis in 2008, Tesla Inc. launched its innovative Roadster sports car with sales of about 2,500 vehicles to 31 countries. The Roadster is capable of accelerating from 0 to 60 mph (0–97 kph) in 3.7 seconds, as well traveling nearly 250 miles (402 km) between charges of its lithium ion battery. This was followed in 2012 by the four-door Model S sedan, capable of covering 265 miles (427 km) between charges and becoming the world's best-selling plug-in electric car in 2015 and 2016.

Supervising development of the Model S was Jérôme Guillen, who had been head-hunted from his success with Freightliner's eCascadia truck. Global sales of the Model S reached the 200,000-unit milestone during the fourth quarter of 2017. Next came the crossover Model X SUV. In addition to its own cars, Tesla sells electric powertrain systems to Daimler for the Smart EV, Mercedes B-Class Electric Drive and Mercedes A Class, and to Toyota for the RAV4 EV. To make an affordable electric sports car, Musk next presented the world with the Model 3, released in July 2017. To recharge his growing fleet, Tesla set up a network of supercharger stations across the North American continent. In addition, Musk announced that Tesla would allow its technology patents to be used by anyone in good faith in a bid to entice automobile manufacturers to speed up development of electric cars. While the Tesla cars are made in a plant in Fremont, California, batteries and battery packs are made in partnership with Panasonic at Gigafactory 1 outside Reno, Nevada, with its 1.9 million sq. ft. (180,000 m²) and 4.9 million sq. ft. (460,000 m²) of usable area across several floors, while the 1.2 million square foot (111, 484 m²) Gigafactory 2, located in Buffalo, New York, assembles full photovoltaic panels and solar roofs.

It was to this background that on November 6, 2017, Musk unveiled the Tesla Class 8 semi-trailer truck, announcing 500 miles (805 km) of range on a full charge as well as new batteries and motors built to last 1 million miles (1,609,344 km); the Semi would be able to run for 400 miles (640 km) after an 80 percent charge in 30 minutes using a solar-powered "Tesla Mega-

Elon Musk's Tesla Semi claims 500 miles (805 km) of range on a full charge as well as new batteries and motors built to last one million miles. The Semi should be able to run for 400 miles (640 km) after an 80 percent charge in 30 minutes using a solar-powered "Tesla Megacharger" charging station (Tesla pp).

charger" charging station. The zero to 60 mph (0–97 kph) time would be five seconds versus 15 seconds for a similar truck with a diesel engine. Reinforced Armor Glass would be used for the wrap-around cab windscreen. Elon Musk indicated that the Semi would come standard with Tesla Autopilot that allows semi-autonomous driving on highways. The Semi prototype was powered by four rear-axle Tesla Model 3 electric motors. Troubleshooting the project, Frenchman Jérôme Guillen, as of April 2017, is Tesla's Vice President of Vehicle Programs.

Some were skeptical about Tesla's ability to deliver such an impressive performance. Daimler's head of trucks suggested that the Tesla Semi specs defied the laws of physics and would be passing them by if they are true. Despite this, initial advance orders soon came from UPS (125 units), Pepsico (100) Sysco (50), and Anheuser-Busch (40), soon reaching a total of 19 interested companies. Musk confirmed that Tesla expects to manufacture as many as 100,000 electric trucks per year. Elon Musk's younger brother, Kimbal, is also planning to use Semis as part of his goal to build 100,000 Learning Gardens across the U.S., where young American students can learn about real food and healthy eating habits; the trucks will be used to haul materials to the sites.

By January 2018, Tesla was taking pre-orders outside America: state-owned Norwegian postal service Posten Norge, with its goal of operating an emissions-free fleet by 2025, placed an order for an unspecified number of the electric semi-trucks. Tesla was soon working with some of its biggest Semi buyers such as PepsiCo, UPS, and Anheuser-Busch, to build on-site charging stations for the electric long-haulers. The chargers, presumably Tesla's high-powered Megachargers, are set to be installed at key locations frequently visited by fleet operators. This system would enable the Semi to travel from one facility to another without compromising its range.

In March 2018, road trials of the Semi prototype began with its transporting trailer carrying battery packs from Gigafactory 1 in Nevada to Tesla's Fremont factory in California, a distance of 250 miles (402 km). Soon after, the same truck was sighted more than 2,000 miles (3,219 km) away at the Anheuser-Busch brewery in St. Louis, Missouri. The massive electric long-hauler was also seen parked at St. Charles, Missouri, roughly 24 miles (39 km) away from the beer giant's facility, later in the day. The brewery would then be able to add a charging station for the 40 Tesla Semis that it has ordered. In May, the Semi was seen near the West Los Angeles Service Center, Tesla releasing a very short video of the Semi on the Golden Gate Bridge heading for Santa Rosa, about 50 miles (80 km) away from the Golden Gate Bridge, 100 miles (160 km) from its plant. For the driverless cab system, Tesla worked on such features as the autopilot's blinker detection for better lane-merging, its ability to detect turn signals from other vehicles and "Mad Max," a blind spot threshold gauging how much distance is allowed between the Semi and cars in other lanes. In March, FedEx pre-ordered 20 units of the vehicle.

Unofficial trials continued with the Semi. It was spotted at the headquarters of trucking company J.B. Hunt, nearly 2,000 miles (3,200 km) away from the Fremont factory at the Catoosa, Oklahoma, Supercharger station, off of Interstate 44. This was one day after it was seen cruising in New Mexico on I-40, more than 600 miles (1,000 km) away. It had of course made the requisite stops at the California Highway Patrol checkpoints along the way. The truck charged via several extension cords, each plugged into its own supercharger stall (these are the chargers used to power Tesla's other vehicles). This will eventually be replaced and speeded up using Megachargers. The following day, the Semi traveled another 580 miles (900 km) or so and stopped at Tesla's Supercharger station in Brush, Colorado. Its next sighting was in Salt Lake City, Utah. In December 2018, the Tesla Semi black prototype was spotted at the Kettleman City Supercharger station between Los Angeles and the Bay Area plugged in to no fewer than five stalls at once. In May 2019, Tesla gave their Semi a maximum weight range test by hitching on a trailer loaded with large concrete blocks and trialing it along the busy 405 freeway in Los Angeles. Elon Musk stated that he expected that the production version would have a range closer to 600 miles.[16]

Musk had also announced that, following its planned Model Y SUV, Tesla would make a Class 3 electric pick-up truck slightly bigger than a Ford F-150, with dual motor all-wheel drive with "crazy" torque and a suspension that dynamically adjusts for the load. Other features under consideration are pivoting rear wheels for parallel parking and a 360-degree camera and sonar. Possible release date would be 2020. SsangYong, the South Korean brand, part of Mahindra & Mahindra, was also planning an electric pickup truck, based on its successful Musso model using its e-SIV (Electronic Smart Interface Vehicle) concept.

Musk's Tesla Semi has a competitor, taking the first name of the same legendary Croatian inventor: Nikola Motor Company, based in Salt Lake City, Utah. It has been founded by Trevor Milton. The son of a railroad man, Milton spent his youth riding locomotives and learning the inner workings of the Union Pacific trains at his father's shop. Milton was fascinated by the electric-diesel hybrid engines in the locomotives, which used a diesel-fueled engine to generate power for the electric motors that made the train move. Milton wondered why trucks did not have the same efficient design.

Milton, fluent in English and Portuguese and semi-fluent in Spanish, having lived in Puerto Rico, was CEO of dHybrid Systems, the second largest natural gas fuel system provider in America that was acquired in October 2014 by Worthington Industries. Milton then took Nikola Motors from startup to more than four billion dollars in pre-order reservations for the Nikola Class 8 electric truck. In 2016, the prototype mode was created, the Nikola Zero, a Utility Task Vehicle, with 72 or 107 kWh battery. It has 555 hp combined from a motor at each wheel. For the Nikola One, a 320 kWhEV battery supplies six traction electric motors with a combined software-limited 1,000 hp (750 kW) and 2,000 lb-ft (2,700 N-m) of torque, nearly 86,000 lb-ft (117,000 N-m) after gear reduction, inspired by electric locomotives. This is sufficient for keeping a speed of 65 mph (105 kph) with a full load of 35 tons (35,000 kg) on a 6 percent grade. The energy source is 300 kW hydrogen fuel cells consuming 10 lbs. (4.6 kg) of H_2 per 62 mi (100 km) from tanks with 220 lbs. (100 kg) of hydrogen, giving a range of 1,200 mi (1,900 km). Consumption is equivalent to 15.4 mpg of diesel. The truck has regenerative brakes to supplement the traditional disc brakes, decreasing stopping distance and fuel usage. The hydrogen version was unveiled in December 2016. In some markets, compressed natural gas to power an on-board gas turbine generator may be used instead. The first 5,000 trucks are to be built by Fitzgerald in Byrdstown, Tennessee; the company is known for its "glider" trucks, which are built without engines. In September 2018, Bosch announced a partnership with Nikola to develop fuel-cell powertrains for long-haul trucks. In April 2019, Nikola showcased its pre-production Nikola Two hydrogen electric semi-truck and its 2.3-megawatt Phoenix hydrogen station hydrogen filling station. The production-ready, zero-emission Two will have a 1,000-mile range, 20 percent lower operating costs per mile, and more horsepower, torque and safety features than any other diesel ever built. By 2028, Nikola is planning on having more than 700 hydrogen stations across the USA and Canada.

In November, Nikola announced R&D on a third version of its 120 kW FCT, the 1,000 hp Nikola Tre (Norwegian for three) with torque vectoring and a range of between 500 and 1,200 kilometers on a single tank (about 310 to 750 miles) with a refuel from empty in about 20 minutes. The Tre was conceived as a fully autonomous, level 5 platform with automated steering and braking. The Tre is aimed at the European and Asia Pacific truck markets. Because of the restrictive length regulations in export markets such as Europe and Asia-Pacific, the Tre will have less maximum range because there is less room to accommodate the hydrogen pressure tanks. Nikola worked with NEL Hydrogen of Oslo, Norway, to have a fueling infrastructure to supply the hydrogen fuel for the range extension electrical generator subsystem by the time the trucks rolled out to the different marketplaces. The Tre would start testing in 2020 with production slated for 2023. By 2028, Nikola planned to have more than 700 hydrogen stations across the USA and Canada, each capable of 2,000 to 8,000 kg of daily hydrogen production. Nikola's European stations are planned to come online around 2022 and are projected

Top: **Nikola One's energy sources are 300 kW hydrogen fuel cells consuming 4.6 kg (10 lbs.) of H$_2$ per 100 km (62 mi.) from tanks with 100 kg (220 lbs.) of hydrogen, giving this Class 8 truck a range of 1,200 mi (1,900 km) (Nikola Motor Press Portal). *Bottom:* Driver controls in the Nikola Two, a hydrogen-powered day cab, a far cry from the controls of the legendary British milk float of the 1960s (Nikola Motor).**

to cover most of the European market by 2030. By the end of 2019, private fleet Anheuser-Busch and truckload carrier U.S. Xpress Enterprises will have begun fleet tests of Nikola trucks.

Nikola then announced that it would refund all deposits it had taken on its battery-electric and hydrogen semi-trucks, the Nikola One and Nikola

Two. In a tweet announcing the refunds, the company said, "We want everyone to know we have never used a dollar of deposit money to operate the company on like other companies do." On April 5, 2018, Nikola followed up with a second tweet, saying, "Over 8+ billion [dollars] in pre-order reservations, so who needs deposits?" The company reportedly took $2.3 billion when it first announced the fuel-cell semi in 2016, which it said amounted to 7,000 pre-orders. The total described might amount to as many as 30,000 pre-orders. Days after Nikola tweeted about the refunds, NEL Hydrogen announced that it had received a $5.5 million order from Nikola Motor for its hydrogen fueling stations, indicating that Nikola may have a big order for its semis waiting in the wings.

It was perhaps inevitable that Nikola would come into conflict with Tesla. Ironically, Tesla, the man and inventor, did not like the litigious side of patents, often refrained from patenting his own inventions and completely avoided suing anyone for infringement. When it was brought to his attention that Marconi was using some of his patents in the development of the radio, he famously said, "Marconi is a good fellow. Let him continue. He is using seventeen of my patents."[17] Such was not the attitude when, in 2018, Nikola filed a $2 billion lawsuit claiming that Tesla had copied the design of their truck for the Tesla Semi. In the complaint, Nikola alleged that Tesla's electric truck design infringed on a series of three specific design patents that they recently obtained for the design of a few features of their Nikola One truck unveiled in 2016—over one year before Tesla unveiled its own electric truck. They alleged that the body of the Tesla Semi is similar to the one that they patented. The second complaint is related to Nikola's patent for a wrap windshield on a semi-truck. The third complaint is related to the fact that Nikola patented a mid-entry door design for their truck and Tesla is also using a mid-entry door for the Tesla Semi truck. Nikola Motors claimed that Tesla's design is creating market confusion that is stealing away orders for their truck and therefore there are damages, which they estimate at more than two billion dollars. Such litigation did not prevent orders. Anheuser-Busch ordered up to 800 hydrogen-fueled semi-trucks from the Nikola Motor Company, which planned to build more than 700 hydrogen stations across the USA and Canada.

By early 2019, Nikola had taken reservations worth $8 billion for its truck—enough to cover the cost of 7,000 vehicles. By contrast, Tesla was believed to have received about 650 pre-orders for its Semi. At this time, neither company has announced when production is expected to begin.

Another new company in competition with Tesla, Nikola and BYD is the start-up Thor Trucks Inc. in North Hollywood, not far from the Los Angeles airport. Named after the Norse god and Marvel hero, Thor has produced an all-electric Class 8 ET-One prototype with 36 ton (32,659 kg) carrying capacity which can travel up to 300 miles (483 km) on a single charge. It was co-founded in 2016 by Giordano Sordoni and 25-year-old Dakota Semler. Semler, who converted his mother's SUV to run on vegetable oil, grew up around the trucking business. His family business, Malibu Wines, owned a fleet of 150 trucks based out of Riverside, California. An electric truck startup seemed like a perfect fit to meet new air quality standards in the state of California. Unlike Tesla, which manufactures its vehicles completely, Thor Trucks plans to partner with existing auto manufacturers to build its trucks. Having hired engineers from Navistar, Boeing Co., electric-car maker Faraday Future Inc., and Chinese electrics leader BYD Auto Co., it has its own battery technology, but otherwise its trucks will use off-the-shelf components and have features that feel familiar to drivers and fleet managers. In August 2018, UPS partnered with Thor to develop and test two Class 6 delivery trucks with a 50 and 100-mile range over six months. Thor teamed up with AxleTech of Troy, Michigan, to use their specialized axle embedded with electric motors as the powertrain for its ET-1 line of electric semi-tractors. A large electric motor was mounted between the frame rails of a Navistar chassis. A deal that Thor has with Wiggins Lift Co. was one example. Thor initially provided battery technology for Wiggins' forklifts with an integrated electric powertrain to follow. Companies leading truck electrification were doing likewise, with axle makers buying electric motors instead of making them. For example, Dana Inc. acquired a 55 percent interest in Hydro-Quebec subsidiary TM4, becoming Dana's source for electric motors, power inverters and control systems. Thor has no plans for autonomous driving.

Robert J. Scaringe graduated from Rensselaer Polytechnic Institute and obtained his PhD in mechanical engineering at Massachusetts Institute of Technology's Sloan Automotive Laboratory. Passionate about fuel-efficient automobiles in general, in 2009 he started up Mainstream Motors, changing its name to Avera Automotive but finally settling on Rivian and diverting his goal to sustainable electric transportation, developing operations in Plymouth, Michigan, San Jose, California, and Irvine, California. Rivian also bought a former Mitsubishi factory in Normal, Illinois. Among the team of specialists hired is Gary Gloceri, a former Magna electric powertrain chief engineer who led the development of the powertrain for the Ford Focus Electric. In late November 2018, Rivian finally revealed its first two products, the R1T, an all-electric pickup truck, and the R1S, a seven-seater electric SUV. Both were ground-up designs, sharing a skateboard platform (common to most battery electric vehicles, with the battery pack living between the axles and underneath the passenger compartment). Rivian offered three different sizes of battery in both vehicles: either 180 kWh (and 400 miles/640 km of range) or 135 kWh (310 miles/500 km) packs, with a third configuration of 105 kWh (240 miles/390km) coming six months after production starts in

Dakota Semler, founder of Thor Trucks in North Hollywood, has a fine sense of history. Here his 2018 all-electric Class 8 ET-One prototype with 80,000 lb. carrying capacity which can travel up to 300 miles on a single charge poses alongside a 1918 Walker electric truck chassis. This represents a century of innovation (Thor Trucks).

2020. The batteries are capable of recharging at up to 160 kW on a DC fast charger and are also equipped with an 11 kW onboard charger.

Both R1T and R1S feature four electric motors—one per wheel—and varying levels of power and torque depending on the battery size. Interestingly, the 135 kWh pack gets the greatest power output (562 kW/754 hp); the 180 kWh vehicles have to make do with a mere 522kW/700hp. Both make an identical 1200 N-m/855 ft·lbs. (The 105 kWh configuration will come with 300 kW/402 hp and 560 N-m/413 ft-lbs.) The R1T will have a payload capacity of 1,763 lbs. (800 kg) and a trailer rating of 11,000 lbs (5,000 kg).

In February 2019, Rivian announced that it had received a $700 million investment led by Amazon. Seven months later, Amazon CEO Jeff Bezos announced his company had ordered 100,000 electric delivery vans of a new design from Rivian, with the first expected to be in service in 2021. Rivian had also secured, in April 2019, a $500 million investment from Ford, and a strategic partnership to co-develop a battery electric vehicle for Ford.

Perhaps inspired by the Rivian vehicles, General Motors announced they were working on an electric truck.

Over in New Zealand, the New World and Pak 'n' Save supermarket brands prepared to roll out 16 fast chargers and four electric trucks after receiving money from a government fund dedicated to expanding New Zealand's electric vehicle fleet. The charging station would build on the company's existing network of 48 fast chargers and 28 electric delivery vans. Student mechanics in New Zealand would be able to get a qualification in electric vehicle maintenance and repair thanks to a new government grant. The previous and current governments aimed to double the number of electric vehicles every year to reach 64,000 by 2022—around 2 percent of the country's fleet.

Chapter One of this book tells of the fierce competition among the first golden generation of over one dozen electric truck builders, a century ago. Chapter Two relates how Henry Ford's gasoline Model T, TT and S virtually destroyed the battery dreams of men like his friend Thomas Edison. How very ironic that in May 2018, Ford CEO Jim Hackett made the announcement during the company's latest financial report:

> By 2030, almost 90 percent of the Ford portfolio in North America will be electric trucks, utilities and commercial vehicles. Given declining consumer demand and product profitability, the company will not invest in next generations of traditional Ford sedans for North America. It will bring 16 battery-electric vehicles to market by 2022.

Even more ironic, when Hackett formed a new internal team to identify and develop electric-vehicle partnerships with other companies, including suppliers, in some global markets, he called it, with perhaps a sense of history, "Team Edison." In July 2018 Ford, celebrating its 155th anniversary, moved Team Edison to the historic and renovated Michigan Central Station in Corktown in Detroit. The Blue Oval also confirmed that approximately 2,500 Ford employees, most from the mobility team, will call Corktown their work home by 2022.[18] In January of 2019, Ford announced that it had changed its strategy from hybrid and would launch an all-electric F-150 Series pickup truck.

NINE

Start-Ups Out
of a Driverless Future

It was rare when science fiction, more concerned with rocketry in outer space, mentioned electric trucks. In 1956, Poul Anderson of Orinda, California, who had authored several works of fantasy, wrote a short story called "The Corkscrew of Space," published by Galaxy Science Fiction, in which one reads:

> As he watched [the spacecraft] entered its cradle and was wheeled off toward the waiting *electro trucks*. Unloading began immediately; the trucks gulped packages and scurried like beetles towards the warehouses.

In the last two decades of the 20th century, Professor Ernst Dieter Dickmanns and a team at Bundeswehr University in Munich, Germany, adapted a Mercedes sedan to practical, driverless technology. In 1986, the Robot Car "VaMoRs" managed to drive all by itself and by 1987 was capable of driving itself at speeds up to 96 kilometers per hour (60 mph). In 1993, Dickmanns' prototype made a 1,758 kilometers (1,092 mi) trip in the fall of 1995 from Munich in Bavaria to Odense in Denmark to a project meeting and back.[1]

Tomorrow's electric trucks may well be working hand-in-hand with electric cargo drones in the business of doorstep delivery. It has already begun. In 2017, Workhorse of Loveland, Ohio, already makers of an electric W-15 pickup truck, and unveiled their 100-mile (160 km) range N-Gen delivery van as part of their concept towards delivery with their integrated HorseFly drone. The latter takes off from the parked N-Gen lifting packages weighing up to 10 lbs. (4.5 kg) and delivering them to a destination within the driver's line of sight. If it can deliver pizzas, then why not fresh produce such as milk? Thus, the definition of a milk float enters the future.[2] In November 2018, Workhorse started production of the N-Gen at its factory in Indiana. Workhorse also struck a deal with Ryder Systems to supply all warranty and maintenance services for its vans. It had about 1,000 orders waiting to be filled.

One feature of the N-Gen was a standard all wheel drive capability using an electric motor for both the front and rear wheels with the capability to achieve 50 MPGe—many times that of a conventional delivery van.

The number of trucks on the roads across the world is constantly growing, yet there are fewer and fewer new entrants to the truck-driving profession. Clearly, the job is stressful, often monotonous and the prospects of promotion are limited, necessitating a long-term rethink. It is very likely that in the years to come, a significant number of electric trucks will be driverless, provided a fail-safe reliable system can be established.

Automated Guided Vehicles (AGVs), which are basically driverless forklifts and other materials handling vehicles, were invented in 1953 by Arthur "Mac" Barret, Jr., of Northbrook, Illinois. He took a modified towing tractor that had been used to pull a trailer and configured it to follow an overhead wire in a grocery warehouse, allowing the vehicle to be operated automatically. Soon afterwards, Barrett Electronics began to market a rudimentary AGV called the Guide-O-Matic. The technology soon proved to be appealing to factory and warehouse owners throughout the U.S. during the late '50s and early '60s.

In 1991, Konecranes Gottwald, a Finnish company, specializing in the manufacture and service of cranes and lifting equipment, developed their first AGV for work in container ports, such as the Hamburger Hafen und Logistik AG (HHLA) Container Terminal Altenwerder (CTA) in Germany. Switching over to lead-acid battery power in 2011, five years later Konecranes built an AGV prototype using li-ion batteries, coupled with an automatic electric charging station. As of August 2018, Hamburg's 100-strong fleet of 14.8-meter (48 ft.) driverless diesel and diesel-electric trucks with a payload of 40 tons will gradually be replaced by li-ion units built at Konecranes Dusseldorf yard. The transition will be complete by the end of 2022.[3]

On July 3, 2014, Daimler Trucks unveiled their Mercedes-Benz Future Truck 2025, calling it the transport system of the future. The truck of tomorrow would drive itself. The road for this is being paved by assistance and telematics systems that are already in use today. These were brought together in a highly intelligent system called "Highway Pilot." The result: increased safety and lower fuel consumption. An improved vehicle/transport management and app-based solutions will enable fleet operators to save money. The Highway Pilot system took a further step towards production maturity with the unveiling of the Freightliner Inspiration truck, already approved for use on public roads. It is based on the Freightliner Cascadia Evolution series production model, thousands of which can be seen on U.S. roads. And it is approved for autonomous driving on public highways in Nevada. But following teething troubles, in June 2018, Martin Daum, chief executive of Daimler Trucks, announced that it would take at least five years before driverless technology becomes commercially available to its customers.

On December 21, 2018, Daimler Trucks North America delivered its first electric Freightliner eM2 to Penske Truck Leasing for trials in everyday commercial applications. This was the first commercially available medium-duty electric truck in the country and became the first of ten such models the leasing company would test in partnership with its own fleet customers over the next two years. Penske would also add the eCascadia to its fleet once available. Daimler planned to begin mass production of its battery-electric trucks in 2021. The eM2 can travel 200 miles per charge and recharge to 80 percent in an hour; the eCascadia will be able to travel 250 miles per charge. In the days leading up to CES, the company announced it would begin offering lane-keeping assist with automated steering capabilities and let industry press test drive its new battery electric models at an off-site event in Las Vegas.

Toyota Motor Corporation's truck-making arm, Hino Motors, is also adding artificial intelligence to large diesel-electric hybrids to improve fuel efficiency. It plans to launch a system in Japan in mid–2019 using GPS and gyro sensors, which sense rotational motion, to assess the best way to manage the power system of its Profia trucks—its largest diesel-hybrid models, marketed abroad as the 700 series. Along with existing automatic cruise-control technology, the system calculates ways to limit the impact of tailgating and other driving habits which can reduce mileage, improving fuel economy by 15 percent over diesel-only counterparts.

Kalmar of Helsinki, Finland, part of Cargotec, is transitioning to autonomous electric propulsion with a 9–18 ton range of forklift trucks, the DCG90–180. Toyota has also produced a versatile electric counterbalanced forklift truck in the Traigo80 with its ergonomically designed driver cab, which also provides very good all-round visibility. Designed for heavy-duty applications, AC-motor Traigo 80 series forklifts have an 80-volt battery and offer lift heights of up to 21 ft. (6.5 meters). Suitable for multiple pallet handling, these four-wheel counterbalanced fork trucks can handle loads weighing up to five tons.

The ZF Innovation Truck, a Class 8 truck equipped with autonomous technology, carried a trailer to a loading zone, unhitched on its own and drove away. It then backed into another space and hitched to a different trailer before driving off. The entire process took less than seven minutes. The demonstration was part of ZF Technology Day, a showcase hosted by the company at its headquarters in Friedrichshafen, Germany, in June 2018. In recent years, ZF has acquired companies such as Lidar producer Ibeo Automotive Systems and Michigan-based electronics specialists TRW Automotive. The supplier, which has never built a vehicle of its own, now has the ability to develop nearly an entire connected truck. The autonomous-friendly supercomputer called ProAI 2.0 will debut for commercial vehicles in 2021.[4]

Volvo Autonomous Solutions is developing a driverless electric truck called VERA, in particular for use in busy hubs like ports and warehouses. A fleet of VERAs operate together in a network and are connected through a Cloud-based service and management center. The concept relies on autonomous, electric-powered, cabless tractors that are wirelessly connected to a control center. The vehicle itself is outfitted with lidar, cameras and radar sensors to detect its surroundings. The chassis itself uses Volvo's existing electric truck powertrain, which has a 185 kW motor and has a range of up to 186 miles. It will also pull a standard trailer with loads of up to 32 tons.[5]

As early as 2016, Volvo was testing autonomous trucks in an underground mine in Sweden, part of an initiative to demonstrate the technology as a means of improving both efficiency and safety in hazardous conditions. In Brazil, Volvo trialed self-steering trucks to help sugarcane farmers improve crop yield, and it has also tested an autonomous garbage collection truck. In 2019, Volvo signed a deal with the Norwegian mine Brønnøy Kalk to transport limestone along five kilometers of roads and tunnels from the mine to a nearby port using self-driving trucks.

In November, Greenlots of Los Angeles, a global provider of EV (electric vehicle) charging software and solutions, began collaboration with Volvo Trucks to deploy charging infrastructure for electric trucks operating out of warehouses in Southern California. All of the charging equipment for the project, including both Level 2 chargers and 150 kW DC fast-chargers, would operate on Greenlots' SKY enterprise software platform to enable seamless management of Volvo's fleet, charging stations and energy storage systems. Greenlots collaborated with ABB and other charging station manufacturers to provide the equipment, while partnering with Burns & McDonnell to engineer, construct and install the new EV charging stations. The project became one of the first in North America to demonstrate a new heavy-duty vehicle charging standard, SAE J3068, in real-world applications.

Stefan Seltz-Axmacher of San Francisco founded Starsky Robotics in 2015. It is named after the trucking slang term for when drivers work in teams, like the title characters of the 1970s TV series *Starsky & Hutch*. The Starsky system plans for big-rigs to be driverless on highway conditions, then for "mission control" human drivers to take remote control when the trucks encounter anything weird or complicated.[6]

Robert Falck, together with Linnea Kornehed and Filip Lilja of Stockholm, Sweden, founded Einride to develop the self-driving T-pod electric truck that is not only able to operate autonomously, but does not even feature a driver's seat. Without the cabin, more space is left for the drivetrain and freight. Instead, it carries a more compact suite of lidar, radar, and camera sensors, feeding information about the environment to Nvidia's AI supercomputer. Powered by a 200 KWh battery, T-pod can cover approximately 125 miles (200 km) on a single charge. Over that distance, it has space for 15

Robert Falck of Einride stands beside his driverless T-pod. Without the cabin for the driver, more space is left for the IT/GPS drivetrain and freight. Powered by a 200 KWh battery, T-pod can cover approximately 125 miles or 200 km on a single charge (Einride pp).

standard pallets, equal to 160 sq. ft. (15 m²). Its maximum weight will be around 20 tons (20,000 kg). In October 2017, Einride released a statement explaining how it is going to support Lidl in its transition towards electric and autonomous transport. The supermarket chain has a goal of reducing its emissions by 40 percent in Sweden by 2035. Lidl planned to start a pilot program using the T-pod by the third quarter of 2018. The vehicle will be driving around the city of Halmstad on the Swedish west coast, carrying real Lidl products and driving through Swedish traffic. At first the T-pod will be monitored at a distance by a human driver, ready to take over the wheel when required. Total autonomy, at least at the start of the pilot, had not yet been reached, but Einride plans to slowly decrease human involvement, going from one to ten trucks per remote driver. By 2020, 200 T-pods will be transporting two million pallets on the route from Helsingborg to Gothenburg.

In July 2018, Einride unveiled the T-log, with a stronger suspension for the logging industry. Acknowledging that computers cannot handle every on-road driving scenario yet, let alone unmarked lanes under heavy tree canopies, Einride will be able to drive its T-logs from a remote location, using teleoperation tech provided by Phantom Auto. Einride plans to put vehicles on the road later this year, starting with a T-pod truck carrying tires between two depots belonging to DB Schenker, one of the world's largest logistics companies, in Jönköping, Sweden.[7]

From November, a single Einride T-Pod began moving pallets of goods between warehouses run by German logistics giant Schenker, in the southern Swedish city of Jönköping. It covered about six miles a day, some of it on public roads, at speeds below 25 mph. Einride and Dubai's Roads and Transport Authority (RTA) have signed a memorandum of understanding, paving the way for autonomous semis to begin hauling freight in the Middle East. Dubai hopes to make 25 percent of vehicle trips within its borders autonomous by 2030. In December, DeepMap, a startup specializing in high-definition (HD) mapping and localization technology for autonomous vehicles, announced that it would be providing HD mapping technology to Einride. The two companies integrated DeepMap's HD mapping software in their autonomous fleets enabling Einride to deploy its first truck using DeepMap's mapping software in 2019.

Slightly smaller than Einride is Nuro, developed by Dave Ferguson and Jiajun Zhu, two of the top engineers in Google's self-driving vehicle group who left the company in 2016 to found Nuro, and managed to convince Waymo, Uber, and Tesla, as well as Stanford and MIT, to produce Nuro R1 (as in Neurological). Using Velodyne Ultra Puck lidar, along with a comprehensive array of cameras all around the vehicle for localization and obstacle avoidance, Nuro R1 is designed to transport goods (a "good" being anything that will fit into its capacious compartments) for delivery, return, or even for purchase. Nuro calls this "last mile transportation," although it seems like it might be more accurate to bump that up to perhaps 16 kilometers (10 miles) to differentiate R1 from sidewalk robots in terms of more than just payload, since R1 is intended to drive autonomously for longer distances on city streets.

Whilst Einride and Nuro are newly conceived vehicles, Embark is about retro-fitting. Embark has been set up by Alex Rodriguez and Brandon Moak, two former students at the University of Waterloo, Ontario, Canada, who in 2015 began work on self-driving technologies together in college, starting a company called Varden. Venture-backed, Moak & Rodriguez formed their now self-driving truck company, Embark, instead of graduating. Their idea was to partner with the trucking industry rather than rolling over it, by using a retro-fitting technology. Embark's retrofitted 18-wheelers were soon driving themselves while on interstate highways. Where it gets tricky is near cities, which are still too complex for driverless trucks to navigate. To compensate, Embark operates hand-off depots, where a skilled human takes over for the last few miles of driving. Currently, the highway portion of the trip, where the truck drives itself, is overseen by a team of two drivers who switch off regularly so they can stay alert while monitoring the system, and an engineer. With improved technology, this backup will no longer be necessary.

In 2017, at the Volvo Group Innovation Summit in Beijing, China, Volvo demonstrated a new self-driving truck designed to travel autonomously from one hub to another. The truck is based on the company's existing FH platform and navigates completely autonomously, using lidar and GPS to continuously scan its surroundings and check its location. It can navigate around fixed and movable obstacles and gather data to optimize its route, traffic safety, and fuel consumption. The truck requires no manual supervision and is part of a total transport solution that controls the entire delivery process. The latest autonomous concept truck was designed for hub-to-hub transportation in semi-confined areas such as harbors and dedicated lanes on highways. The company previously showed similar autonomous concepts for confined areas such as mines, quarries, and sugarcane fields, and this new solution takes those ideas into an over-the-road setting, as well as one in refuse collection and another one at a sugar plantation in Brazil.

Following trials in California in 2017, Waymo, the self-driving vehicle tech development division of Alphabet/Google, launched a new self-driving truck pilot program in Atlanta, Georgia. The self-driving trucks in question will be operating in support of local Google data centers, with the trucks carrying cargo to and from the data centers.[8] In 2018, using Anthony Levandowski's Otto system, Uber's self-driving truck drove itself 344 miles (554 km) across Arizona from the Midwest to southern California.

At the IAA Commercial Vehicles 2018 conference in Hannover, Germany, Robert Bosch GmbH of Gerlingen, Germany, endorsed that the U.S. and Europe showed the greatest potential for hub-to-hub automation, or driverless trucks shuttling between depots. Also unveiled at this show was the streamlined Ford F-Vision Future Truck, as designed by Team Edison in Detroit and built by Ford Ottosan. The legacy automaker's Turkey-based vehicle production base will also involve electric propulsion linked to autonomous and connected drive.

PDDs

As related in Chapter Five, during the 1950s, fleets of British-built Harbilt 551 pedestrian-controlled electric prams, just 3 feet (1 m) tall, were in daily use for milk and postal deliveries. With the advance of AI robotics, the electric delivery pram has been transformed into a Personal Delivery Device (PDD).

In 2014, Starship Technologies was started up in Estonia by Ahti Heinla and Janus Friis, inventors of Skype, to design and produce PDDs. Trials began with delivering food with Postmates in Washington, D.C., and DoorDash in Redwood City, California. Further trials involved a fleet of 25 PDDs to deliver coffee and pizza to college students at George Mason University in Fairfax,

Virginia, who wanted late-night food from on-campus retailers—including a grocery store and the local Starbucks—with their order delivered by one of 25 ADDs. Starship PDDs also went into in use at Intuit's corporate campus in the Bay Area, as well as north of London in the town of Milton Keynes, where they now deliver groceries and packages to around 5,000 homes. Using a suite of sensors, including ten cameras, ultrasound, and radar, and using artificial intelligence to make decisions, the bots can navigate through the city autonomously.

The idea soon caught on. In March 2016, in Brisbane, Australia, the Domino's pizza company teamed up with Marathon Robotics to build a PDD which, besides transporting pizza and drinks (in separate hot and cold compartments), can also accept payments and chat with customers. It uses GPS and lasers to get around, and can reach speeds of 12 mph (18 kph).

Dispatch, a team with expertise in robotics and artificial intelligence from MIT, UPenn, USC, UIUC, and UC Berkeley, built their PDD, christened Carry for trials around Menlo College and California State University, where it mostly interacts with pedestrians and completes various kinds of deliveries. A mobile app lets customers interact with Carry, such as by opening one of its four compartments to grab their parcels, while a software tool will let its eventual customers easily send delivery orders to Dispatch's fleet of these robots. Carry can transport up to 100 pounds. They envision a world in which PDDs can replace cars for many deliveries in cities everywhere, helping cut traffic and pollution.

Marble was founded in 2015 by Matt Delaney, Jason Calaiaro and Kevin Peterson, at Carnegie Mellon University (CMU) in Pittsburgh, Pennsylvania, the world's most prestigious computer science department and robotics institution. Marble built a fleet of PDDs, which began trial use in 2017 around San Francisco's relatively flat Mission and Potrero Hill districts in a new partnership with Yelp's Eat24. Almost immediately San Franciscans, already perturbed by the growing glut of electric scooters, were questioning how safe it was to share the pavement with them. In December 2017, city supervisor Norman Yee introduced legislation to restrict their use, including capping the number of permits issued at three per company and requiring the PDDs to only operate at 3 mph and within certain neighborhoods. They must also be accompanied by a human at all times.

Amazon's research and development lab in Seattle has produced a version of a PDD, the six-wheeler Scout. In January 2019, six of these devices began delivering to customers in a neighborhood in Snohomish County, Washington.

There are an increasing number of PDDs: Cleveron, an Estonian logistics company, mostly known for its pickup towers installed in some Wal-Mart stores across the United States, has produced the Generation R PDD. Felipe

Chavez, the founder of a robot food-delivery company called Kiwi, worked with students at the MLK Student Union of UC Berkeley to produce a food delivery PDD able to travel almost anywhere in the area bounded by Cedar and Sacramento streets and Ashby and Piedmont avenues, including to UC Berkeley residence halls and campus buildings. PepsiCo, working with Robby Technologies in the Bay Area, are trialing a fleet of snack-carrying PDDs on the University of the Pacific's campus in California. The robots—or "snackbots"—carry snacks and beverages from the company's Hello Goodness portfolio, which includes choices like Smartfood Delight popcorn, Baked Lays, Pure Leaf Tea, and Starbucks Cold Brew drinks. Students can place their orders on the iOS app and have them delivered to select locations around the 175-acre campus between 9 a.m. and 5 p.m.

Another PDD is the Robomart, which brings groceries and dairy products to the door. Consumers tap a button to request the closest available vehicle, which is small and streamlined. Once it arrives, the van doors unlock, and consumers pick the products they want. Robomart tracks what customers have taken using patent pending "grab and go" checkout-free technology, charges them, and sends a receipt accordingly. Then the Robomart moves back out onto the road and heads to another waiting consumer. The company is deploying its initial fleet in 2019 commercial pilots with their first customer, Stop & Shop.

In February 2019, lawmakers in both the U.S. House and Senate introduced bills that would define and regulate PDDs. The bills' definition of the devices includes a 120-pound (55 kg) weight limit (before goods are added) and a maximum speed of 10 mph (16 kph). Other jurisdictions that have adopted laws or regulations "governing automated ground-based delivery devices," according to House Transportation Committee fiscal coordinator Mark Matteson, are "Utah, Arizona, Ohio, Idaho, Virginia, Florida, Wisconsin, and the District of Columbia."[9]

Concerning PDD versus UAV drone-delivery, one might use an old phrase, "horses for courses," except that it may be more about dogs.

Continental of Hanover, Germany (established in 1871), wants to use a system of autonomous vans packed with dog-like four-legged robots to deliver packages. The concept is based around Continental's driverless electric vehicle, the Continental Urban Mobility Experience (CUbE), a minibus-sized pod whose interior can be reconfigured to suit different functions. The company has paired the vehicle with PDDs except that in the last yards of the parcel delivery chain, the wheels are replaced by quadrupeds. Continental says that an efficient autonomous mobility system could focus on moving passengers during the day and switch to delivering goods at night, when people are more likely to be at home to receive their packages. The system could be almost 24/7.

Batteries

Although it does not fall within the brief of this transport history, one would be accused of looking through rose-tinted spectacles if one did not play devil's advocate with three questions. What to do so that the carbon footprint of an electric vehicle battery does not become an ecological disaster? What to do so that its recycling does not become an ecological disaster? How to find sufficient raw materials to make the cells and the chemicals for batteries in the longterm? If the history and the future of the electric truck is to have a beneficial impact, such questions must be addressed by those responsible.

In 2016, I researched a 270-page book about innovators in battery technology. I was fully aware that with the worldwide race to provide batteries of ever greater energy density, my book would be out of date days after the printer had stopped. Three years on, it is the same with this book about electric trucks. When, in May 2018, the author asked Professor John Goodenough, aged 95, one of the electrochemists who led the successful quest for the lithium-ion battery, his view of the future, he replied:

> Modern society runs on the energy stored in a fossil fuel; this dependence is not sustainable. A fossil fuel, once burned, is not recyclable, and the gaseous exhausts of their combustion add to global warming and are already choking large populations in China and India. The li-ion battery of the wireless revolution will not provide an all-electric road vehicle that is competitive in safety, cost, and convenience with today's road vehicles powered by a fossil fuel in an internal combustion engine. However, we and others are working on the development of an all-solid-state lithium or sodium battery that will compete, I believe, with the internal combustion engine to get rid of the distributed air pollution from the highways of the world as well as the oceans and many other applications. I believe the new battery products will become available within 5 years, which is why the automotive industry is panicking about how to plan for the future.[10]

Professor Goodenough was referring to work carried out with Portuguese physicist Maria Helena Braga at the Cockrell School of Engineering at the University of Texas, Austin. In the laboratory they have developed a battery made entirely from a special glass which can handle up to 15,000 recharge cycles, is not flammable and offers three times as much energy density as a conventional li-ion battery.

But Professors Goodenough and Braga are not alone in seeking improvements. Solid-state batteries are one Holy Grail of battery researchers around the world.

It has been realized that when the entire transport world switches over to electric transport (eight million vehicles), there will not be enough lithium, cobalt and other rare earths to meet the demand, a situation threatening a monopolistic ownership situation similar to that of OPEC in the 1970s. To take just one example, the Tesla Motors "giga factory" plans to produce enough lithium-cobalt-ion batteries to power 500,000 electric cars by 2020. Global cobalt prices shot up from $34,600 per ton in January 2017 to $81,360 in early 2018. The given reason is ongoing low-level conflict in the Democratic Republic of Congo. On February 9, 2018, China Molybdenum announced it was purchasing the Tenka Fungurume mine in the Democratic Republic of Congo, so becoming owner of 62 percent of global refined cobalt production. Hitting back, Samsung SDI of South Korea is developing batteries raising the proportion of nickel to over 90 percent, with cobalt down to 5 percent. Then there is BYD's proprietary lithium-iron-phosphate. But there are other alternatives.

In November 2013, Elton Cairns, aged 86, another veteran electrochemist, a Faculty Senior Scientist at Lawrence Berkeley National Laboratory, with co-workers Min-Kyu Song (Molecular Foundry, Berkeley Lab), and Yuegang Zhang (Suzhou Institute of Nano-Tech and Nano-Bionics, Chinese Academy of Sciences) announced their innovation of an advanced lithium/sulfur (Li/S) cell that can provide 500 Wh/kg (2 kg/kWh), more than twice the output of a li-ion battery, and have already shown that it can do 1,500 charge cycles without significant deterioration. This is a sulfur-graphene oxide nanocomposite with styrene-butadiene-carboxymethyl cellulose copolymer binder.

In June 2017, researchers at the Argonne National Laboratory and Oregon State University made a new cathode architecture for lithium-sulphide batteries that consists of crystalline di-lithium sulphide nanoparticles encapsulated in few-layer graphene. Lithium-sulphur (Li-S) batteries are promising for future energy-storage applications thanks to their extremely high theoretical energy density of 2600 Wh/kg, which is three to five-fold higher than that of state-of-the-art lithium-ion batteries.

Another alternative is the rechargeable lithium-titanate battery ($Li_4Ti_5O_{12}$, referred to as LTO in the battery industry) which has the advantage of being faster to charge than other lithium-ion batteries.

Graphene, which had been produced unintentionally in small quantities for centuries through the use of lead pencils and other similar graphite applications, was observed in electron microscopes in 1962 and then isolated and characterized in 2004 by André Geim and Konstantin Novolselov at Manchester University. In 2016, Henrik Fisker, a Danish automotive designer and entrepreneur residing in Los Angeles, announced development of an electric car whose graphene supercapacitors, instead of lithium-ion batteries, would give it a range of 400-plus miles and four-minute charge time. Research had been led by Dr. Fabio Albano, VP of battery systems at Fisker, the co-founder of Sakti3. In November 2017, Fisker announced that the commercial version, the Fisker Orbit battery, would be ready for automotive production around 2023.

Meanwhile, Eun-kyung Lee, Byoung-Lyong Choi, Jae-Hyun Lee and Dong-mok Whang, researchers at the Samsung Advanced Institute of Technology (SAIT) in Gyeonggi-do, South Korea, working with a team from Seoul National University's School of Chemical and Biological Engineering, announced a mechanism to mass synthesize graphene into a 3D form like popcorn using affordable silica (SiO_2). This "graphene ball" was utilized for both the anode protective layer and cathode materials in lithium-ion batteries. The graphene ball enables a 45 percent increase in capacity, and five times faster charging speeds than standard lithium-ion batteries; i.e., 12 minutes. Graphene balls hit energy densities of nearly 800 Wh/L, around the same as Li-ion batteries today used by Tesla. SAIT has also filed two applications for the "graphene ball" technology patent in the U.S. and Korea. Already with many years' experience in manufacturing, Samsung's researchers soon figured out how to coat the electrodes using the Nobilta, a high performance powder processing machine used for particle design developed by the Hosokawa Microon Corporation of Japan. Following the marketing of graphene ball smartphones, it may not be long before the technology is applied to electric vehicles, including trucks.

Avevai, a startup working with e-Synergy, both in Singapore, has produced the Iona commercial vehicle using a patented graphene-infused supercapacitor technology. This energy management system (GEMS) allows for what Avevai calls an "unrivalled range" of 330 km for the Iona Van and 300 km for the Iona electric truck. Controlled by a smart algorithm, GEMS allows charging and discharging cycles to run in nanoseconds. Avevai claims up to 85 percent of energy is captured through regenerative braking, allowing battery technology to take faster charging and discharging cycles with less damage. Avevai specified a 200,000 km or five-year warranty and says a 22 kW AC charging station will fully charge the Iona Truck in two hours, while the electric van takes less than four hours to be fully charged. For the custom chassis, Avevai turned to Daimler and Foton in Germany, longstanding partners, to incorporate all performance and safety related components such as brakes, bearings, drive and control systems, as well as insulation and NVH, to comply with international standards. Foton of China will take over production of the electric vehicles for Avevai. The Iona went on sale in February 2019 in China, while other markets such as Europe and the U.S. followed later that year.

In the race to build a better electric vehicle battery, another option is silicon, which has a higher energy density than the graphite traditionally used as part of battery anodes. Researchers at Vrije University in Brussels estimate that using silicon can cut the cost per kilowatt hour of EVs by 30 percent. Sila Nanotechnologies of California, which started at a laboratory at Georgia Institute of Technology, is preparing a commercial product for its key customers, BMW AG and Amperex Technology Limited—the world's largest producer of batteries for consumer goods—with EV application by 2023. While Sila's product replaces graphite entirely, Canadian graphite material producer Elcora Advanced Materials Corp (ERA.V) is one of a number of companies working on boosting the capacity of graphite anode powders by adding silicon.

Researchers led by Arve Holt at Norway's Department of Energy Technology (IFE) in Kjeller have perfected a way to substitute silicon for the graphite commonly used in the anodes of lithium ion batteries. They have found a way to mix silicon with other elements to create an anode that is stable and long lasting and which has three to five times higher capacity than a conventional graphite anode. The discovery will lead to batteries that can power an electric truck for 600 miles (967 km) or more. Kjeller Innovation works to commercialize research results from IFE, in trials by both material manufacturers and battery manufacturers to determine if it can be marketed successfully.

But what if the body panels of an electric truck could form part of its battery? Researchers at Sweden's Chalmers University of Technology have been exploring the possibility of using carbon fiber as a structural battery. The team has studied the relationship between carbon fiber's microstructure and electrochemical capacity, and is working to develop a combination that is both mechanically sound and energy-dense. The team has discovered that carbon fiber's electrical and mechanical properties can be controlled by carefully rearranging its graphitic order and crystallite sites. Fibers with small, disorganized crystals have better electrical characteristics and are slightly stiffer than steel. Large, highly oriented crystals provide even better stiffness (over twice that of steel), but the electrochemical properties are not adequate for practical use as a battery. The team then experimented with ways to increase the composite thickness in order to overcome the mechanical challenges while boosting total energy storage capacity. "The key is to optimize vehicles at system level—based on the weight, strength, stiffness and electrochemical properties," says Chalmers Professor Leif Asp.[11]

However, when it comes to industrialization of the latest research, costs are important. It is possible to make better batteries than those on the market today, but they are often too expensive to pay off.

In May 2018, Felix von Borck and a team at Akasol GmbH of Darmstadt, Germany, launched their extra high 221 Wh/kg capacity cylindrical cell battery, the CYC 60, for trucks and buses. This is added to their innovative OEM lithium-manganese-cobalt-oxide battery product line, which ranges in energy storage capacity from 10 watts and 25 kilowatt-hours to 30 watts and 73.2 kilowatt-hours per unit. With capacity for 600 megawatt-hours of lithium-ion battery production a year, the Akasol plant is the largest of its kind in Europe.

In March 2018, Samsung SDI and Webasto signed a letter of intent to build high voltage batteries together for the commercial vehicle sector. Samsung is developing a battery module using its prismatic battery cells for Webasto to integrate. Webasto already offers battery packs for commercial vehicles that again can be packed together to serve various systems. The cooperation between the German and the Korean company aims to offer customized battery systems to manufacturers of commercial vehicles.

In December 2018, Daimler bought more than $20 billion in battery cells to support their electric vehicle plans. The company was planning a total of 130 electrified variants at Mercedes-Benz Cars by 2022, as well as electric vans, buses and trucks. The batteries were purchased from manufacturers such as China's CATL, South Korea's SK Innovation and Japan's Panasonic. However, to break the dependence on Asia, Stuttgart battery manufacturer Varta and the Fraunhofer Institute joined forces in a research partnership intended to lead into the manufacture of large-format lithium-ion batteries within Germany. The arrangement was backed by funding from the German state of Baden-Württemberg and in the European effort to target mass production of lithium-ion battery cells for electric cars. The German government had set aside one billion euros to support companies. In addition, Mercedes-Benz invested billions in a plan to convert six factories to electric vehicle production and so create a "global battery network" within the country.

Fuel Cells

Ballard Power Systems are now working with Weichai Power Co Ltd. of Weifang to support China's Fuel Cell Electric Vehicle (FCEV) market using Ballard's next-generation LCS fuel cell stack and power models for commercial truck applications in the Republic. Weichai has committed to building and supply at least 2,000 fuel cell modules for commercial vehicles in China.

An Australian-Israeli startup has innovated a water-based fuel it claims will offer zero emissions with a lower cost and greater range than current battery or fuel cell tech. Electriq-Fuel is 60 percent water, and releases hydrogen when it reacts with an onboard catalyst. The fuel cost is as low as 50 percent of other fuel types, and Fuel-Cell Electric Vehicles' total-cost-of-ownership is reduced by about 30 percent compared to other clean vehicles. Spent fuel is recaptured and taken to a plant for recycling. Electriq-Global (formerly Terragenic), based in Tirat Carmel, Israel, is claiming that their potentially revolutionary hydrogen on-demand technology enables 15 times (x15) the energy density of standard automotive batteries and with only a few minutes of refueling time which would be done at a pump, much like a car powered by fossil fuels or conventional gaseous hydrogen for fuel cell vehicles. The fuel is liquid-stable, non-flammable, non-explosive and safe at ambient pressure and temperature. The technology includes a patented hydrogen liquid carrier type fuel (T-Fuel™), a process for producing and recycling the fuel (T-Pot™), and a catalyst that allows hydrogen to be extracted on demand (T-Cat™).

Its inventor, Dr. Alex Silberman, having studied electrochemistry in the Ural, moved to Israel, where he started his applied research on borohydride in 2006. Three years later, he cracked the kinetics (fast release of hydrogen) process, the stability of the solution and the recycling of the spent fuel. He patented the controlled generation, storage and transportation of hydrogen for mobility in 2009. He also patented the catalyst that released the hydrogen from the solution quickly enough. Silberman added another patent for the second-generation hydrogen solution with double the energy content.

Electriq-Global first tested its Electriq~Fuel technology with a hydrogen e-bike. The fuel cell was mounted on the rear. But there was no pressure tank for the hydrogen. Instead, the e-bike had a small plastic fuel tank and a metal vessel that generated hydrogen from the liquid. Additional studies the company conducted showed a transport bus covered 621 miles on a single tank compared to an electric bus's 155-mile range. The same technology could also be used in trucks. The company plans to commission its first fuel recycling plant in Israel in 2019. In April 2019, it plans for samples of its next-generation of the fuel. Total commercialization of the fuel has a targeted 2022 release date, likely at a small scale in either Israel or Australia.

Solar power

While it is unlikely that photovoltaic energy will play a major part in the propulsion of electric trucks, it will certainly provide supplementary power.

In 1998, the Solar Car Corporation in Melbourne, Florida, equipped its S-10 Chevrolet pickup Electro-Chevy with a solar panel to supplement its electrical system. Alkè XT was founded in 1992 by Achille Salvan in Padua, northeast Italy. Their 6 kW CargoHopper II solar delivery trucks are in use for deliveries of up to 2.5 tons (2,500 kg) around the historic center of Utrecht city and have a maximum range of 37 mi (60 km). This Alkè vehicle is designed for the delivery of packages and is able, in a working day, to do the work of five to eight standard vans in areas where gas-engined vehicles are not permitted. It continues with deliveries to shops, then once empty, it collects from shops dry waste, in particular paperboard, paper and empty packaging, for recycling in order to take advantage of the homeward journey. The three trailers are driven on both axles, giving the vehicle great maneuverability. It is a completely ecologically sound vehicle.

VIA Motors in Utah and Mexico have produced the "XTRUX," or X-Truck extended-range electric pickup. This is essentially a 4 × 4 Escalade Class-S SUV converted to hybrid-electric drive that comes in two models, averages about 100 miles per gallon (160 kmpg) and can drive approximately the first 40 miles (64 km) in all-electric mode. The XTRUX has 800 horsepower in two 402-horsepower electric motors, and a 5.3-liter Chevrolet V-8 engine. VIA Motors' business plan is to take big General Motors vehicles like the Chevy Silverado and "electrify" them by turning them into plug-in hybrid utility vehicles. VIA also extends the mileage of these trucks by covering them with industrial-grade 800- or 400- watt solar panels. The panels help power the car's battery and even power tools hooked up to the truck's outboard power outlet. Parking the truck in the sun all day can add up to six (with the 400-watt model) and ten (800-watt) miles of range (10–16 km) to the battery pack.

Finally, Shell Lubricants, working with Robert Sliwa of the AirFlow Truck Company in Newington, Connecticut, have created a "hyper fuel-efficient" semi-truck called the Starship. It has a nose more resembling a high-speed train made of carbon fiber, a streamlined body and an aerodynamic boat tail for streamlined airflow and drag reduction. The trailer also has a 5,000-watt solar array, which helps power electrical components. Underneath the sleek bodywork sits a Cummins X15 six-cylinder diesel engine, rated at 400 horsepower and 1,850 pound-feet of torque. The engine uses Shell Rotella T6 Ultra 5W-30, a new low-viscosity, fully synthetic oil, and is mated to an Eaton 18-speed automated manual transmission. The engine and transmission have been calibrated to run at speeds as low as 800 rpm, which Shell claims will improve efficiency and pulling power. In April 2018, Starship appeared at the Shell Eco-Marathon at Sonoma Raceway. The following month the Starship made a six-day 2,300-mile (3,701 km) journey across southern United States from San Diego, California, to the Jacksonville Convention Center in Florida. The truck achieved 178.4 ton-miles per gallon for freight ton efficiency while the average North American freight ton efficiency is 72 ton-miles per gallon. AirFlow and Shell also plan to install a hybrid system in the Starship, by replacing the tractor's non-driven rear axle with a new axle that sports an integrated electric motor. The motor will provide a power boost on hills, and will get its energy from an onboard battery pack. Energy will be harvested during braking. Cummins, which built the Starship's engine, has also demonstrated an all-electric truck.

In a similar way that this sustainable power source is being used at airports around the world, solar has also been seen as an advantage for truck recharging depots. In Amsterdam, a fleet of eight electric trucks in service for the brewer Heineken, as deployed by carrier Simon Loos, run on electricity that is generated by solar panels located on the roof of their distribution

Shell International's Starship truck, built by AirFlow Truck Company in Newington, Connecticut, is not merely aerodynamic; its trailer has a 5,000-watt solar array, which helps power electrical components (Shell International).

center in the city. Due to a load capacity of five tons (5,000 kg) and a range of up to 75 mi (120 km), they are ideal for urban distribution. By 2020, Heineken is planning to make full use of zero emissions transportation for its hospitality and distribution in all major cities in the Randstad (Amsterdam, Rotterdam, Utrecht, and The Hague).

In 2009, Minneapolis–St. Paul International Airport installed ten 1 kW AeroVironment wind turbines on top of the airport fire station to harness the power of prevailing northwest winds. The turbines generated 10 kilowatts of electricity an hour and have since been used to recharge their fleet of Cushman utility vehicles.

Tesla is partnering with PepsiCo's Frito-Lay to design a new "near zero-emission" distribution facility that will involve a whole fleet of Tesla Semi electric trucks, along with a few other electric vehicles, a charging system, some Tesla energy storage systems and a solar array. The project is part of the California Air Resources Board and San Joaquin Valley's effort to reduce air pollution, which has been a real issue in the region.

Voice Control—Silence Not Preferable

For centuries, packs of horses and mules towing wagons had heard the command of their drivers ("Whoa" or "Woah!"). For voice control of trucks,

Mercedes-Benz User Experience (MBUX) developed a system powered by the SoundHound Houndify platform and activated by saying "Hey Mercedes," while BMW launched an assistant that can respond when you say you're tired.

The Bosch voice assistant "Casey" uses a similar principle. It recognizes commands in 30 different languages and is trained to understand natural speech patterns. It can also be renamed, meaning that drivers can finally name their own car. Ford Motor announced that owners of its cars would soon be able to use Amazon's Alexa voice-activated assistant in their vehicles. Drivers will be able to ask for a weather report, stream music from Amazon Music or add appointments to their calendars. They will also be able to use Alexa from home to start or unlock their cars remotely. But that's not enough for the Japanese manufacturer Nissan, which is why it wants to literally read the driver's thoughts by tapping into their brain waves with so-called "brain-to-vehicle" technology. The system should be able to predict movements for braking and steering and thus be able to implement them more quickly.

In November 2016, *The Verge* journalist Andrew J. Hawkins reported, "Electric cars are now required to make noise at low speeds so they don't sneak up and kill us."

In the United Kingdom, the Locomotive Acts of 1865 required self-propelled vehicles to be led by a pedestrian waving a red flag or carrying a lantern to warn bystanders of the vehicle's approach. "Firstly, at least three persons must be employed to drive or conduct such locomotive, and if more than two wagons or carriages be attached thereto, an additional person must be employed, to take charge of such wagons or carriages. Secondly, one of such persons, while any locomotive is in motion, shall precede such locomotive on foot by not less than sixty yards, and shall carry a red flag constantly displayed, and shall warn the riders and drivers of horses of the approach of such locomotives, and shall signal the driver thereof when it shall be necessary to stop, and shall assist horses, and carriages drawn by horses, passing the same."[12]

In his research, this author came across an uncorroborated report of how, in the early 1900s, the driver of an electric vehicle in New York City had been tried for a double manslaughter. He had run over an unsuspecting pedestrian and reversed only to run over a second unsuspecting pedestrian. When in the 1980s, those of us promoting the Electric Boat Association attempted to persuade narrowboat owners on the British Canal System to convert to silent electric power, the owners complained that they would no longer enjoy the "dugga-dugga-dugga" of their Gardener or Lister oil engine. We suggested that they take an audio-cassette player on board with them which would play the familiar sound they feared missing. We were, of course, only joking.

For 20 years the objective has always been to make trucks quieter. Now things are in part too quiet and EVs are obliged to become louder again. Beginning in summer 2019, electric and hybrid-fuel cars, as well as scooters and motorcycles, in the USA are required to produce noise when traveling at low speeds under a new rule issued by the U.S. National Highway Traffic Safety Administration. This is to prevent these vehicles from injuring pedestrians, especially people who are blind or visually impaired. The new rule requires all newly manufactured electric vehicles 10,000 pounds (4,500 kg) or less, including motorcycles, to make an audible noise when traveling forward or in reverse at speeds of 19 mph (30 kph) or less. NHTSA says the sound alert is not required at higher speeds because other factors, such as tire and wind noise, "provide adequate audible warning to pedestrians." It doesn't explain what kind of alert automakers use, so whether it's a fake engine noise or a "beeping" noise will be up to the manufacturers of electric vehicles.

Psycho-acousticians at the Technical University of Munich (TUM) are building up the comparing sounds. It should sound like a motorcycle—yet not precisely the same as a gas motorcycle. In spite of the fact that playing a tune isn't permitted, the nature of the sound is up to the makers, who have already been working on the challenge for almost a decade. Advanced technology cars available in the market with manually activated electric warning sounds for automobiles include the Nissan Leaf, Chevrolet Volt, Honda FCX Clarity, Nissan Fuga Hybrid/Infiniti M35, Hyundai Sonata Hybrid, and the Toyota Prius (Japan only).[13]

There are different approaches to this problem. ECTunes is developing a system that utilizes directional sound equipment to emit noise when and where it is needed. According to the company, its technology sends audible signals only in the direction of travel, thus allowing the vehicle to be heard by those who may be in its path. On the other hand, SoundRacer AB of Sweden have presented their Electric Vehicle Electronic Engine Sound System which uses only real engine sound recordings as the base for the sounds it emits.

In 2016, Volvo equipped its electric buses with a "Honk at Them" system that monitors the road ahead, and if it detects somebody in its path, it sounds an alert, similar to the beeping sound made by a reversing bus or truck. It also sounds an alert inside the cab, along with a flashing light, to wake up the driver. If the pedestrian still doesn't get the message, the bus honks at them. This meets the minimum noise level demands introduced for all electrified vehicles in the EU in July 2019, even when traveling at slow speeds. The "Acoustic Vehicle Alerting Systems" requirements shall ensure that only adequate sound-generating devices are used. As one example, the all-electric yellow school buses which went into service at White Plains, New

York, must regularly play a four-tone melody for safety as they roam the streets. Schoolchildren are calling them "singing buses."

According to the rule, automakers will be required to have 50 percent of their electric car fleets equipped with the technology to create low-level noise by September 2019. That percentage goes up to 100 percent, or all EV cars on the road, in 2020. With the rules in place, automakers are now required to install at least one external speaker on electric and hybrid vehicles to emit a constant sound that is recognizable as "a motor vehicle in operation" at speeds below 30 kph, or 18.6 mph. This particular rule has been reviewed and confirmed by the Department of Transportation. As such, automakers will need to take the new rule into account when they're developing their hybrid and electric vehicles. That said, the rule only applies to light-duty cars and trucks with a gross vehicle weight rating of under 10,000 pounds.

Cycle Trucks

As I chronicled in my book *Electric Motorcycles and Bicycles*,[14] electrically assisted or pedelec cargo delivery bicycles have been around for a century. In 2010, Sparta of Apeldoorn, Netherlands, launched their E-Kargo while Markus Riese and Heiko Müller of Darmstadt launched their Delite pedelec cargo bike. Neil Saiki, the founder of Zero Motorcycles, having developed the Lifetime Rebuildable Battery Technology, whereby a new battery can be rebuilt if the lithium ion cells go bad, innovated the LockerCycle, a 2 × 4 electric cargo bike with a carrying capacity of 100 lbs. of groceries, a top range of 40 miles and an innovative front-axle steering system. The company logo featured a simple six-petal design from the Saiki family crest. The bike had a USB charger for GPS or cellphones. The following year, Saiki produced the NTS SunCycle where the solar panel with a rated power of 60 watts was on top of the cargo carrier.

In January 2018, the City of London Corporation's Environment Committee announced that a cargo bike scheme run jointly with zero-emission delivery operator Zedify formed from established cargo bike delivery companies Recharge Cargo and Outspoken Delivery who currently provide services across six UK cities, would be rolled out to all local businesses in the Smithfield and Farringdon areas. Couriers would use electric cargo pedelecs and trikes with load capacities of 100 and 250 kg (220 and 550 lb.) to make deliveries to and from a hub located at West Smithfield. The cargo bikes could drop the goods off anywhere within the Congestion Charge zone. The aim is to fill a gap diesel vans may leave as running one through the city center is becoming increasingly costly.

In January 2019, at the Consumer Electronics Show, the German auto supplier Schaeffler unveiled their bio-hybrid, a four-wheel bicycle with electric assist. There are two versions for cargo and passengers, sharing a modular platform. Its four wheels give the concept exceptional driving stability, the company says. Another vehicle being showcased in Las Vegas is sort of a miniature pickup truck. The modular body allows the bio-hybrid to serve as a refrigeration vehicle, coffee shop or locked stowage compartment.

Trucking by Hyperloop

In 1799, George Medhurst, a clockmaker of London, conceived of and patented his "Aeolian" atmospheric railway, a wind pump for compressing air to obtain motive power that could convey people or cargo through pressurized or evacuated tubes. In his pamphlet on the properties, power, and application of the Aeolian engine, with a plan and particulars for carrying it into execution, Medhurst proposed the establishment of Aeolian truck services, operated by pumping stations along the route. A hundred years later, in 1904, Robert Goddard, as a freshman at Worcester Polytechnic Institute in the United States, proposed a "vactrain" for very-high-speed rail transportation. Another hundred years later, in 2013, Tesla electric sports car maker Elon Musk re-invented the vactrain calling it Hyperloop. It incorporates reduced-pressure tubes in which pressurized capsules, traveling at up to 620 mph, ride on air bearings driven by linear induction motors and axial compressors. Musk proposed a route running from the Los Angeles region to the San Francisco Bay Area, roughly following the Interstate 5 corridor. An agreement was signed in 2017 to co-develop a Hyperloop line between Seoul and Busan in South Korea.

Although Musk referred to the transportation of people in automobiles, before long the advantage of Hyperloop could be seen for ultra-speed trucking. One such cargo Hyperloop would connect Hunchun in northeastern China to the Port of Zarubino, near Vladivostok, and the North Korean border on Russia's Far East. In 2018, British architecture practice Foster + Partners teamed up with Virgin Hyperloop One and Dubai-based transport and infrastructure company DP World to imagine a Hyperloop system devoted to cargo transportation at DP World's flagship port of Jebel Ali in Dubai. Hyperloop would form a backbone of a fully integrated transport chain that could also include autonomous delivery drones. Automated warehouses would be an interface between different modes of cargo delivery. Foster + Partners propose to use renewable energy sources, like solar, to power the Hyperloop network and claim that the system could operate at "the cost of trucking and the speed of flight." To develop the pod, Musk's SpaceX developed a competition that drew hundreds of entrants. The main two, TU Delft in the Netherlands and WARR of Munich University, have built up speeds of over 400 kph. The ultimate target would be 1,000 kph.

Other firms are developing their version of hyperloop. TransPod Inc. in Toronto, Canada, will use fully electric propulsion with zero need for fossil fuels. To achieve fossil-fuel-free propulsion, TransPod "pods" take advantage of electrically driven linear induction motor technology, with active real-time control and sense-space systems. The cargo transport TransPod pods will be able to carry payloads of 10–15 tons and have compatibility with wooden pallets, as well as various unit load devices such as LD3 containers and AAA containers. Following its U.S. $15 million seed round, TransPod is opening offices in Canada, Italy, and France to position the company for increased global growth as it focuses on producing a commercially viable product by 2020.

When 45th U.S. President Donald Trump announced that fuel-efficiency regulations for cars and light trucks set by former President Obama were too stringent and must be revised, a process sought by the U.S. auto industry began to roll back anti-pollution targets. In August 2018, California and 18 other U.S. states promised to fight the proposal, arguing the United States has an obligation to protect the environment for future generations. They announced they would sue to halt the proposed rollback, touching off what will likely be a heated legal showdown, possibly making it to the Supreme Court. It could also become a polarizing issue in future elections. "The Trump Administration has launched a brazen attack, no matter how it is cloaked, on our nation's Clean Car Standards," said California's attorney general, Xavier Becerra, quoted in *Reuters*, August 2, 2018. California "will use every legal tool at its disposal" to defend strict standards, he said in a statement. Former EPA Administrator Scott Pruitt signaled that he wanted to freeze fuel-economy standards at 2020 levels, while Koch-funded groups are fighting EV incentives and blocking public-transit projects around the country. And low oil prices have kept gas prices down, which means American consumers are once again opting for SUVs and trucks.

There are numerous reasons why electric trucks may continue to take a backseat when private transportation fleets and for-hire carriers are developing their truck procurement strategies. Fuel economy, cost of investment, range and charging station infrastructure are at the top of the list of apprehensions for fleet managers.

In terms of electric or hydrogen fuel-cell trucks, only 4 percent of respondents said they are currently procuring these types of trucks, and 53 percent said they neither see the value nor will they consider the technology for at least another 10 years. Nearly a quarter of respondents (21 percent) also said they believe electric or hydrogen fuel-cell trucks will never be widely used for over-the-road operations. As for their reasons, 39.4 percent said they will not consider the technology because of limited fueling or charging station infrastructure, and 33.3 percent have concerns over the vehicle's range or distance.[15]

Yet in 2019 Bosch of Stuttgart (established in 1888) has predicted that one-quarter of commercial vehicles worldwide will be "electrically driven." Bosch also said the U.S. and Europe showed the greatest potential for hub-to-hub automation, or "driverless trucks shuttling between depots." To reach this future, Bosch is investing to develop products that embrace "electrification, automation and connectivity." It committed to hiring 5,000 more R&D associates by the end of the year.[16]

At the last hour of the COP 24 held in Katowice, Poland, in December 2018, with the disturbing rise in global temperatures of 1.5° C, despite reticence from the U.S., Saudi Arabia, Russia and Kuwait to do more than take note, a road map was agreed on in the final hour targeting zero net carbon emissions by 2045 and involving even greater investment in electric vehicles. South Korea's government planned to supply 1 million electric vehicles by 2021.

The United Kingdom and France planned to ban all new sales of petrol or diesel vehicles after 2040. Jian Liu of China emphasized the contribution electric vehicles (EVs) will make when he predicted 95 percent of Chinese vehicles will be EVs, PHEVs (plug-in hybrids) or fuel cell powered by 2050 and that electricity would meet more than half the nation's power demand.

As nearly all types of transport—airplanes, drones, ships, boats, buses, tractors and trucks—enter this challenging, disruptive new era, the increasing cross-fertilization from innovations in battery energy density, motors, management, recharging and driverless systems can only benefit all concerned, in a way that our pioneering ancestors never dreamed of. Time will tell.

Appendix A: Trolley Trucks and Electrified Roads

If a road truck picks up its electric energy from above or below, battery capacity is no longer a problem.

To understand trolley trucks or trackless railways we must look at the origins of streetcars. Ernst Werner von Siemens engineered Eleketromote, the first trolleybus, in 1882. During the first half of the 20th century, and especially from the 1930s, the streetcar was a success story. Around 1950, there were some 900 streetcar systems operating worldwide. A large share of these were done away with in the 1960s and 1970s, mostly to the advantage of private cars and diesel buses.

German engineer Max Schiemann was among the first engineers to develop a commercial trolleybus system for passengers at the turn of the 20th century; he also created some unique cargo systems. Born on September 10, 1866, in Wroclaw, Prussia, after studying electrical engineering at the Technical University (Berlin) Charlottenburg, Schiemann worked at Siemens & Halske in Berlin with electric trams: the Fa. Bachstein in Berlin and the Dresden tram. He then worked for Herrmann Bachstein, who had founded the Central Administration for Secundairbahnen in 1879, and the Dresdner Straßenbahn. In 1900, Schiemann founded his own engineering office in Dresden and in 1901 in Wurzen, together with Fritz Momber, he established a company for trackless railways, Geselschaftfürgleislose Bahnen Max Schiemann & Co.

The first system built by Schiemann and his company was the Bielatalbahn, a 1.7-mile (2.8 km) track in Sachsen. From that summer for the next four years, it carried both passengers and cargo (mainly for a paper factory). The Bielatalbahn infrastructure was reused to build part of a new line close to Leipzig: the Industriebahn Wurzen, where an exclusive cargo line was in operation from 1905 until 1928. It was 2.63 miles (4.23 km) long up to 1914, when an extra track was in use, and 2.15 miles (3.46 km) long afterward. The cargo

Between 1905 and 1928, German engineer Max Schiemann's trackless trolley trucks, or "Bielatalbahns," were not only used in Sachsen, Altona and Hamburg, but in France (Lyon-Charbonnières), Italy (Pirona), Norway (Drammen) and England (Leeds, Bradford) (Kris De Decker).

system consisted of two trolley trucks, ten wagons for coal transport, each with a capacity of six tons, and 27 wagons for flour transport, each with a capacity of five tons. Each truck had a power output of 25 hp and could pull a maximum of three wagons with a total weight of 15 tons.

The most successful (and most remarkable) trolley truck network designed and constructed by Schiemann was the Hafenschleppbahn in Altona, today an area in Hamburg. The road from the port to the town was so steep that horses had severe difficulty climbing it. Trolley truck technology came to the rescue, but the electric trucks on the 0.6 mile (1 km) long track up and down did not replace the horses. The trucks were used as an assisting power source. The trolley truck pushed or pulled one or more horse cars, while other wagons (handcarts included) were also attached to the convoy. Fees were collected during the trip. The service was initially exploited by the Gesellschaft für gleislose Bahnen Max Schiemann & Co., but from 1922 it was run by the town of Altona, and later by the city of Hamburg. Other trackless railways were built by Schiemann's companies in Blankensee near Mecklenburg, also in France (Lyon-Charbonnières), Italy (Pirona), Norway (Drammen) and England (Leeds, Bradford).

Trams and trackless cars shared common overhead lines 1910. Contemporaries of Schiemann, building or experimenting with trolley truck systems, were Werner von Siemens, Hans-Ludwig Stoll and Lloyd-Köhler in Germany, Lombard et Guérin, Carl Stoll and Charles Nithard in France and E. Cantono in Italy, though World War I slowed down the further development of trolley systems. Trolley trucks were used in Gümmenen and Mühleberg, Switzerland, between 1918 and 1922 during the construction of the dam that retains Lake Wohlen. The trucks were built by Tribelhorn, and they used the Stoll system of current collection.

The Valtellina trolley system was built in 1938 and operated until 1962 by AEM (Milano Power Company), the owner of hydro-electric power plants in Valtellina. A total of 20 trolley trucks were used to carry concrete, sand and equipment for construction of the San Giacomo and Cancano II dams in the high Valtellina valley in northern Italy. The electric power was (and still is) sent to Milan to supply the needs of the city. Trolley trucks were used in St. Lambrecht, Austria, by the Nobel Industries' dynamite factory from November 16, 1945, to April 21, 1951. Trolley trucks were used to carry dynamite over the Alps just after World War II due to the shortages of material that for a time prevented the use of diesel trucks.

In 1941, in the USSR, the first converted trolley trucks appeared on the streets of a Moscow in the ruins after bombing. The cargo trolleybus, unlike the passenger trolleybus, should have some degree of autonomy—the ability to move away from the contact network for at least several kilometers. Consequently, 20 years later, 12 prototype 7-tonner trolley trucks were manufactured by SVARZ TG1. Their battery was automatically charged when operating under the contact network, although the trolley truck could only be away from that contact for a limiting distance of 1.86 mi (3 km). Because of the rapid aging of the batteries, their heavy weight (about three tons/3,000 kg) and low speed of 12–16 mph (20–25 kph), the first batch were excluded from the inventory and transferred to other Soviet cities.[1]

Revival

The trolley truck system has begun its revival in the second decade of the 21st century, by none other than Max Schiemann's former employer, Siemens, who installed an overhead pantograph-equipped e-Highway on the north- and south-bound sections of Alameda Street where it intersects with Sepulveda Boulevard in Carson, California. Supervised by the South Coast Air Quality Management District (SCAQMD), this two-mile (3.2 km) stretch of road is in the area served by the two largest U.S. Ports of Los Angeles and Long Beach, California. When the three Mack trucks (a battery-electric truck, a natural gas-augmented electric and a diesel-hybrid truck) are traveling the e-Highway, they can run on diesel, compressed natural gas (CNG), battery or other energy source. Demonstration runs began in November 2017. Siemens is hoping to propose a longer test route on the 710 freeway, which is wall-to-wall with trucks from those Californian ports to inland distribution centers.

Sweden's target of achieving independence from fossil fuel by 2030 requires a 70 percent reduction in the transport sector. For several years, the Swedish Transport Administration has been working on two test projects involving heavy-duty trucks that receive electricity outside the vehicle. One of these, a trolley truck system, is located on 1.2 mi (2 km) of Highway E16 near the city of Gävle in Sandviken. The pantograph system feeds 750 volts DC to a Scania G 360 truck's hybrid biofuel-electric system, while the stretch of road includes posts that are about 200 feet (61 meters) apart. The special trucks can connect at speeds as fast as 56 mph (90 kph). The testing system is operated by a partnership between Scania and Region Gävleborg. The system went into operation with a fleet of trucks on June 22, 2016. The Swedish government began talks with Berlin about a future network.

VW began partnering with Siemens on a pilot project in 2019. Volkswa-

Since 2017, Siemens' e-Highway system is being trialed by trucks both in California and Sandviken (Siemens AG).

gen will supply trucks from its Swedish Scania division, while Siemens will build the hardware to collect electricity from overhead wires. The German environmental ministry has given the green light for the eHighway pilot. Two Scania trucks will be used with different electrification voltages on the hybrid motor on three different test tracks in Germany: sections of Germany's A5 autobahn south of Frankfurt, followed by sections of the A1, near Lübeck, as well as the B442 highway near Gaggenau.

Electrified Roads

On October 11, 1884, the last day of the Edinburgh International Forestry Exhibition, Austrian-born inventor Henry Bock Binko fitted the steam-electric propulsion system from his exhibition railway into an ordinary horse car and ran it along the street from the exhibition gates to the Haymarket railway station, a distance of about 700 yards. The tramcar picked up the current via a wheeled collector running along two lines of copper plate laid between the tracks. It worked as a one-off trial but was completely unsuitable for wider work on street tramways with its dangerously exposed live electrics. Binko was already seriously in debt and one month later he was declared bankrupt.

The concept of electric vehicles using energy transmitted wirelessly was also considered by the visionary Nikola Tesla. But it was not until 1972 that Don V. Otto, professor of electrical engineering at the University of Auckland, New Zealand, tested a small trolley powered by induction at 10 kHz. Six years later, J.G. Bolger, F.A. Kirsten, and S. Ng at Lawrence Berkeley Laboratory, Berkeley, California, made an electric vehicle powered with a system at 180 Hz with 20 kW. The paper they delivered on March 28, 1978, at the Vehicular Technology Conference held at Arlington Heights, Illinois, reported:

A Dual Mode Electric Transportation (DMET) system is under development in which energy is electromagnetically transferred from a powered roadway to moving vehicles. Energy from the roadway can be used for high-speed, long-range travel and for replenishing energy stored in the vehicle in batteries or flywheels. The stored energy is then available for short-range travel off the powered highway network.

Indeed, U.S. patent 4,007,817, taken out by Bolger, is titled "Roadway for supplying power to vehicle and method of using the same."

Thirty years later, in 2009, Gunnar Asplund of Solna, Sweden, an engineer and inventor specializing in High Voltage Direct Current (HVDC), set up a company called Elways to develop systems for supplying vehicles with electricity while in motion, more simply known as an "electrified road." Backed by Sweden's state-owned energy provider Vatenfall, by 2012, an initial total of 656 feet (200 meters) of electrified road had been installed along Test Track 2 in Driveland, near Arlanda, Stockholm. This was increased to 1,148 ft. (350 m) by 2014 and 1,312 ft. (400 m) by 2017. The innovations made by Asplund for eRoadArlanda took his score to 52 individual patents, 187 in total and among his awards, finalist for the Prix de l'Inventeur Européen. By 2018, eArlanda, linking Stockholm Arlanda airport to a logistics site outside the capital city about 35 miles (56 km) north, had grown to about 1.2 miles (2 km) of electric rail embedded in a public road. The electrified road is divided into 164 ft. (50 m) sections, with an individual section powered only when a vehicle is above it. When a vehicle stops, the current is disconnected. The system is able to calculate the vehicle's energy consumption, which enables electricity costs to be debited per vehicle and user. The "dynamic charging," as opposed to the use of roadside charging posts, means the vehicle's batteries can be smaller, along with their manufacturing costs. A former diesel-fueled truck owned by the logistics firm PostNord was the first to use the road. In Sweden there are roughly 311,000 miles (half a million kilometers) of roadway, of which 12,427 mi (20,000 km) are highways. The distance between two highways is never more than 28 mi (45 km) and electric vehicles can already travel that distance without needing to be recharged. Some believe it would be enough to electrify 3,100 mi (5,000 km).

In Malvern, a suburb of Philadelphia, since 2009, Andrew Daga and a team at Momentum Dynamics have developed a 5-minute wireless recharging system for electric vehicles in which energy is transferred from a panel embedded in the pavement, through the air, into an EV. Daga, who was trained as an architect and an aerospace engineer, got the idea for EV charging after participating in an Air Force study on wireless power transfers for orbital spacecraft when he saw potential applications for terrestrial motor vehicles. He and his cofounders, Jonathan Sawyer, vice president of product design, and the late Bruce Long, vice president of research and development, decided to aim at developing the technology to deliver high power, especially for the bus market, which they believed would be one of the first sectors to electrify on a big scale. Their system can also be applied to industrial vehicles such as forklifts or short-haul trucks in ports.

The trolley-truck system has also been revived for mining, again in Sweden. Located near the northern tip of Sweden is the Aitik mine, the largest open pit copper mine in the country. There, enormous Caterpillar 795F mining trucks as designed by Michael Betz, with tires 15 feet tall (4.5 m), haul 310-ton (310,000 kg) loads of rocks up steep inclines 24 hours a day, 365 days a year. The bottom of the mine is 1,500 feet (457 m) below the surface of the earth. Combined, a fleet of 30 trucks moves 70 million tons (70,000 million kg) of earth each year. From that total, 97,500 tons (99,065 kg) of copper are obtained, along with 2.9 tons (2,900 kg) of gold and 62 tons (62,000 kg) of silver. The mining trucks are marvels of modern engineering, but they have one drawback. Each one consumes over 100 gallons (380 liters) an hour of diesel fuel. To address that issue, Caterpillar is converting some of the trucks to run exclusively on electric power taken from overhead wires. Batteries large enough to supply the enormous amount of power needed would simply be too large and heavy to work on individual trucks, but putting the energy needed into overhead wires solves the problem. The overhead wiring is being constructed by ABB and Eitech, two companies with considerable experience building electrified railways and tram systems. The work is supported by a grant of $1.2 million (€1,025,992) from the Swedish Energy Agency. The Caterpillar 795F mining trucks are already powered by diesel electric powertrains, so converting them to exclusively electric power will be fairly straightforward and Caterpillar has already started on the conversions.

Initially, the electrified trucks will only be used to haul non-ore bearing rocks to a 200 foot (61 m) high area a half mile away, but if the system proves reliable and cost effective, it could be added to the road leading from the bottom of the mine. Such equipment has never been used in such harsh winter conditions before, so a "proof of concept" period of time is needed to make sure the trucks will not break down on the way up or down, which could bring the entire mining operation to a halt. Each truck will be capable of handling up to 4.75 megawatts of power. With that much energy on tap, they can actually move twice as fast as the diesel electric trucks in use today, which struggle to reach ten miles per hour (16 kph) on the uphill climb from the bottom. Faster speeds could lead to significantly higher production from the mine, leading to more revenue for the operators. Economics is the principal reason to make the switch to all electric power, but eliminating the emissions from 30 diesel powered trucks burning 100 gallons of diesel fuel an hour (380 liters) into the pristine atmosphere near the Arctic Circle is a benefit the entire world can celebrate.

Appendix B: Speed Records

In my previous histories of electric boats, aircraft and motorcycles, I have always reserved a place for speed records—so why not do the same for electric trucks?

One of the thousands of milkmen driving British-built delivery e-trucks was Alfred "Benny" Hawthorne, working for James Hann of Dorset Dairies, Eastleigh. Hill would later become a famous comedian and among his songs was "Ernie, the Fastest Milkman in the West," an innuendo-laden comedy or novelty song, originally written in 1955 as the introduction to an un-filmed screenplay about Hill's milkman experiences. The song was first performed on television in 1970, and released as a successful recording, topping the UK Singles Chart in 1971, reaching the Christmas number one spot. Ironically, Ernie's milk cart was horse drawn.

In fact, Guinness World Records has a category for the fastest average speed that a truck powered by electricity can achieve over one mile (1.6 km) from a standing start.

On August 27, 2003, two teams met at Bruntingthorpe Aerodrome in Leicestershire for a competition to set the first World Milk Float Land Speed Record. CBL Electric Vehicles of Bampton, Oxfordshire, were the brains behind the Electric Dream Team, led by driver Daniel Hoffmann-Gill from Nottingham. Their vehicle was a Morrison Electricar dating from the 1950s, with a much-altered driveline and control equipment, extra cell packs and safety equipment. Called the Electric Blue, this milk float was made in Birmingham in 1969 (as a Morrison Type F) and refitted with batteries supplied by Chloride Motive Power. The opposition came from EV engineering firm VXL Automotive, a subsidiary of Symonds Hydroclean, based near Newport, Gwent. Their entry was a development vehicle for their latest model, the Electron E150. It was powered by a 12000 rpm AC motor and featured rapid exchange battery packs to allow near continuous use. Design consultancy was provided by Bluebird Automotive Group Ltd. of Swansea. The winner was the VXL float with a recorded average speed of 73.39 mph (118.12 kph); the CBL float managed an average of just 47.61 mph (76.62 kph), although the maximum recorded was around 52 mph (84 kph). It had, in fact, achieved higher speeds on test, but most unfortunately had caught fire a few days before the event, and had not been quite the same since. The belts driving the pulleys also proved troublesome, with noticeable slipping taking place.

In 2013, eBay Motors challenged British Touring Car Championship star Tom Onslow-Cole and TV motoring expert Edd China to transform an electric milk float into a high performance speed machine using only parts and accessories purchased on eBay Motors; the result was a hi-speed float, piloted by Onslow-Cole, who reached 77.53 mph (124.78 kph) at the Transport Research Laboratory, for the fastest milk float, according to the World Record Academy. Tom and Edd worked with the eBay Motors team of race engineers to develop the vehicle; this even included fitting a V8 engine from an old ambulance and a using a milk churn as a fuel tank. This was of course not a purely electric record.

In another class, in June 2011, a 2100 bhp D16 Volvo diesel/electric power-

In 2016, Boije Ovebrink drives the Volvo *Iron Knight,* equipped with special Goodyear tires, down the single runway of the former Skellefteå airfield in Sweden to record an average speed of 131.29 kph (81.58 mph) and a time of 13.71 seconds over 500 m (1,640 ft.). This breaks the record with the special Goodyear tires (Goodyear-Dunlop pp).

train called *Mean Green* was driven by 1994 European Truck Racing Champion Boije Ovebrink and established its first records of 135.943 mph (218.780 kph) for the flying kilometer at Hultsfred Airport in Sweden. It was then taken out to Wendover Airfield, Utah, where sanctioned by the United States Auto Club, it raised the flying kilometer record to 147.002 mph (236.577 kph) and the standing start record to an average 95.245 mph (153.252 kph). This is an enormous feat of acceleration for the motor which produces 6,780 N-m (5,000 lb-ft) torque, of which, 1,200 N-m (885 lb-ft) of torque comes from the 200 bhp electric motor. The same Volvo hybrid drive system is being used by hundreds of Volvo buses throughout the world.

Records are there to be broken or raised. Volvo's next step was to custom-build *Iron Knight,* a five-ton (5,000 kg) fiberglass cab, 2,205 lb. (1,000 kg) lighter than *Mean Green* and with 600 hp (447 kW) more power. In June of 2016, Boije Ovebrink took the e-truck *N°26* out on the single runway of the former Skellefteå airfield, Sweden, and recorded an average speed of 81.58 mph (131.29 kph) and a time of 13.71 seconds over 1,640 ft. (500 m) and 105 mph (169 kph) with a time of 21.29 seconds over 3,281 ft. (1,000 m), both from a standing start. Zero to 62 mph (100 kph) took 4.6 seconds.

One wonders whether an e-truck will ever average 200 mph (322 kph).

Appendix C: Antique and Classic Truck Conservation

Like any other form of transport, antique and classic (or veteran and vintage) electric trucks have been saved and restored around the world. The following incomplete appreciation does not take into account individual e-trucks in private collections.

USA

Of his fine collection of e-trucks in Manchester, Pennsylvania, Jay K. Crist explains:

I have been around cars and trucks from the time that I was able to ride with my Dad in a milk truck without someone holding me. My Dad and one of my uncles were owners of a family dairy, riding in a milk truck was almost our regular means of travel until my brother and I got our drivers' license and a car. From the time that I was still in elementary school and throughout my whole working career, I was around all kinds of vehicles and enjoyed keeping things running in top condition as well as taking things apart that didn't work and repairing them back to a working condition. My interest in vehicles hasn't changed and today I like to work on the restoration of vehicles from the past that have special meaning to me. One of my main interests is the searching for and the restoration of different types of milk truck that were known as "Stand & Drive" delivery trucks. The real fun comes when the trucks are restored and we can take them to Truck & Car Shows. There we can bring back memories to lots of people on how milk used to be delivered to the houses and also inform the younger folks of the way things were done in the past.[1]

Jay Crist's 1919 LA-10 Walker truck was owned by a man in Ohio for over 40 years. He painted the truck, installed new tires, replaced some wood panels and installed new batteries.

After we bought the truck and got it back to my shop to check out the truck, we found the body's wooden frame to be rotten and termite infested. Since wooden frames aren't easy to patch and weld like metal frames and because a lot of patch work had been done to the truck over the years of being in service, I had a local cabinet company make a new duplicate wooden body for the truck. All of the electric power components and wiring parts were replaced and/or restored. The electric motor is 3.5 HP (for its size it looks like it should be 30 HP to 40 HP). The control box has a shift lever (for forward and reverse directions). We had Motor Technology of York, Pa completely rebuild these two units to a like new condition. The manufacturer states that the truck can travel approximately 12 MPH for 30 to 35 miles on a hard and level road with a capacity of 36 cases of milk. To start the restoration process, we removed the wooden body from the chassis. The chassis was cleaned and sand blasted. We replaced parts of the frame that were rusted or missing. After all repairs were made to the frame and suspension, it was painted.

All of Jay Crist's restored "Stand & Drive" trucks have been lettered as milk trucks because he was in the dairy business. But since this was a 1919 truck, he decided to letter it in memory of his grandfather and father. The truck was shown at Antique Automobile Club of America meets in 2017. It has been awarded the Junior 1st Award, the Senior Award, received the 2017 AACA Cup Award, made the cover of the AACA July/August magazine, been

Jay Crist's Walker truck during its rebuild in Manchester, Pennsylvania, during 2008 (Jay Crist).

Jay Crist's fully restored Walker truck (Jay Crist).

featured as the "Vehicle for October" on the AACA 2018 calendar and was one of the 16 nominees for the 2018 AACA Zenith Award.

Of all the Walker Electric (battery operated) trucks built from 1907 to 1942, at the present time there are ten Walker Electric trucks known to be in existence. All ten of these trucks appear to be of different models. The International Electric Vehicle Museum in Kingman, Arizona, as organized by the Historic Electric Vehicle Foundation (HEVF), includes a 1912 CT truck loaned by Bob Oldfather. The I-80 Trucking Museum in Walcott, Iowa, has a 1911 Walker Model 43 formerly in service with Bowman's Dairies. Its 100th birthday was celebrated at the Walcott Truckers Jamboree in 2011. It also has an unrestored 1918 Walker. A 1918 Walker is displayed at the Thor Electric Truck company alongside their state-of-the-art Thor ET-One Class 8 li-ion truck in Los Angeles. A 1914 Walker used by the Dwinell-Wright Coffee Company in Chicago was photographed at Edaville Railroad in Carver, Massachusetts, circa 1966. A freight truck is displayed at the National Automotive and Truck Museum (NATMUS) in Auburn, Indiana. A 1921 Walker is on show at the Seashore Trolley Museum in Maine, which also has two big ice delivery trucks, plus a 1918 Walker truck for parts only. A 1918 Walker Model P 3.5-ton open cab version (serial number 1686) is on display at the Hays Antique Truck Museum at Woodland, California, alongside a 1916 C.T. Electric.

As an example of trucks kept in a private collection, one Commercial Truck Company Model A10 Standard, built in Philadelphia in 1912, had been used locally by the Curtis Publishing Company for more than 50 years to deliver *The Saturday Evening Post, Ladies' Home Journal,* and other publications to the post office and area newsstands, according to the seller's representative. Retired in 1964, it eventually came into the private collection of Carroll Hutton of Winfield, West Virginia. In 2018 Hutton sold it and his other antique vehicles to donate to a local children's charity.

A 1912 Westinghouse electric truck motor is exhibited at the Smithsonian Collection. An Edison Electric Company Electric Generator Truck made by Thomas Edison Industries of Orange, New Jersey, is on show at the Boyertown Museum in Boyertown, Pennsylvania, which claims to have the world's largest collection of electric vehicles. They also exhibit a Commercial Truck Company of America machine that served in the Curtis Publishing Company's fleet in New York City. A Ford Escort panel truck is sitting comfortably on the bed of the Commercial, to provide the visitor with a sense of scale and size.

General Motors tried to give their prototype 1966 Electrovan to the Smithsonian Institution, but they declined the vehicle for reasons that are still not clear. For years, the Electrovan sat in cold storage in a warehouse in Pontiac, Michigan, avoiding the crusher on several occasions. Then it was transported to the General Motors Heritage Center near Detroit. Recently, the GM Electrovan was taken for display and shown off at the Petersen Automotive Museum in Los Angeles, California.

Finally, a 1972 Battronic delivery van has been conserved. As is chronicled in Chapter Five, the Battronic Truck Corporation built electric trucks, vans and buses during the 1970s on the very location which now houses the museum. The Boyertown Museum's Battronic sports the colors of the Cinnaminson High School, which was known for several electric vehicle projects through the 1970s and '80s. Finally, a 1940s Divco Helms Bakery Truck is displayed at the Lyon Air Museum in Santa Ana, California.

Great Britain

The preservation of old trucks and buses in the British Midlands began in 1964. The veterans were kept in factory and farm yards, wherever a kindly soul could be found. Unfortunately, kindly souls would move on or local authorities turn unfriendly and the search would begin again for another home. Every so often ideas ran out and a vintage truck, priceless today, would have to be scrapped. To care for old trucks and buses, the Birmingham Omnibus Preservation Society was formed in 1973 and originally had to use such sites for its vehicles but realized it was no way to carry on. Another home was found in Wythall, Worcestershire, and a transport museum created.

Alongside its buses, due to the initiative of enthusiasts including Paul Gray, it has a collection of some 29 milk floats and other BEVs dating from 1935 to 1982 and representing 14 different manufacturers.

My background had nothing to do with vehicles. As a youngster I liked all forms of commercial road transport—local lorry fleets (Birmingham and Black Country), Midland Red, Birmingham City Transport, etc. Many years later, when our children were a bit older I fancied a small vehicle to work on for the museum. By chance I heard that a Wales & Edwards 3-wheeler was available. This ended up in the garage at home where the necessary work was undertaken—with the help of an experienced e.v. man. Prior to this, the first problem for us was how to move a 3-wheeler. I decided to approach its original owner—Handsworth (later Birmingham) Dairies. They were more than happy to move it, no cost, and then, after that offered us a Smiths milk truck that had just been withdrawn from service. It sort of snowballed from then on—the local Post Office workshops offered a Harbilt p.c.v., then the old Birmingham Co-op let us have an M-E which had started life as a bakery van and, like almost all such vehicles in the fleet, later converted to milk truck. This was rebuilt to original form with lots of help from the Co-op. Again, no transport or other costs were requested.

The Transport Museum Wythall has the finest collection of electric trucks and milk floats in the world (Wythall/de Astui).

Later, Unigate moved a derelict Midland (that was "found" in a factory) to the museum and then offered us one their standard M-E trucks, which again they delivered to the museum—no charge for anything. Unigate at Eastbourne donated the last surviving W&E artic. and again, delivered to museum gratis. We have paid for a few and met the transport costs, these are generally privately-owned vehicles. The local dairies (there are others not mentioned) were all very friendly, helpful and generous—we were rather lucky in that respect. I should also add that the other museum Trustees were happy (therefore supportive) to see the expansion of the e.v. collection. At the time (1986) there were very few such vehicles in the care of museums.[2]

Examples include the Lewis-designed Rider Pram (immensely popular in the London area), a Post Office parcels van, and a unique Victor; each has its story. The 1947 Brush 10/14 cwt (508/711 kg) was selected from a collection of battery-electric vehicles being disposed of by an enthusiast at Blandford, Dorset, in 1987, who also waived the purchase price.

The 1935 Electricar CY2 Airline van was used to deliver dairy products

Awaiting restoration. What remains of this 1947 10/14 cwt Brush truck was selected from a collection of battery electric vehicles being disposed of by an enthusiast in Blandford, Dorset, who waived the purchase price given its condition (Transport Museum Wythall).

for 20 years. During the next 32 years it was moved only once by its new owner to a barn in Nottinghamshire. Its exceptionally good and original condition is due to the fact that it was locked away, unnoticed and untouched for so long.

Thanks to the enthusiasm of Brian Dyes during the 1960s, there are five battery-electric road vehicles in the collection at the Ipswich Transport Museum in Suffolk: among them, a 1916 Ransomes, Sims and Jeffries 50 cwt (2,032 kg) Orwell truck (Registration DX 166) which was returned to Ransomes in December of 1919 and became part of their works fleet, numbered "1." It has been much rebuilt over its life, although it retains the original chassis layout with motors driving the front wheels. The original solid tires were changed to pneumatic and the original open cab was enclosed, although it has since been converted back to an open cab. It was withdrawn in 1963, placed on loan to an enthusiast in Southend, then returned to Ipswich in 1966. The museum also has an Ipswich Cooperative milk float, built in 1948, in service for 27 years, being withdrawn when it was donated to the museum. An Ipswich Cooperative coal truck, in service from 1951 to 1983, had been stored in the open, when it was presented to the Museum in 1989 where it is currently being restored.

In Dublin, Ireland, there is a Smith's electric milk float at the National Transport Museum, Howth Castle.

Alongside these important collections, various electric trucks are housed around the UK. One of the fleets of Walker trucks used by Harrods Ltd. Department Store in Knightsbridge, London, Y-29/1 remained in service until 1967 when, having covered about 350,000 miles (563,270 km), it was withdrawn from service and presented to the National Motor Museum in Beaulieu, Hampshire. When not exhibited there, it takes part in the annual London-to-Brighton run for veteran motor vehicles. Beaulieu also has a 1947 Brush Pony milk float operated by United Dairies Ltd. Another Walker was restored by Harrods before being presented to the Science Museum, London.

East Anglia Transport Museum at Carlton Colville, Suffolk, has a 1922 Ransomes electric tower wagon, a 1934 Electricar, a 1943 Ransomes forklift truck and a 1948 NCB milk float. Before it was closed in 2012, the Snibston Discovery Museum in Leicestershire housed a 1928 Electricar with wooden refuse collection body (now almost totally rotted away), originally supplied to Birmingham Salvage Department; this is now at the Abbey Pumping Station, Leicestershire, which also shelters two Harbilts: a 735 milk float and a 770 factory truck. The National Forklift Truck Museum in Derbyshire has a Harbilt 731 stacker pedestrian.

A conversion of a Royal Mail Harbilt PEDT used as a publicity vehicle for Postman Pat "and his black & white cat" was bought in UK and has finished up in the Dezer Collection of automobile oddities in Miami. When parcels were separated to Parcel Force, the PEDTs were redundant and the ingenious engineers converted many into publicity modules featuring Postman Pat. A Harbilt conversion was chosen for Dezer.

Aston Manor Road Transport Museum at Walsall houses one Wales & Edwards milk float. The Riverside Museum of Transport in Glasgow houses one Smith's Cabanac. The Kelham Island Museum in Sheffield exhibits a green 1940 "Crompton-style" Metrovick 18/22 S&E Cooperative milk float, originally in service until the 1990s for the Sheffield & Ecclesall Cooperative Society, after which it was used to move things around on the museum site.

The only one to have been preserved of the 72 Electricar DV4 4-ton (4,000 kg) refuse vehicles bought by the City of Birmingham between 1938 and 1948, Number 184 (Registration EOA 956) was in use until 1971 and is now at the Collections Centre of the Birmingham Museum of Science and Industry, which houses objects that are not currently on display. Their batteries were recharged with electricity generated from steam produced by burning the refuse which they collected.

One toy inspired by the full-scale electric milk floats described in Chapter Five was part of the Dinky Toy range, the brand name for die-cast Mazak zinc alloy miniature vehicles produced by Meccano Ltd. in Liverpool. In 1960, Dinky Toys launched the No. 490 electric milk float with "Express Dairy" livery and the No. 491 with NCB livery. In August 1960, Job's Dairy ordered 3,000 models of the toy, but blank, without the usual decals. The Job's Dairy decals were added at Jensen Transfers Division. Because of serious troubles with the very worn-out tooling, Meccano could only deliver 1,176 models. The transfers were applied individually, by hand, by the milk factory staff. The first examples were available to the staff themselves, and the rest were meant as presents for business relations. Still in their original boxes, such Dinky toys would become collector's items. A number of these were included in the North West Durham Collection of 999 toy cars which, valued at £100,000, went up for auction in 2013. The vendor, who did not wish to be identified, had started the collection some 60 years ago in the North East after he became interested in the public service and commercial cars and vans he saw on the streets as a child. The collection netted £134,000.

Australasia

In 1918, a Walker half-ton truck was exported to New Zealand where it entered into service for the Christchurch Electricity Network Company. One hundred years later, having been restored by Neville Digby at Orion New Zealand Ltd., it has become one of the most prized examples of motoring heritage in New Zealand.

A Lucas Bedford electric van was donated to Museums Victoria in Melbourne by Lucas Industries Australia in 1984. The museum's van is one of two such electric vans used during the 1982 Brisbane Commonwealth Games marathon. The other Lucas van is held by the Queensland Energy Museum. The museum's van was registered AUY585 and completed 3,157 miles (5,080 km) during the trial period, which ended in October of 1983. This included a month spent with Telecom as a line service vehicle in the Dandenong Ranges near Melbourne.

Europe

Like Walker, between 1926 and 1966 the Lyon-based company SOVEL built over one thousand e-trucks. At the beginning of the 1960s the city truck operator SLEVE bought land at Vaulx-en-Velin to begin to park electric trucks that had become obsolete. A hangar was built and a graveyard of over one hundred trucks accumulated there, awaiting demolition.

This 1918 Walker, restored by Neville Digby at Orion New Zealand Ltd., has become one of the most prized examples of motoring heritage in New Zealand (Digby Collection).

At the beginning of the 1960s, the Lyon city truck operator SLEVE bought land at Vaulx-en-Velin to begin to park electric trucks that had become obsolete. A hangar was built and a graveyard of more than 100 trucks accumulated there, awaiting demolition. Only a handful of SOVEL trucks have survived (Collection J-N Raymond).

Only a handful of SOVEL trucks have survived. Alongside the Berliet Museum, the Heavy Vehicle Museum at Montrichard has one AB delivery truck of 1940 in use until 1984 and then donated by the Poulain chocolate firm in 1984. A 1938 Sovel Poulain is also on show at the Dufresne Museum in Azay-le-Rideau in the Centre-Val-de-Loire region. A 1942 seven-tonner which had trucked for more than 50 years for a livestock food producer called Collet at Ramilly, restored in 1992, was donated to the Gambrinus Drivers Museum in Belgium in 1999. Collet still has three SOVELs while the city of Lyon has restored a SOVEL for their museum. In Germany a 1935 Hansa-Lloyd Werke AG "Electrolastwagen" is conserved at the Deutschen Technikmuseum in Berlin while a Hansa-Lloyd truck 1923 is also housed at the Auto und Technikmuseum, Sinsheim.

Appendix D: Electric Truck and Battery Builders (Past and Present)

TRUCKS

Alden Sampson
AM General
Anderson
Argo
Arrival
Artisan
Atlantic
Atlas Copco
Automatic Transportation
Bailey
Baker
Baker, Rauch & Lang
Battronic
Bergmann
Berliet
Borland
Brush
Bucyrus
BYD
Carter Paterson
Champion
Citroën
Cleco

Columbia
Commercial Truck
Crescent
Crochat
DAF
Daimler-Benz
DaimlerChrysler
De Dion et Bouton
Detroit Electric
Deutsche Eleketromobil
Diamond
Dodge
Einride
Electric Carriage and Wagon Company
Electric Vehicle Company
Electrix
Electro Mobile Co
Electruck
Elwell-Parker
Emoss Mobile
FDG
Fenwick
Fischer Equipment Company

Ford
Fritschle
Garrett and Sons
General Motors
General Vehicle
GGT
GMC Electrics
Goupil
Govecs
Grumman
Harbilt
Harrods
Hewitt-Lindstrom Motor Co
Sidney Holes
Isuzu
Jatco
Jeantaud
Jet Industries
Karsan Otomotive
Kenworth
Kreisel
Kriéger
Lansden, Lansing Bagnall
Laporte-Bergmann

Lektro
T.H. Lewis
Leyland
Linde
Lohner-Porsche
Maserati
Mercedes-Benz
Mercury
Metrovick
Midland
Mildé
MIP
Mitsubishi
Morrison-Electricar
NAMI
Nikola
Nissan
Nordco
Norddeutsche
Opel
Otis
Partridge, Wilson
Peterbilt
Peugeot
PVI
Ransomes, Sims &
  Jefferies
Renault
Republic Motor Vehicle
  Company
Riker Electric Motor
  Company
Satmé
SCEMT
Schiemann

Sebring-Vanguard
Siemens-Schuckert
Smith
SOVEL
STAE
Steinmetz
Still
StreetScooter
Studebaker
Tesla
Tevva
Thor
Tokyo Electric
Toledo
Tomlinson
Toyota
TransPower
Tribelhorn
Tropos
Universal Electric
  Carriage Syndicate
Urban
Vauxhall-Bedford
Vehicle Electric
  Company
Vetra
Victor
Volkswagen
Volvo
Wales & Edwards
Walker
Walter
Ward
Waverley
West Coast Machinery

Woods Motor Vehicle
  Company
Workhorse
Yale & Towne

BATTERIES

A.E.M.
Alkaline
Britannia
Chloride
DP
Edison
Electra
Electric Storage (Exide)
Exxon
Faure-Sellon-Volckmar
Fulmen
Liotech
Lucas
Oldham-Crompton
Ovonic
SAFT
Sony
Svenska Ackumulator
Tudor
Varta

MOTORS

Bosch
Cummins
Lundell
Siemens
Westinghouse

Chapter Notes

Prelude

1. "'World's Oldest Railway Tunnel' Awarded Protected Status," *BBC*, 19 March 2015.
2. Leonardo de Vinci, *Codex Atlanticus* Fol 812r.
3. Carl Lira, "Biography of James Watt" (2001), https://www.egr.msu.edu/~lira/supp/steam/wattbio.html.
4. "Pre-1825 locomotives-2," *Locos in Profile*, March 2008, https://web.archive.org/web/20080306101936/http:/www.locos-in-profile.co.uk/Articles/Early_Locos/early2.html.
5. Hunter Davies, *George Stephenson*, Weidenfeld & Nicolson (1975). The development of electric passenger carriers or omnibuses is narrated in a separate work: Kevin Desmond, *Electric Buses: A History*, McFarland (2019).
6. *The Manufacturer and Builder* IV (2): 32, February 1872.

Chapter One

1. W.H., letter to the editor, "Electromagnetism," *The Penny Mechanic and Chemist*, vol. 5, 1840.
2. "The American Railroad: Its Inception, Evolution and Results," *The National Magazine*, vol. 11, April 1890, 176.
3. Dr. Antony Anderson, *Robert Davidson, Pioneer of Electric Locomotion*, Scotland, Alford, The Grampian Transport Museum (2018).
4. Charles G. Page, M.D., "Magneto-Electric and Electro-Magnetic Apparatus and Experiments," *American Journal of Science*, vol. XXXV, 1839.
5. Information supplied by Pavel Yalyshev, the Saint Petersburg Museum of Transport.
6. Dieter Bäzold, Brain Rampp, and Christian Tietze, "Elektrische Lokomotiven deutscher Eisenbahnen" (Eisenbahn-Fahrzeug-Archiv; Bd. 4), Düsseldorf 1993.
7. Kevin Desmond, *Gustave Trouvé: French Electrical Genius*, McFarland (2015), 64.
8. Desmond, *Gustave* Trouvé, 58–60.
9. Henri de Parville, *The Official*, 20 April 1881.
10. L'AbbéMoigno, *Les Mondes*, 20 May 1881.
11. *The Electrician* (London), 27 May 1882, 28–29.
12. alondoninheritance.com/eventsandceremonies
13. *The Horseless Age*, vol. 1, no. 12, October 1896, 47.
14. "The Bersey Carriage," *The Automotor and Horseless Vehicle Journal*, November 1896.
15. Joseph Seymour Currey, and Juergen Beck, *Chicago, Its History and Its Builders*, vol. 4.
16. Г. Нартов, "Монорельс: Москва—Париж—Нью-Йорк," *Юный Техник* (1962), 46.
17. "The Riker Electric Delivery Wagon," *The Automotor and Horseless Vehicle Journal*, April 1899; "Some American Delivery Trucks," *The Automotor Journal* (1901).

18. K.R. Coker, and C.E. Rios, "A Concise History of the US Army Signals Corps," *SDTICD*, 1988.

19. Kevin Desmond, *Innovators in Battery Technology: Profiles of 95 Influential Electrochemists*, McFarland (2016), 64.

20. Thatcher's Milk Bottle, potsdampublicmuseum.org.

21. Hershey Company archives.

22. Kathryn Gemperle, "13-year-old Girl Wins Auto Race," *Edgewater Historical Society*, vol. XXVI, no. 2, Summer, 2015.

23. Abhilash Gaur, "Amex and Budweiser Rode on Electric Trucks 100 Years Ago," Lectronomy, Medium.com, 30 March 2017.

24. With Westinghouse Vehicle units.

25. Henry Francis Joel, "Electric Automobiles," *Minutes of the Proceedings of The Institution of Civil Engineers*, London, 1903.

26. "The Fischer 1-Ton Petrol-Electric Truck," *The Automotor Journal*, 21 March 1903.

27. D-03–01 *Selected Automobile—Edison TA Family*, Thomas Edison National Historical Park.

28. Catalog, *Westinghouse Motor Applications—Westinghouse Electric Vehicle Equipment Catalogue 3002-A Section 3223*: Senator John Heinz History Center, in association with the Smithsonian Institution, Pittsburgh, PA.

29. E114 *Edison General File. Battery Storage Delivery Wagons*: Thomas Edison National Historical Park.

30. E1310 *Battery Storage Delivery Wagon Endurance Tests*: Thomas Edison National Historical Park.

31. "Canadian Government Advertising Wagon," *The Commercial Motor*, 11 May 1905.

32. "An Interesting American Road Train," *The Commercial Motor*, 5 December 1907.

33. *Harper's Weekly*, 7 December 1912.

34. Howard L. Applegate, "The 1902 Studebaker Electric," *Syracuse University Library*.

35. "Walker Balance Gear Electric Trucks," *Cycle and Automobile Trade Journal*, December 1910, 197–200.

36. Reed L. Parker, "Auto Concerns Report Increasing Trade," *Chicago Daily Tribune*, 27 December 1914.

37. Afterward the vehicle was put on display at Edaville Heritage Railroad in South Carver, Massachusetts.

Chapter Two

1. Mougeot was better known for his "mougeoes" or green-bronze mailboxes situated across the across the Capital.

2. Tragically Jeantaud took his own life in November 1906 following the bankruptcy of his EV firm, by poisoning himself with carbon monoxide in his Paris office.

3. Erwin Maderholz, "Elektrofahrzeuge in Postdienst," *Archive für deutsche Postgeschichte*, Heft 2/1981.

4. Wencer, David. "Historicist: The Dawn of the Horseless Era," *Torontoist*, 26 May 2012.

5. "From Our Berlin Correspondent," *The Commercial Motor*, 19 May 1910.

6. *New York Times*, 7 February 1915.

7. Gisj Mom, *The Electric Vehicle: Technology and Expectations in the Automobile Age*, Johns Hopkins University Press (2004), 195.

8. "Four 'Electrics' on Tour," *Motor Traction*, 28 October 1914.

Chapter Three

1. Gisj Mom, *The Electric Vehicle: Technology and Expectations in the Automobile Age*, Johns Hopkins University Press (2004), 241.

2. Heinz Rusterholz, Tribelhorn, *Erste Elektrofahrzeuge vom Zürichsee* Exhibition Brochure 2012/2013 Uetiker Museum, Uetikon, Switzerland.

3. Grace's Guide to British Industrial History.

4. "Olympia Show—Electric Vehicles," *Motor Transport*, 2 November 1925.

5. Maurice E. Fox, Electrical Engineer, Edison Storage Battery Co. in London and Paris: *Report on Messrs Harrods Ltd Electric Trucks*, May 2013.

6. "Electric Vehicle Notes: The Harrods Fleet of Electrics," *The Electrical Times*, 6 December 1917.

7. "Mechanical Biscuits Leaflet," Reading Borough Council (Reading Museum Service).

8. "Moving Heavy Weights Short Distances," *Motor Transport*, 20 August 1923.

9. *Power Wagon—Journal of the Motor Truck Industry*, published in Chicago.

10. "Les Véhicules électriques à accumulateurs: Les Essais controlés de Bellevue," *La Vie Automobile*, 25 February 1924.

11. Not to be confused with SOCOVEL, who manufactured electric motorcycles in Brussels during World War II.

12. Jean-Noël Raymond. *SOVEL Camions Electriques 1925–1977 La SLEVE*. France, Brignais Raymond, 2016.

13. Vétra, the "Société des Véhicules et Tracteurs Electriques" was better known for its streetcars and electric locomotives.

14. Kfz der Wehrmacht.de

15. "Elektro-Kleinwagen 'Omnobil,'" *Klein MotorSport No 10*.

16. Jonathan Norton Leonard, *Loki: The Life of Charles Proteus Steinmetz*, New York: Doubleday (1929).

17. "Leoni Light Electric Vehicle Follows Gasoline Truck Practice," *Automotive Industries*, August 27, 1925.

18. Gijs P. A. Mom, and David A. Kirsch, "Technologies in Tension: Horses, Electric Trucks, and the Motorization of American Cities, 1900–1925," *Technology and Culture*, vol. 42, no. 3 (July 2001).

Chapter Four

1. Jean-Noël Raymond, *SOVEL Camions Electriques 1925–1977 La SLEVE*. France, Brignais Raymond (2016).

2. "A Battery-Electric Halted by War," *The Commercial Motor*, 30 July 1943.

3. J.A. Gregoire, *50 ans d'automobile*, tome 2, "La voiture électrique," C Flammarion, Paris 1981, 175–179.

Chapter Five

1. Advert from the British National Milk Publicity Council 1958.

2. "News and Views: Britain's Electric Vehicles," *Autocar*, vol. 127, no. 3729, 3 August 1967, 55.

3. Keith Roberts, "Electric Avenue: The Story of Morrison-Electricar," Bryngold Books (2010).

4. "The Municipal Exhibition," *Motor Transport*, November 26, 1923.

5. "Chassisless Construction in a Prototype Electric," *The Commercial Motor*, 27 April 1945.

6. "Electric Billposting Halves Labour Costs," *The Commercial Motor*, 6 February 1948.

7. "A New Battery-Electric Announced," *The Commercial Motor*, 22 January 1937.

8. "A New Type Battery-Electric Vehicle," *The Commercial Motor*, 25 October 1940, 24.

9. "A New Battery-Electric Vehicle," *The Commercial Motor*, 8 January 1937.

10. "Streamlined Electric Vans," *The Commercial Motor*, 26 October 1934, 38.

11. "A Platform-Steered Industrial Truck," *The Commercial Motor*, 8 December 1944; SOVEL in France had a similar design approach: 26 October 1934, 38.
12. "Battery Electric Marathon," *Commercial Motor*, 24 August 1951.
13. Bob Hakewill, "Harbilt Electric Trucks," Harborough Museum (2011).
14. "Milk & More Adds 200 Electric *StreetScooter* Vans to Fleet," CommercialFleet.org, 30 May 2018.

Chapter Six

1. Kevin Danchisko, "Machines or Bust: Post Office Department Research and Development, 1945–1970," postalmuseum.si.edu.
2. Jean-Noël Raymond, *SOVEL Camions Electriques 1925–1977 La SLEVE*. France, Brignais: Raymond (2016).
3. *Wall Street Journal*, October 3, 1973.
4. Kevin Desmond, *Innovators in Battery Technology: Profiles of 95 Influential Electrochemists*, McFarland (2016), 237.
5. "Geoffrey Ballard, founder of fuel-cell firm Ballard Power Systems, dies," *Canadian Press newswire* CBC.ca, 6 August 2008.
6. Kevin Desmond, *Innovators in Battery Technology: Profiles of 95 Influential Electrochemists*, McFarland (2016), 4.
7. Kevin Kantola, "1966 GM Electrovan," hydrogencarsnow.com; "Craig Marks," *The National Academies Press Memorial Tributes*, vol. 14 (2011).
8. www.lektro.com.
9. "The US Gov't Shares the Cost of Electric Vehicle Programs," *The Rotarian*, February 1981.
10. Philippe B. de l'Arc, "Histoire de la Voiture Électrique" boursinp.free.fr/velec.
11. "Bedford Electric: A Model of Quiet Efficiency," vauxpedianet.uk.
12. James Bradbury, "When Britain was in the Forefront of Electric Vehicle (EV) Technology," Greenbarrel.com.
13. Bedford CF website.
14. "Leyland Terrier takes over from heavier Ms," *The Commercial Motor*, 28 August 1970.
15. Bedford CF website.
16. Richard Stepler, "Coming: Speedy Electric Delivery," *Popular Science*, January 1993.
17. Tariq Malik, "Fuel Cell Pioneer: An Interview with Geoffrey Ballard," *Scientific American*, 18 November 2002.
18. Kevin Desmond, *Innovators in Battery Technology: Profiles of 95 Influential Electrochemists*, McFarland (2016), 148.

Chapter Seven

1. Kevin Desmond, *Innovators in Battery Technology: Profiles of 95 Influential Electrochemists*, McFarland (2016), 104.
2. mitsubishi-fuso.com.
3. PVI website, http://www.pvi.fr/?lang=fr.
4. See Wikipedia entry on Smiths, particularly endnotes.

Chapter Eight

1. Stanley, M. Hills "Battery-Electric Vehicles." UK, London: George Newnes Ltd. 1943.
2. unfccc.int/news/the-paris-declaration-on-electro-mobility-and-climate-change-and-call-to-action
3. Kevin Desmond, *Electric Motorcycles and Bicycles: A History Including Scooters, Tricycles, Segways and Monocycles*, McFarland (2019).

4. Although this is true for the 21st century, earlier chapters of this book show that companies in both the USA and Europe had already achieved serial production even if for limited range.

5. daimler.com

6. Jérôme Guillen profile, Linkedin.com.

7. Fred Lambert, "Daimler to Deliver Fleet of eCascadia Electric Trucks to Partners by End of the Year," *electrek*, 28 June 2018.

8. "Germany Supporting Truck Platooning Project with Nearly €2M," *Green Car Congress*, 13 July 2017.

9. toyota-global.com

10. Yuki Hanai, "Volkswagen Truck Teams with Toyota's Hino Despite Parents' Rivalry," *Nikkei Asian Review*, 12 April 2018.

11. Ryan ZumMallen, "1,000 Hyundai Fuel Cell Electric Trucks Headed for Switzerland," trucks.com, 21 September 2018.

12. corporate.walmart.com

13. "Mayor Launches New Taskforce to Expand Electric Vehicle Infrastructure," *London Assembly*, 31 May 2018.

14. "GOVECS AG Signs Letter of Intent for 6,000 E-scooters for the London Shared-Vehicles Market," DGAP News, businessinsider.com, 25 September 2018.

15. Norihiko Shirouzu, "A Slew of Electric Truck Plans May Deliver the Goods for China's EV Ambitionism," *Reuters*, 16 November 2018.

16. Fred Lambert, "Tesla Semi Production Version Will Have Closer to 600 Miles of Range, Says Elon Musk," *electrek*, 2 May 2018.

17. Nikola Tesla, *My Inventions and Other Writings*, Penguin (2011).

18. Joe Borràs, "Ford Team Edison, Ford's EV Team, Moves to Corktown, Detroit," cleantechnica.com, 6 July 2018.

Chapter Nine

1. Ernst D. Dickmanns, *Dynamic Vision for Perception and Control of Motion*, Springer (2007).

2. workhorse.com.

3. konecranes.com/equipment/container-handling-equipment/automated-guided-vehicles.

4. zf.com.

5. volvotrucks.com.

6. starsky.io.

7. einride.tech.

8. waymo.com.

9. Sara Gentzler, "Robot Crossing: Delivery Bots Allowed on Washington Sidewalks, If Bill Passes," *Washington State Wire*, 28 January 2019.

10. Communication to the author, 30 August 2018.

11. Rishab Rangarajan, "Structural Battery Composites in Electric Vehicle Design A Feasibility Study," Department of Industrial and Materials Science Chalmer University of Technology, Gothenburg, Sweden, 2018.

12. "Parliamentary Intelligence: House of Commons," *The Times*, 24 April 1865.

13. Amit Malewar, "Artificial Sounds for Traffic Safety," *TechExplorist*, 24 January 2018.

14. Kevin Desmond, *Electric Motorcycles and Bicycles: A History Including Scooters, Tricycles, Segways and Monocycles*, McFarland (2019).

15. Brian Holland, "Are Fleets Implementing Electric Trucks Soon?" *FreightWaves*, 22 January 2019.

16. Edwin Lopez, "Bosch Predicts a Future of Electric, Hub-to-Hub Trucks," Supplychaindrive, 24 September 2018.

Appendix A

1. One of them was kept in Simferopol until 2006, but then it was cut up, although they had wanted to take it to the MGT Museum.

Appendix C

1. Communication from Jay Crist, January 2018.
2. Communication from Paul Gray, August 2018.

Bibliography

Books

Anderson, Antony. *Robert Davidson, Pioneer of Electric Locomotion*. Scotland: Alford, The Grampian Transport Museum, 2018.

Baldwin, Nick. *Old Delivery Vans*. Buckinghamshire, UK: Shire Publications, 1987.

Bersey, Walter C. *Electrically-Propelled Carriages*. London: Morgan, Thompson, & Jamieson, 1898.

Burton, Nigel. *A History of Electric Cars*. Ramsbury, England: Crowood, 2013.

Cushing, H. R., Jr., and Frank Smith. *The Electric Vehicle Hand-Book*. New York: H. C. Cushing, Jr., 1914.

Desmond, Kevin. *Gustave Trouvé: French Electrical Genius*. Jefferson, NC: McFarland, 2015.

Desmond, Kevin. *Innovators in Battery Technology: Profiles of 93 Influential Electrochemists*. Jefferson, NC: McFarland, 2016.

Electric Vehicles in the Postal Service. usps.com, 2014.

Gregoire, Jean-Albert. *50 Ans d'Automobile, tome 2: La Voiture Électrique*. Paris: C Flammarion, 1981.

Hakewill, Bob. *Harbilt Electric Trucks*, vols. 1 (2011) and 2 (2013). Harborough Museum.

Havard, Patrice. *La Fabuleuse Histoire des Sapeurs-Pompiers (de Paris)*. Talandier, 2002.

Hills, Stanley, M. *Battery-Electric Vehicles*. London: George Newnes, 1943.

Kirsch, David A. *The Electric Vehicle and the Burden of History*. New Jersey: Rutgers University Press, 2000.

Kriéger, Louis, et al. *Le Vehicule Electrique Utilitaire à Accumulateurs: Conférences Données à la Société des Ingénieurs de l'Automobile*. Paris: Dunod, 1947.

Lecouturier, Y, and P-S Proust. *La Poste Automobile et les Véhicules des PTT: 1897–1970*. Paris: Union Marcophilie, 1998.

Mom, Gijs. *The Electric Vehicle: Technology and Expectations in the Automobile Age*. Baltimore: Johns Hopkins University Press, 2004.

Payne, Harold J. *Profitable Application of Electric Industrial Trucks and Tractors*. Survey Committee of the Society of Electrical Development Inc., New York, December 1927.

Petit, Henri. *La Voiture Electrique à Accumulateurs*. Paris: Dunod, 1943.

Raymond, Jean-Noël. *SOVEL Camions Elecriques 1925–1977 La SLEVE*. France: Brignais Raymond, 2016.

Roberts, Keith. *Electric Avenue: The Story of Morrison-Electricar*. Neath, UK: Bryngold Books, 2010.

Rusterholz, Heinz. *Tribelhorn: Erste Elektrofahrzeuge vom Zürichsee*. Exhibition Brochure 2012/2013, Uetiker Museum, Uetikon, Switzerland.

Test, Charles D. *Chuck's Toyland: An Historical Preservation*. South Minneapolis, Minnesota.

Valentine, J. H. *Registered Vehicles of Southern Californian Origin in 1917*. Motor Vehicle Department of Sacramento.

Wakefield, Ernest H. *History of the Electric Automobile: Battery-Only Powered Cars*. Pennsylvania: Society of Automotive Engineers, 1994.

Wood, Donald F. *Delivery Trucks: The Crestline Series*. Wisconsin: MBI Publishing, 1999.

Wren, Genevieve J., and James A. Wren. *Motor Trucks of America*. Ann Arbor: University of Michigan Press, 1979.

Periodicals

Autocar
Automobile Engineer
Automotive Industries
The Automotor and Horseless Vehicle Journal
Charge Utile Magazine
Commercial Motor
Cycle and Automobile Trade Journal
The Electric Vehicle
Electrical Times
La Genie Civile
The Horseless Age
The Motor Age
The Motor-Car Journal
Motor Traction
Motor Transport
La Nature
The New York Times
Omnia
Penny Mechanic and Chemist
Le Petit Journal
Power Wagon—Journal of the Motor Truck Industry
The Railway Journal
Le Vie Automobile
Voitures Legères
The Wall Street Journal

Index

Numbers in *bold italics* indicate pages with illustrations